GRIEF, MOURNING AND DEATH RITUAL

FACING DEATH

Series editor: David Clark, Professor of Medical Sociology,
University of Sheffield

The subject of death in late modern culture has become a rich field of theoretical, clinical and policy interest. Widely regarded as a taboo until recent times, death now engages a growing interest among social scientists, practitioners and those responsible for the organization and delivery of human services. Indeed, how we die has become a powerful commentary on how we live and the specialized care of dying people holds an important place within modern health and social care.

This series captures such developments in a collection of volumes which has much to say about death, dying, end of life care and bereavement in contemporary society. Among the contributors are leading experts in death studies, from sociology, anthropology, social psychology, ethics, nursing, medicine and pastoral care. A particular feature of the series is its attention to the developing field of palliative care, viewed from the perspectives of practitioners, planners and policy analysts; here several authors adopt a multi-disciplinary approach, drawing on recent research, policy and organizational commentary, and reviews of evidence-based practice. Written in a clear, accessible style, the entire series will be essential reading for students of death, dying and bereavement and for anyone with an involvement in palliative care research, service delivery or policy making.

Current and forthcoming titles:

David Clark, Jo Hockley and Sam Ahmedzai (eds): *New Themes in Palliative Care*
David Clark and Jane Seymour: *Reflections on Palliative Care: Sociological and Policy Perspectives*
Mark Cobb: *The Dying Soul: Spiritual Care at the End of Life*
Kirsten Costain Schou and Jenny Hewison: *Experiencing Cancer: The Quality of Life in Treatment*
Catherine Exley: *Living with Cancer, Living with Dying*
David Field, David Clark, Jessica Corner and Carol Davis (eds): *Researching Palliative Care*
Jenny Hockey, Jeanne Katz and Neil Small (eds): *Grief, Mourning and Death Ritual*
David Kissane and Sidney Bloch: *Family Grief Therapy*
Gordon Riches and Pamela Dawson: *An Intimate Loneliness: Supporting Bereaved Parents and Siblings*
Jane E. Seymour: *Critical Moments – Death and Dying in Intensive Care*
Tony Walter: *On Bereavement: The Culture of Grief*

GRIEF, MOURNING AND DEATH RITUAL

Edited by
JENNY HOCKEY
JEANNE KATZ
NEIL SMALL

OPEN UNIVERSITY PRESS
Buckingham · Philadelphia

Open University Press
Celtic Court
22 Ballmoor
Buckingham
MK18 1XW

email: enquiries@openup.co.uk
world wide web: www.openup.co.uk

and
325 Chestnut Street
Philadelphia, PA 19106, USA

First Published 2001

A catalogue record of this book is available from the British Library

ISBN 0 335 20501 1 (pb)   0 335 20502 X (hb)

Library of Congress Cataloging-in-Publication Data available

Typeset by Graphicraft Limited, Hong Kong
Printed in Great Britain by Biddles Limited, Guildford and Kings Lynn

CONTENTS

List of contributors

Arnar Árnason studied anthropology at the University of Iceland and the University of Durham where he finished a PhD on death, grief and bereavement counselling in the North East of England. He is currently a researcher at Ibaraki University, doing research on death and grief in Japan.

Michael Anderson is a social anthropologist and Senior Research Associate at the Newcastle Centre for Family Studies in the University of Newcastle upon Tyne. His teaching interests are in the anthropology of identity and selfhood, and the anthropology of childhood. His research interests cover death and bereavement, communication in families and childhood. He is author of articles and reports on all of these topics.

Mary Bradbury is the author of *Representations of Death: A Social Psychological Perspective*. She is currently training at the Institute of Psychoanalysis. She lives in North London with her partner and their two children.

Caroline Currer is a social worker and sociologist, currently working at Anglia Polytechnic University in the Social Work Department. She is also a supervisor with CRUSE Bereavement Care. Previously, she worked as a psychiatric social worker in Pakistan, and then in the Sociology Department at the University of Warwick. With Meg Stacey, she is co-editor of *Concepts of Health, Illness and Disease: a Comparative Perspective*, and has just completed a textbook entitled *Responding to Grief: Dying, Bereavement and Social Care*.

Anne Eyre is Lecturer in Disaster Studies and Management at the Centre for Disaster Management, Coventry. Her research interests include the psychosocial dimensions of disaster planning, preparedness and response, the needs and rights of disaster victims and human aspects of disaster management.

She sits on a range of research and practitioner committees and on the committees of Disaster Action and Victims Voice. In addition, she has published studies based on the experience of disaster in the UK and overseas.

Shirley Firth teaches Death and Dying for The Open University and Death in Indian Religious Traditions at Reading University. She gives seminars on cross-cultural perspectives on palliative care, death and bereavement on various palliative care courses. Her doctoral research was published as *Dying, Death and Bereavement in a British Hindu Community*.

Doris Francis is a social anthropologist and author of *Will You Still Need Me, Will You Still Feed Me, When I'm 84?*, and co-editor of *Workers' Expression: Beyond Accommodation and Resistance*. Between 1995 and 1998, she was Visiting Professor and Principal Research Officer at The Centre for Environmental and Social Studies in Ageing, University of North London. She is currently writing a book (with Leonie Kellaher) on the comparative cemetery behaviour of different ethnic groups in London entitled *The Secret Cemetery: Cultural Meanings of Cemetery*.

Philip Gore is a director of the family funeral firm in Margate and a part-time research student at Goldsmiths College London. He is interested in local funeral history and is an examiner for the British Institute of Embalmers.

Joanna Heslop is a Macmillan Lecturer in Palliative Care in the Social Work department at the University of Hull. Having worked as a social work practitioner on the Regional Paediatric Oncology Unit, one of her main research interests is in the area of children with life-threatening illnesses. She also has an interest in disaster work and is a consultant to Humber Response, the multi-disciplinary disaster response team based in North Lincolnshire and East Yorkshire.

Jenny Hockey is Senior Lecturer at Hull University. A social anthropologist, her publications include *Death, Gender and Ethnicity* (with D. Field and N. Small); *Beyond the Body: Death and Social Identity* (with E. Hallam and G. Howarth). She is a member of the editorial board of *Mortality*, the journal of death studies.

Glennys Howarth is based at the University of Bath. Prior to that she was Associate Professor of Sociology at the University of Sydney. Glennys has been researching in the field of death and dying for over ten years and is currently working on a study of policy making around euthanasia. She is author of *Last Rites* and co-author (with E. Hallam and J. Hockey) of *Beyond the Body*. She is a founding editor of *Mortality*, the first major international journal of death studies outside the United States.

Jeanne Katz teaches at The Open University in the school of Health and Social Welfare. She chairs the Death and Dying course and has contributed to other courses including Health Promotion and Human Biology and Health. Her research focuses on caring for people of different ages dying in a variety of settings.

Leonie Kellaher is a principal research officer at the University of North London where she directs the Centre for Environmental & Social Studies in Ageing. A social anthropologist by discipline, her research has focused on the organizational, built and material environments in which older people live. A recent publication, *Re-evaluating Residential Care* represents the culmination of nearly two decades' work in this field with colleagues S. Peace and D. Willcocks. She is co-author with Doris Francis of the forthcoming text, *The Secret Cemetery: Cultural Meanings of Cemetery.*

Carol Komaromy works as a lecturer in Health Studies at the School of Health and Social Welfare at The Open University. She previously worked for five years on two large Department of Health funded projects investigating the case for palliative care in residential and nursing homes for older people. She also works as an associate lecturer for The Open University on the Death and Dying Course and is a member of that course team. Previously she worked in the health service as a nurse and midwife and is a qualified counsellor.

Jane Littlewood, BSc, PhD is a senior lecturer in social policy at Goldsmiths College, University of London. Her research interests include bereavement, loss and socio-cultural factors affecting social change.

Miriam S. Moss, MA, a research sociologist, has been Senior Research Scientist at the Philadelphia Geriatric Center for over 30 years. Her interests have been on family caregiving, quality of life of the very old, and the interface between old age and dying, death and bereavement. She is Co-principal Investigator of a major study of Bereavement in Long Term Care funded by the US Institute on Aging.

Sidney Z. Moss, DCSW, is a clinical social worker and family therapist, and is currently Research Analyst at the Philadelphia Geriatric Center in a continuing study of the meaning and role of death, dying and bereavement in long-term care facilities in the US. His writings have emphasized issues of separation and loss across the life course, and most recently have focused on end-of-life issues in old age.

Georgina Neophytou conducted the study of Greek Orthodox cemeteries for the ESRC funded research project, Cemetery as Garden, carried out at the University of North London. She is a doctoral candidate in Sociology at the London School of Economics.

Jean Simons trained as a social worker and has worked with children with cancer and their families since 1982. She is Bereavement Services Coordinator and Joint Coordinator of the Child Death Helpline at Great Ormond Street Hospital in London, having held these posts since 1995. She is Vice-Chair of the London Bereavement Network.

Neil Small is Professor of Community and Primary Care at Bradford University. In this position his focus is on the relationship between policy innovation and practice development. This fits well with longer term interests in theory and evidence in health and social care and with research into service user involvement.

Series editor's preface

This latest addition to the Facing Death series will catch the attention of a great variety of readers. For the editors of *Grief, Mourning and Death Ritual* have provided us with a rich array of chapters organized around some key debates in the understanding of human mortality in late modern culture. As Jenny Hockey, Jeanne Katz and Neil Small acknowledge, this is also a book with both a past and a context. It has grown out of a small but lively forum of social scientists and practitioners who, meeting in Britain since the early 1990s, have done much to foster research and writing on the social aspects of death, dying and bereavement.

As a result we have been fortunate in seeing social analysis relating to mortality engaged on two parallel fronts. First it has been concerned with processes of reflection about tradition, modernity and postmodernity and has shown how the meanings, social practices and values surrounding death and dying are reflective of deeper social characteristics. Second it has engaged with practitioners, policy makers, planners and providers of human services to look at how practical issues of the day might be illuminated and addressed through the lens of social science. The results of these two, linked, endeavours are brought together in this volume.

Each section of the book begins with a sustained and critical analysis of a single theme. Neil Small's review of theories of grief provides an excellent theoretical introduction to understanding a subject which for too long has only been visible through the prism of a single discipline (psychology); he shows us something of the cultural dimensions of grief and how they relate to postmodern narratives of the self. Building on this, part two opens with an exploration of the practice implications of current theories of bereavement, showing how in some instances these develop into strategies of power and inscription, but also offering examples of resistance on the part of bereaved people themselves. The third and final part of the book moves us on to questions of ritual and memorialization and here Jenny Hockey provides us with an elegant and thoughtful review of the historical anthropology of this subject, contrasting the separate influences of romanticism and modernism.

So much for the book's organizing framework. Following each of these splendid scene-setting chapters we are then offered a wide range of contributions, written from several professional and disciplinary perspectives. We are presented with evidence from new empirical studies. There are further explorations of the book's key theoretical themes. Examples are given of new approaches to intervention and service provision relating to dying and bereaved people.

The Facing Death series has of course already introduced its readers to some of these topics. We have seen sociological analyses of research and practice in the field of palliative care. There have been sustained theoretical expositions relating to loss and bereavement as well as direct accounts of the experience of life-threatening illness. We have also provided a platform for multi-disciplinary explorations of policy and service development in these areas. In *Grief, Mourning and Death Ritual*, Jenny Hockey, Jeanne Katz and Neil Small capture exactly the practical and intellectual purpose of the series. Their book deserves to be widely read within that increasingly diverse constituency which concerns itself with death, dying and grief in personal and social context.

David Clark

Acknowledgements

The inspiration for this book has come out of our joint work as organizers of the annual symposia on the Social Aspects of Death Dying and Bereavement during the mid 1990s. As such it is the third book to emerge from this series, the first being *The Sociology of Death*, edited by David Clark in 1993 and the second being *Death, Gender and Ethnicity*, edited by David Field, Jenny Hockey and Neil Small in 1997. Since its inception at the University of Leicester in 1990 by David Clark, David Field and Nicky James, this annual meeting has proved an invaluable source of intellectual support for an international group of new and established social science researchers in the fields of death, dying and bereavement. Alongside more recent innovations such as the large scale Death, Dying and Disposal conferences and the European journal of death studies, *Mortality*, this relatively small one-day workshop continues to provide an informal, supportive platform for new work from around the world. Many of the contributions in the current collection stem directly from the symposia and its publication fortuitously coincides with the tenth anniversary meeting in November 2000 at the University of Leicester.

Introduction

JEANNE KATZ

The opening lines of Douglas Dunn's poem 'December' bid the reader to write their grief into their poetry until there is none left, a task which may take many years. His lines indicate a sea change in the attitudes of the English speaking Western world to grief and mourning. It reflects an emergent postmodern view that grief can accompany what remains of a lifetime. The message here is clear, that grief is work, and that this is not necessarily bad, nor time limited. On the contrary it suggests that it might fruitfully occupy the time of mourners and even be productive in some way.

The explicit expression of this perspective (the assumption that grieving could be productive and indeed constitute legitimate creativity) is something of a departure from the popular assumption that grieving should be time limited and that one can expect to recover from loss. This latter view was based on Freud's claim that recovery usually includes transferring the emotional energy previously invested in the deceased into a new relationship. It also included the concept that grief is a process; one moves through stages of accepting one's fate or stages of grief (Kübler-Ross 1969; Worden 1991). This was in many ways contrary to the cultural tradition, encompassed in art, music and literature, which has enriched Western society for centuries. Requiem masses were commissioned for monarchs and other luminaries of the age; composers, poets and artists gave expression to their own grief through works that focused specifically on their personal losses – Mahler's *kindertotenliede* is a notable example. In very few of these artistic forms was there any suggestion that the deceased could be replaced.

In contrast, within Anglophone Western societies, the late twentieth century saw much attention being given to grief and mourning as mental health 'problems' that could be 'solved'. This is often thought to represent an attitudinal shift in these areas. However, throughout the whole of the twentieth century considerable attention had been paid to grief and mourning, although the focus of this attention was not constant. Following the First World War, society celebrated the contribution that fallen soldiers had made to the war effort despite the powerful, critical poetry of those such as Siegfried Sassoon and Rupert Brooke. By the end of the Second World War the atrocities perpetrated by the Nazis (and indeed the Japanese) were more the focus of attention, rather than the impact these had on the survivors. For the survivors of the concentration camps, and those rendered homeless by the war, the focus was on building a safe future. Looking back was far too painful and many of those who found it difficult to project a safe future became paralysed by emotion and unable to function.

The middle of the twentieth century was accompanied by many changes in attitudes towards caring for dying people, as well as those in mourning. Death was removed from the domestic to technologically superior institutional settings where professionals strove to 'cure' the dying and, when this was unsuccessful, were seen by critics to isolate those for whom 'nothing more can be done'. In the UK caring for the corpse was still mostly the province of small family firms of undertakers who provided a personalized service for bereaved relatives and made respect for the deceased the central plank of their marketing (see Gore's chapter in this volume). In the United States, critics argued that death was being denied. This was exemplified by American undertakers' attempts to make the deceased look as lifelike as possible, practices which were highlighted by Jessica Mitford in *The American Way of Death* (1963). Gorer in the UK made a similar assertion that British society had lost the art of grieving (1965).

In addition to this emphasis on the denial of death, also exemplified in the work of Philippe Ariès (1981), there was a considerable focus on grief, mourning and death ritual amongst researchers from a wide range of disciplines in the middle of the twentieth century. Scholarly and lay articles on different aspects of grief and mourning continued to proliferate throughout the second half of the century. Many of these were collected in an annotated bibliography by Michael Simpson (1979) to challenge the myth that little was published in this area.

Looking back it is evident that since the late 1950s there has been a growing body of literature on bereavement and loss. Practitioners, researchers and academics saw this as an increasingly important area for study, which paralleled a growing interest in the experience of general and specific stress, as well as concern about the psychological outcomes of disasters for those who survived them. Lay interest in this field can arguably be seen to be fuelled by the media exposure given to disasters and the gory deaths that are so much the hallmark of mass media entertainment. In the US, for example, children are believed to have watched several thousand mostly fictional deaths on television by the time they reach adolescence.

Not only does the viewer see, in their living room, the details of mass murders and natural disasters but also the emotional consequences for the bereaved. The latter is encapsulated in concern with post-traumatic stress disorder (PTSD), which became the subject of considerable academic as well as practice research (see Eyre's chapter in this volume). The emotional consequences of death have also become a focus for the attention of the media. They have promoted the importance of counselling for bereaved people following the Paddington rail disaster in London and the Egyptair disaster in New York, both of which occurred at the end of 1999. Post-traumatic stress disorder is now seen as nothing particularly new as it was first 'discovered' following the First World War and was then described as 'shell shock'.

Why this book now?

Books on loss, grief and bereavement abound for all types of readerships. Their existence challenges the thesis that death is a 'taboo' subject, a view that predominated for much of the middle part of the twentieth century. Another predominant view expressed in the literature focusing on grief in the twentieth century, which has now been widely challenged, is the concept of normal or abnormal grief. This was usually explained and treated by psychological and psychoanalytical approaches.

Two recent publications by Open University Press have continued to challenge these perspectives, critically evaluating different theoretical approaches to loss, grief and bereavement. Sheila Payne and colleagues, using broadly a health psychology perspective in their book *Loss and Bereavement*, present the reader with contemporary and historical theoretical perspectives and explore models of adapting to loss (1999). Similar to the accounts we present in this book, Payne *et al.* assume that the processes of loss and change occur in a variety of social and cultural contexts, which are mediated by historical and other perspectives. In particular, they look at the role of the family and changes over the life course. Their work shows how models of adaptation to loss have developed over the twentieth century, starting with Lindemann (1944) who first observed that grief seemed to follow a prescribed pattern. Payne *et al.* go on to illustrate how these models have been used in different types of interventions, and in clinical and community settings.

Tony Walter's *On Bereavement*, also published at the end of 1999 by Open University Press, takes a more sociological approach to this topic. Instead of focusing primarily on models of grief, he looks at how culture affects grief as well as mourning. Walter explores the interaction between the living and the dead in certain cultures and focuses predominantly on problematizing the response to death of the host societies in the UK and the

US. Walter's approach is refreshing insofar as it challenges the tensions between the dominant theories of integration and regulation. He questions the concept of the 'social integration of the dead' by positing two inter-pretations. 'One is that the living must leave the dead behind and move on without them. The other is that the dead are always with us and the bereaved continue to bond with them; indeed the dead must be incorpor-ated in some way if families, other groups and indeed entire societies are to have any sense of their past' (Walter 1999: 205).

Our book, similarly, draws on the strengths of sociological and anthro-pological perspectives. Through a critical use of postmodern theory it examines the production of knowledge, of theories of bereavement, demon-strating a Foucauldian elision of knowledge/power via an examination of the diversity of practices that constitute bereavement care. In this way we address both personal and professional responses to death, so broadening perspectives on death and dying. Drawing on social theory, the volume explores what we assume to be a 'universal' human response within the unique set of cultural, social and historical circumstances that characterized the end of the twentieth century in Anglophone societies. We ask whether Gorer's assertion in the 1960s that British society had lost the art of griev-ing still pertains, or is relevant even to small sections of this society. We recognize the contribution made by ethnic minorities who have enriched the experience of living in postmodern Britain in relation to both bereave-ment and death ritual. We consider whether 'death in the living room' brought to us by the media might have enabled us to acknowledge death as a final state of being.

Although the terms grief, mourning and bereavement are used extensively in this book, we have adopted a critical stance towards their meanings and the meaning of the variety of concepts associated with them. Meanings can be culturally mediated and socially understood; for example construc-tions of 'mourning' will carry implications for what might be termed as 'adjustment'. We undertake the task of examining these terms with refer-ence to a number of key researchers and authors in this field and where possible their definitions will be presented. Here we begin by introducing some key definitions, which will be debated throughout the book. As argued, there is little consensus about these definitions and once one crosses language and cultural boundaries the terms can be both confusing and limiting.

Bereavement is seen by Stroebe and Schut (1998) to be '. . . the situation of a person who has recently experienced the loss of someone significant through that person's death'. According to this definition, 'bereavement' could be seen as 'time limited' and relating solely to the loss of the life of a significant other. A wider definition could encompass a variety of additional losses across a longer time frame. This perspective is provided by Corr *et al.* (1997) who suggest that;

The term *bereavement* refers to the state of being bereaved or deprived of something; that is, bereavement identifies the objective situation of individuals who have experienced a loss. Both the noun *bereavement* and the adjective bereaved derive from a less-familiar root verb, *reave*, which means 'to despoil, rob or forcibly deprive' (Simpson and Wiener 1989 Vol. 13, p. 295). In short a bereaved person is one who has been deprived, robbed, plundered or stripped of something.

(Corr *et al.* 1997: 220 original emphasis)

Grief is defined in a variety of ways and is often recognized as an activity rather than a state of being. Corr *et al.* define it as follows:

Grief is the *response to loss*. When one suffers a loss, one grieves. The word *grief* signifies one's reaction, both internally and externally, to the impact of loss . . . The term *grief* is often defined as 'the emotional response to loss' . . . As Elias (1991) noted, 'Broadly speaking, emotions have three components, a somatic, a behavioural and a feeling component' (p. 117). As a result 'the term *emotion*, even in professional discussions, is used with two different meanings. It is used in a wider and in a narrower sense at the same time. In the wider sense the term *emotion* refers to the feeling component of the syndrome only' (Elias 1991: 119).

(Corr *et al.* 1997: 221, original emphasis)

Parkes, in a recent publication (1998: 6), defines grief as 'the normal reaction to a loss and is the means by which people begin to accept the reality of an event which will change their lives. The term *psycho-social transition* covers the complex process of learning which then takes place'. Grief is therefore twinned with change and implies that the individual is engaged in 'work', which is geared to making sense of the loss. Parkes notes that the allied concepts of 'grief work' (Freud 1917) and 'worry work' (Janis and Leventhal 1965) 'have been proposed to reflect the idea that *it takes time and effort to come to terms with painful realities* but that this is a job that is worth doing' (1998: 8).

Corr *et al.* (1997) emphasize that conceptualizing grief as a 'matter of feelings' could lead to a narrowing of the concept that risks marginalizing the full range of responses to loss (physical, psychological (affective/cognitive), behavioural, spiritual and social).

Mourning usually indicates the process of coping with loss and grief and the ways in which individuals and societies incorporate this process into their new reality (Corr *et al.* 1997). Mourning is not the same as grief but is associated with it. Stroebe and Schut note that 'Mourning refers to the social expressions or acts expressive of grief, which are shaped by the practices of a given society or cultural group' (1998). Using this definition, we can see that whilst bereavement and grieving are often described as individual states or processes (even if they are shaped by society in some form), they are often differentiated from mourning, which 'refers to shared, socially pre-scribed practices' (Currer in press). *Mourning* can therefore be conceptual-ized as a site or context for the grief felt in response to a bereavement. Defined as a set of cultural and social practices rather than an individual phenomenon, it has been a focus for social anthropologists and historians. However, this book explores arguments which suggest that the apparently 'internal', individualized emotions encapsulated by the term 'grief' can them-selves be seen to have been produced through the discursive practices of members of particular societies, categories and groups. Thus, whilst the book divides itself into three parts, beginning with theories of grief, moving on to the practices of bereavement care and finishing with mourning and death rituals, we attend to the *social* nature of this material in each of the three parts.

Death ritual is easier to define than bereavement and mourning because it describes what people do when they have experienced the loss of an individual. Death rituals can be public or private, or both, and work in this area clearly has roots in the social anthropology of cultural traditions, whether long standing or devised for the occasion. Although there are many traditions where the death ritual is 'laid down' for generations, it is none-theless constantly being redefined and reconceptualized within most socie-ties in ways that reflect the contemporary reality. Examples of this are to be found in Firth's chapter on Hindu death rituals and Heslop's chapter on the candle service, 'invented' for those bereaved of a child.

The organization of the book

As noted, this book comprises three long and 15 short chapters, all of which aim to advance thinking about grief, mourning and death ritual. We not only document and make sense of contemporary practice, but also offer a critical review of the way in which thinking about bereavement and loss is constantly changing and being refined as different theoretical frameworks and practical experiences are applied.

It was in order to focus on different types of theory that we chose to separate grief and mourning from bereavement work and death ritual. However, as noted already, there is an ambiguity here. Grief and mourning are seen to relate primarily, though not exclusively, to issues dealing with the internal world. Theorists in this area draw primarily on psychological and psychiatric perspectives but also, to an extent, on social psychology and sociology. Bereavement care and death ritual are both areas where public behaviour takes precedence. In our review of bereavement work we highlight its theoretical underpinning in psychoanalysis; in our exploration of death ritual, we draw on the theoretical insights offered by social anthropologists in this area. According to some definitions, mourning is seen as the 'expression' of grief and therefore closer, conceptually, to death ritual rather than grief.

Each part of the book begins with a substantial review of our understanding of the particular area covered, and is then followed by illustrations from theory and practice as they are manifest in specific circumstances or with defined groups. Although these shorter chapters are offered as exemplars, we make no attempt to be inclusive of all possible trends or types of circumstance. Rather we seek to illustrate certain themes so that readers can extrapolate to a wider variety of experiences and social groups.

The first part of the book begins with Neil Small's extended chapter 'Theories of grief: a critical review'. This explores the extent to which the development of bereavement theories can be seen to have ushered in hard and fast definitions of the experiences of bereavement. Are we seeking to impose scientific structures on experiences better represented through poetic language or other artistic forms and if so, might our arrogance mean we do a disservice to those we seek to understand or help?

Small charts the phases in the development of a discourse on death and dying during the twentieth century, focusing primarily on the post-war period. He describes the way modernity has shaped attachment and psychoanalytic theories and in particular the contributions of major figures in this field, such as John Bowlby and Colin Murray Parkes. He notes the changing use and meanings of terms such as anticipatory grief, grief-work and mourning. He considers the assumptions and limitations of stage theories (Kübler Ross 1969), which, along with 'task' approaches to grief and mourning (Worden 1991), dominated the 1970s and 1980s. Theoretical approaches that subsequently emerged to challenge attachment and stage theories are then considered. Margaret Stroebe and her colleagues, Tony Walter and the 'Continuing Bonds' approach of Dennis Klass, Phyllis Silverman and Steven Nickman, all locate their approaches in relation to prevailing social theory and incorporate a reflexivity that, in Small's view, is to be welcomed. His chapter situates these new approaches within a historical context where thinking about bereavement was undergoing rapid developments and shifts and suggests that we can go even further towards a theoretical position that recognizes diversity and is not framed by a wish to categorize and control.

In his exposition of these developments, Small uses modern and postmodern social theory to unpack existing theoretical work and to suggest alternative narratives. In particular he asks whether the phenomena of bereavement are measurable and whether they should be understood using scales or stages. Can bereavements be compared and can their impact, or the impact of responses to them, be measured?

Critically, Small argues that the way we understand and respond to grief and bereavement contributes to, and is shaped by, the prevailing discourse.

Further, he highlights an important mismatch between those models of bereavement and grief which draw on notions of sequential time and time-defined lives and the way bereavement fractures the modernist understanding of time as linear. In conclusion, he challenges modernist approaches to bereavement that are prescriptive and not tailored to the individual's feelings and needs.

The shorter chapters that follow Small's critical review cover a range of theoretical issues, and address a number of practical agendas. The first, by Caroline Currer, focuses on the process of grieving. She notes that sociological research has only recently turned its attention to the study of grief and mourning, despite considerable disciplinary interest in dying people and their experiences. In contrast to Small, who used social theory as an explanatory device to look at research and practice in relation to grief and mourning, Currer's analysis of some of the same theoretical contributions asks whether understandings from studies of concepts of health and illness could provide some answers. In the context of the influential work by Walter (1994) and Stroebe and Schut (1998), she demonstrates how models of the way health is conceptualized, which have been applied to illness and disease, could be a useful approach when studying grieving.

The following two chapters by Miriam and Sidney Moss and Carol Komaromy and Jenny Hockey explore the concepts of modal or normal deaths, first from the points of view of the surviving children, and second from the points of view of professional carers. Moss and Moss explore the meaning of deaths within a generational context. Instead of looking at a dyadic individual–deceased relationship they consider the family perspective by getting to grips with the meaning of the death of a parent from the viewpoints of several bereaved siblings. They explore family members' perception of the changed 'family' following the mother's death and the impact of this loss on the individual's role within the family. These authors conclude that the family perspective should be the focus of further research.

Komaromy and Hockey examine the concepts of grieving from the perspective of the professional providing support. They explore the assumptions of care staff about what death means to residents in homes for older people and focus on the 'natural' landscape of grief and mourning as perceived by the professionals. This sense of naturalness was related primarily to the concept of 'timely' deaths. Staff believed that older people are resigned to their own deaths and those of their peers, and this was linked partly to a generational perspective.

Like the previous two chapters, Jane Littlewood also considers the impact on survivors of the death of older people but in the context of its meaning for the deceased's surviving spouse. Strategies that widows use to cope with their loss are explored, particularly their attempts to retain their relationships with their deceased husbands. Like other chapters in this volume, the evidence collected by Littlewood suggests that for many such women the concept of 'moving on' was inappropriate. The security and self-definition of these widows was bound up in their wedded status, which was intact, despite the fact that their husbands had died.

The second part of this book opens with 'Discourse into practice: the production of bereavement care'. Small and Hockey explore the implications of what Chapter 1 expounded as the dominant Western discourse of grief for the practice and behaviour of those who work professionally or voluntarily with bereaved people. First they show how modernity elevates both the individual and the expression of feelings. A focus on the work of Foucault then permits a foray into the emergence of a dominant discourse of grief in Western societies.

Small and Hockey ask whether models of grief, which were intended to provide simply a set of interpretive frameworks through which a death might be given meaning, have been inappropriately translated into strategies to deal with grief. Using Foucault's notion of the elision of knowledge/power, they go on to question whether bereavement counselling constitutes a set of prescriptive strategies, or alternatively a range of interpretations. They note how modernity has encouraged each person to take responsibility for their own health and how society regulates emotion through what Walter terms 'policing' (1999: 120ff). Small and Hockey suggest that whilst this challenges the notion of a 'natural' response to loss it simultaneously provides a reassuring structure for bereaved people to assess their 'progress'. Using Lupton's critique of the idea that emotions are innate, 'a set of basic emotions with which all humans are born' (1998: 10), they examine bereavement guides from both practical, theoretical and academic perspectives.

Basing their argument on Foucauldian post-structuralism, they demonstrate how the disciplines that underpin bereavement counselling act to produce their own subjects, the problematic 'emotions' which we know as grief. In exploring the role of mutual help groups, they ask whether caring for bereaved people should incorporate externally focused political action, for example the Snowdrop campaign, (see Katz's chapter in this volume).

Small and Hockey detail the modernist approach to self-monitoring in grief, first in terms of the concept of the 'good death' (e.g. Kellehear 1990; Bradbury 1999), and then in terms of 'anticipatory grief'. They demonstrate how both of these evolved out of theoretical expositions, then to become prescriptive patterns of practice. The impact of legitimated discourses of this kind, they argue, could also be applied to Ariès's (1981) claims that discussion of death was unacceptable for a hundred years and Armstrong's (1987) (and Simpson's 1979) observations about when this trend was reversed.

Small and Hockey then move on to consider how practices of bereavement counselling have changed and indeed been re-invented as theoretical perspectives have evolved. Noting that these practices have been influenced by a variety of disciplines and a range of theoretical perspectives, they show, for example, that Worden's approach can be linked to both psycho-analytic and attachment theory as developed by Bowlby (1961) and Parkes (1972) (this is discussed further in Chapter 1). An example of this is the impact on large organizations, such as Cruse, which have changed their approaches to counselling training from emphasizing largely practical goals, to exploring the psychological and psychodynamic components of grieving (as described in Árnason's chapter in this volume). In addition, the site of death may also contribute to the type of bereavement counselling adopted, hospices being proactive whilst mutual help groups may be seen as reactive. Although developments in family and other systems type therapy acknow-ledge the needs of small groupings, Small and Hockey note that regardless of site or orientation, bereavement counselling is still mainly focused on the individual.

This chapter concludes with an examination of the relevance of research and notes that this has not fed into the training of those providing bereave-ment counselling and care. An alternative site of bereavement care, mutual help groups, are seen by Small and Hockey to share the professional's goals of attempting to minimize suffering, but, as described eloquently by Walter (1999), represent a counter-culture in a number of ways. It is in this setting that we find some of the most radical rethinking about the models of grief which advocated severance of the bonds between the living and dead. This chapter finishes by suggesting that bereavement has empowering dimen-sions, which are often excluded from models of grief. For example, express-ing strong emotion represents a challenge to prevailing social mores, whilst experiencing intense pain, albeit involuntarily, undermines the modernist commitment to the eradication or control of suffering.

The two illustrative chapters that follow Small and Hockey's extended discussion of bereavement care focus on the counsellors' roles in helping bereaved clients to deal with their feelings. Árnason looks at the training philosophy embedded in Cruse services and at the specific counselling tech-niques that are being taught. He describes the 'empathetic understanding', which underpins the strategies volunteer counsellors are encouraged to fol-low. Like Árnason and Komaromy and Hockey in Part I, Anderson's chap-ter on concepts of grieving examines them from the perspective of the professional providing the support. His work extends some of Currer's assertions by looking in depth at conceptions of the nature of grief through deconstructing the words and language used to describe it. He makes Raphael's conversational stages the focus of his study of how bereavement counselling acts to reconstruct grief (Raphael 1983). As a therapeutic de-vice, the so-called 'talking cure' aims to help the bereaved person 'resolve' the emotional trauma that they have suffered. By interrogating words, meta-phors and concepts employed by counsellors both in the clinical practice, as well as in the defence of their profession, this ethnographic account attempts to articulate and interpret the grieving identities of the counselled as seen from the perspective of the counselling culture.

The next three chapters in Part II focus on children. The first by Jeanne Katz examines perceptions of appropriate services for bereaved children in educational settings, and explores how children of different ages who have experienced different kinds of loss vary in their needs. Suggestions are made about how to redress the dearth of loss and bereavement education for teachers. Jean Simons also looks at children and loss, but from the perspective of parents and other relatives bereaved of a child. Her chapter chronicles the development of the Child Death Helpline and the kinds of issues confronted by volunteers counselling the callers.

Having interviewed a cluster of parents who had been bereaved in a variety of ways, Jo Heslop examines the ways in which children's memories can be sustained through death ritual. She describes the annual candle service set up in Liverpool, which enables families to celebrate their memories of their children, a form of commemoration that is rare for adults within British society. The service also provides a forum for parents to gather together to share their memories with one another, a stark contrast with a former imperative to 'deny' the existence of a previously living (or still-born) child – and therefore to stifle emotional expression.

In Part III of this volume we move on to consider death rituals in greater depth and here illustrative case study chapters are introduced by an extended chapter by Jenny Hockey. She explores the ways in which death rituals have changed in the twentieth century primarily amongst host populations in Western societies, so setting the scene for the subsequent accounts of selected areas of practice within the UK. These do not in any way reflect single, overarching patterns of change or dominant ideas but instead present a variety of views, each of which give an indication of change within a particular practice. Hockey's comprehensive historical account of evolving death rituals details the social, economic and environmental changes that have influenced them. She highlights the professionalization of the disposal of the dead and both secularization and the diversification of religious belief and practice.

Her starting points are the impact of two world wars and changing notions of masculinity on death rituals and, in particular, on perceptions of the decaying body. Evolving gender relations and less gender-specific attitudes towards emotional expression have gone hand in hand with a resurgence of Romantic ideology where the display of men's feelings (for whatever reason) has become more acceptable. Although Europe probably entered the twentieth century believing that the body of the deceased was the preserve of the family, Hockey supports Walter's view that the community-based grief, which had been prevalent in previous centuries, was 'revived' in public discourses throughout the course of the twentieth century. She

cites the work of Walter (1994) and Ariès (1981) who note that ownership of the body is central to the professionalization of death ritual. The
question of who owns, or has responsibility for, the body therefore begins
before death, during the dying phase, and this is exemplified in the élite
professional status of the person permitted to provide information about
the dying person to relatives or friends. Hockey suggests that ceding responsibility for the dying person (or deceased) is not necessarily problematic for families since they may be relieved to be offered expert help. In fact
handing over responsibility for the care of the dead is a new development
only insofar as the fact that contemporary experts are now 'professionals';
previously informal care was (and continues to be in many ethnic communities in the UK) professional in every sense other than economic. Hockey
traces the development of the different professionals' role and responsibilities in relation to the deceased. She notes how the responsibility for the
dying person (body) is transferred from the doctor to the undertaker and
how the clergy's previously pivotal role has been eroded.

The second half of Hockey's chapter questions the definitions of mourning and grief that have come to prevail in the second half of the twentieth
century. She contends that in contrast with the considerable body of evidence about the internal process of grief amongst Westerners, we have
only limited knowledge of their mourning practices and death rituals. She
excludes some ethnic minorities who have practised the same rituals for
millennia, for example Jewish rituals that are well documented and observable and which seek to incorporate both internal private and external public
expressions of grief. Hockey's argument, however, is not that rituals do not
exist and cannot be found in historical documentation, but that they were
not analysed in anything like the same depth or extent as psychoanalytic
work on grief. Further, they were represented very much from an outsider's
perspective, with little attempt being made to understand them from a
phenomenological perspective. Where observed emotional responses are
recorded it still remains difficult to know what someone else is actually
feeling, nor can we assume that voluble expression of emotions reflects the
same feelings in different cultures.

Hockey concludes her chapter by exploring further contradictory evidence about what constitutes death ritual. Is it simply the set of symbolic
actions and gestures that surround the period of disposal or does it include
all the events and processes which make up the dying/death period? Her
chapter questions the contemporary belief that death rituals are stark, meaningless and of short duration, instead highlighting the diversity of practices
which may not be recognized as 'death ritual', as well as acknowledging the
proliferation of more individualistic approaches to disposal.

The shorter chapters which follow this discussion describe death rituals
that have evolved to meet particular needs at the end of the twentieth
century. In some ways these chapters provide evidence for the contention

that contemporary death rituals in the host society have not adequately met the requirements of bereaved people.

Phil Gore chronicles the changing role of funeral directors and the impact of the demise of small family businesses of undertakers on the profession and, by inference, on the client population. In the past, undertakers had a role within the local community and saw respect for the dead as central to their professional integrity. Undertakers were also explicit about the content of their role; that is caring for dead bodies and arranging funerals. Even the names of the companies were sometimes explicit. I grew up in a colonial city where the main family firm of undertakers was called 'Human and Pitt' – no one was in doubt as to their function. Gore provides evidence from former employees of now extinct family firms to describe the values implicit in their interaction with clients and the explicit changes in contemporary ethos. This work confirms the views of Clark (1982) and Albery (1998) that the professionalization of this occupation has had a range of implications for mourners.

The next two chapters look at ways in which bereaved people sustain memories of the dead within the cemetery setting. Mary Bradbury's chapter focuses on memorialization in cemeteries and the ways in which mourners make decisions about how to remember their loved ones. She explores the way people are encouraged to develop their own brand of memorial. This obviously has implications for those who would have preferred the security of the 'guidance' provided by the 'benevolent' funeral director.

Doris Francis, Leonie Kellaher and Georgina Neophytou use an ethnographic approach to explore the ongoing relationship between survivors and the deceased. They interviewed 'visitors' to the cemetery to ascertain the significance that specific activities at the site of the grave had for these visitors.

The following three chapters consider different kinds of rituals in a variety of settings. Shirley Firth describes the ways in which Hindu rituals have been modified by British Hindus in an attempt to make sense of the migration experience and the changing roles of Hindu women in the UK. This chapter is reminiscent of the adaptation of Afro-Caribbean rituals as well as Greek Orthodox practices when communities are dislocated from their original locations.

The final two chapters in this book explore the way bereaved people make sense of what is perceived to be 'unnatural death'. Glennys Howarth demonstrates unrecognized manifestations of public grief in her account of families' demeanour in the coroner's court. Although coroners investigate all forms of sudden death, commonly they explore those with an accidental or violent nature. Bereaved relatives and friends use the coroner's inquest to acquire information about the causes of the death as well as to attract the sympathy of the wider public. Howarth suggests that the behaviour of mourners in the courtroom constitutes a way of making sense of a bereavement, which parallels the 'griefwork' undertaken with a counsellor or confidante.

The last chapter by Anne Eyre sustains Howarth's theme – that death rituals particularly following sudden or accidental death have had to be re-invented to adapt to late twentieth century beliefs and attitudes about the appropriateness of expressions of grief. She does this through exploring the United Kingdom during the 1980s, which she terms the 'decade of disasters'. She examines the various kinds of death rituals that grew up in the wake of these disasters, and particularly the interrelationship between the support provided for the mourners and the form that rituals took. The practical implications of mass disasters are considerable and before the 1980s few 'disaster plans' were available. As a result, responses were *ad hoc* and for many bereaved people quite inadequate. The psychological implications for those providing the support were also not anticipated and by the end of the century it became apparent that this too has concomitant issues.

The contributors to this book come from diverse academic and practitioner backgrounds, including anthropology, sociology, social policy, social work, nursing and funeral directing. We have brought this rich diversity of experience together in order to provide readers with an opportunity to consider many different perspectives in relation to the impact of loss. We have striven to demonstrate the relevance of theory to practice and hope that readers will find both the theoretical debates and practical examples stimulating and useful.

References

Albery, N. (1998) *What a Way to Go*. School of Health and Social Welfare, in conjunction with the BBC, radio programme July.

Ariès, P. (1981) *The Hour of Our Death*. London: Allen Lane.

Armstrong, D. (1987) Silence and truth in death and dying. *Social Science and Medicine*, 24: 651–7.

Bowlby, J. (1961) Processes of mourning. *International Journal of Psychoanalysis*, 42: 317–40.

Bradbury, M. (1999) *Representations of Death*. London: Routledge.

Clark, D. (1982) *Between Pulpit and Pew*. Cambridge: Cambridge University Press.

Corr, C.A., Nabe, C.M. and Corr, D.M. (1997) *Death and Dying, Life and Living*. Pacific Grove, CA: Brooks/Cole.

Currer, C. (in press) *Responding to Grief: Dying, Bereavement and Social Care*. London: Palgrave.

Dunn, D. (1985) *Elegies*. London: Faber and Faber.

Elias, N. (1991) On human beings and their emotions: a process-sociological essay, in M. Featherstone, M. Hepworth and B.S. Turner (eds) *The Body: Social Process and Cultural Theory*. London: Sage.

Freud, S. (1917) Mourning and melancholia, in J. Strachey (ed.) *The Standard Edition of the Complete Psychological Works of Sigmund Freud,* Vol. 14. London: Hogarth Press and Institute of Psycho-Analysis.

Gorer, G. (1965) *Death, Grief and Mourning in Contemporary Britain.* London: Cresset Press.

Janis, I.L. and Leventhal, H. (1965) Psychological aspects of physical illness and hospital care, in *Handbook of Clinical Psychology.* New York: McGraw-Hill.

Kellehear, A. (1990) *Dying of Cancer: The Final Year of Life,* Reading: Harwood Academic Publisher.

Kübler-Ross, E. (1969) *On Death and Dying.* New York: Macmillan.

Lindemann, E. (1944) Symptomatology and management of acute grief. *American Journal of Psychiatry,* 101: 141–8.

Lupton, D. (1998) *The Emotional Self: A Sociocultural Exploration.* London: Sage.

Mitford, J. (1963) *The American Way of Death.* New York: Simon and Schuster.

Parkes, C.M. (1972) *Bereavement.* Harmondsworth: Penguin.

Parkes, C.M. (1998) Introduction, in C.M. Parkes and A. Markus (eds) *Coping with Loss.* London: BMJ Books.

Payne, S., Horn, S. and Relf, M. (1999) *Loss and Bereavement.* Buckingham: Open University Press.

Raphael, B. (1983) *The Anatomy of Bereavement.* New York: Basic Books.

Simpson, J.A. and Wiener, E.S.C. (1989) *The Oxford English Dictionary,* 2nd edn. Oxford: Clarendon Press.

Simpson, M. (1979) *Dying, Death and Grief: A Critical Bibliography.* New York: Plenum.

Stroebe, M. and Schut, H. (1998) Culture and grief. *Bereavement Care,* 17(1): 7–11.

Walter, T. (1994) *The Revival of Death.* London: Routledge.

Walter, T. (1999) *On Bereavement: The Culture of Grief.* Buckingham: Open University Press.

Worden, J.W. (1991) *Grief Counselling and Grief Therapy: A Handbook for the Mental Health Practitioner,* 2nd edn. New York: Springer.

PART I

Theories of grief:
a critical review

NEIL SMALL

> No shortage of explanations for life's mysteries. Explanations are two a
> penny these days. The truth, however, is altogether harder to find
> (Salman Rushdie 1999: 74)

Introduction

Procrustes welcomed any guest to his home. But if they did not fit his guest
bed they were either stretched if they were too short or, if they were too
tall, they were cut down to size. Philosopher Thomas Nagel asked, 'What is
it like to be a bat?' He argued that while we can understand how bats fly,
how they do not bump into the walls of their caves and so on (we can even
try and harness bat technology to our human ends), what we do not know
is what it is like to see the world as a bat (see Nagel 1987). Together, this
ancient Greek and twentieth-century academic offer a warning to those
who would build models and seek to fit people into them (see Wortman
and Silver 1989).

While there are dangers in assuming we can incorporate experience into
neat models or convenient analogies we should not go to the other extreme
of believing that we can never even approach the experience of another.
Baudrillard (1990), for example, argues for the impossibility of considering
death. His case is that you can only conceive of death from the perspective
of an onlooker and nobody can be with you, looking on, when you are
dead. Postmodern relativism of this kind can go too far. While it is true
(but trite) to say that we cannot know death, we can certainly look on
dying and bereavement with the knowledge that all of us will experience
both of them, Further, we know that we will experience them within a
specific social context.

In this chapter I tread a fine line between modernist model building and postmodern relativism as I examine the emergence of theoretical understandings of the grief process. Dominant views have changed over time. These changes illustrate, and contribute to, wider social changes. Indeed the emergence of the 'continuing bonds' (Klass *et al.* 1996) model is overtly linked by its proponents to a crisis in modernity. While this degree of theoretical self-consciousness is rare, I argue that the ways different understandings come to prominence is always linked with changes at the level of the social.

Subjectivity and social practices

Borrowing from Raphael (1983) we can define loss as the state of being deprived of, or being without, something one has had. Grief is the pain and suffering experienced after loss; mourning is a period of time during which signs of grief are made visible; and bereavement is the process of losing a close relationship. This chapter, and Part I of the book, is concerned with how the feelings of grief and loss associated with bereavement following a death have been understood. As such its concern is predominately with emotionality. The ways in which that emotionality generates action are examined in the second part of the book whilst the cultural, ostensibly time-bound, phenomenon of mourning will be considered in Part III. While the structure of this book mirrors the divisions between inner emotion and outer behaviour it also considers some of the problems and limitations of making this 'commonsense' division. For example, as this chapter outlines, the terms grief and mourning have been used interchangeably, mourning referring both to an emotional process and formal rituals for the expression of grief. This chapter therefore questions the way 'inner' feelings and 'outer' behaviours have been differentiated and argues that bereavement and grief also need to be understood culturally in that the physical, spiritual and intellectual effects of bereavement and grief are manifest in a cultural context. Further, it is our culture that provides the resources through which we make sense of, or theorize, our emotional reactions to loss. There is, therefore, a complex and reflexive relationship between emotionality, subjectivity and social practice.

When we look at the different ways in which feelings of grief and the experience of bereavement have been conceptualized, not surprisingly, we can see a reflection of the dominant explanatory construct we have lived within, that of modernity. Modernity builds on the twin pillars of reason and progress. It is the child of the Enlightenment and is exemplified in the search to study, write down, see connections and aim for the all embracing explanation. The earliest examples of this new approach to understanding human beings in society was found in the 28 volumes of Diderot's *Encyclopaedia*, published between 1751 and 1772, the work that to some degree 'replaced the word divine with the word social' (Bierstedt 1978: 18).

But within modernist theory the historically or culturally distant have always been made an exception. The belief that they did things differently then, or that they do things differently there, has been preserved by being assigned to the category of 'the exotic'. In this chapter universalism is critiqued and a plea for the more widespread acceptance of difference is made. Indeed, although an examination of grief allows us an insight into 'just how deeply social arrangements penetrate into private emotion: just how moulded by culture and history even intimate internal experiences may be' (Lofland 1985: 172), it also allows us to recognize how far grief can open up fissures in the modern. These fissures reveal both individual narratives of grief and opposition to the conventional. It is in the domain of fiction, crime fiction in particular, that we are made aware that we do not know what goes on behind our next door neighbour's curtains, or what thoughts pass through the mind of the ordinary-looking person down the street. It is this mystery, this acceptance of the strangeness of the apparently familiar, that we should bring to bear on others' experience of grief and bereavement. It is in allowing exoticism nearer home that we best understand the experience of grief. If we do this then we can approach bereavement not as a prompt for 'tasks' or as a 'problem' but as part of the sociality of our existence.

Stages in the development of a discourse on death and dying

Systematic research on death and dying appeared in the aftermath of the Second World War. Until then there had been anthropological accounts of death customs in 'primitive' societies (Tylor 1871; Frazer 1890; Hertz 1907; Van Gennep 1909; Durkheim 1912) and there had been an exploration of death by Freud (1917) and others of the psychoanalytic school, in part prompted by the mass death of the First World War. Isolated articles and books had considered the need for a social psychology of bereavement (Eliot 1933) and had considered aspects of the care of the dying (Worcester 1935). However, by the 1950s, as Benoliel argues:

> In the aftermath of war, interest in death and dying as subjects for scientific investigation was stimulated by a number of factors: the rapid expansion of organized sciences and societal funded research; the appearance of the mental health movement with a central focus on suicide prevention; a depersonalization of many aspects of human existence associated with new technologies; and a powerful death anxiety that has been attributed to the use of atomic weapons at Hiroshima and Nagasaki.
>
> (Benoliel 1994: 4)

Benoliel offers a periodization of the modernist emergence of death and dying as a field of enquiry. (For reviews of this period see also Walter 1993 and Miles and Demi 1994.) She identifies four phases of development between 1940 and 1990. I offer a fifth phase, taking us to the present day. I have also added some events and publications not included in her review but noted by other chroniclers. To break things down into phases risks underplaying the continuity evident in some areas across the second half of the century, for example a continuing and developing concern with sociological approaches, or a development of practice-led initiatives, or of self-help group development. There is also a danger in a history of events and dates that they come to represent the wrong thing. For example Clark (1998) has pointed out that the opening of the first modern hospice, St Christopher's, in 1967 was not the start of something but a significant point along a journey that had begun in the time-consuming preparatory work that Cicely Saunders and supporters had been undertaking during the previous 20 years. Clark also reminds us that we need to look at developments in fields adjacent to that of death and dying. Specifically, the development of the understanding of the physiological/neurological nature of pain and the development of more effective means of responding to it were necessary preconditions for much of the scholarship of death and dying as well as service development in hospices and palliative care (Clark 1999). Without the means to control this pervasive symptom, considerations of say, existential or relational aspects of dying would have appeared less relevant.

1940–60: Opening the field

In the 1940s there were pioneering studies, notably Anthony (1940) on children's awareness of death and Lindemann (1944) on acute grief processes in the survivors of a nightclub fire. Wass and Neimeyer locate the 'grounding of thanatology in Lindemann's (1944) investigation of the impact of the Coconut Grove fire on the Boston community' (Wass and Neimeyer 1995: 440). In the 1950s there were three main areas of advance: first, a critical perspective exemplified in Gorer's work on the avoidance of death (1955); second, empirical studies like that of Marris (1958) on London widows; third, Feifel's (1959) contribution that legitimized work on death, via an appeal to its multidisciplinary relevance and potential for empirical verification.

1960–70: Service development, disciplinary progress and informal networks

This period was characterized by an expansion of concern about the care of dying people. Hinton (1967), Saunders (1969), Kübler-Ross (1969) and Quint (1969) all made lasting impacts on service provision and on the views of service providers, doctors and nurses in particular in the case of the later two. St Christopher's, the first modern hospice opened in London in 1967. Innovations in bereavement care included, in the UK, Margaret Torrie's Cruse Bereavement Care, the first national organization for widows and their children, set up in 1959 (Torrie 1970). Phyllis Silverman set up Widow-to-Widow in Boston in 1967 (see review in Lieberman and Borman (1979) on emerging self-help movements). These developments are also discussed in more detail in Part II of this volume.

In 1961 Bowlby published work on the process of mourning (Bowlby 1961), which looked back to Marris's study of widows (1958, see also Marris 1974 on loss and change). Gorer's 1955 article on death avoidance was made more widely available in 1965. Glaser and Strauss (1965; 1968) and Fulton and Bendiksen (1965) contributed from sociology. There were also emerging contacts between academics and practitioners, such as those recognized and fostered by Kalish and Kastenbaum via a newsletter started in 1966, which became the journal *Omega* in 1970.

1970–80: Formalization of networks and building on the past

The International Work Group on Death and Dying was set up, with an international membership, following a meeting in Columbia, Maryland, USA, in 1974. The Forum on Death Education and Counselling (later the Association) was set up soon after and the National Hospice Organization was formed in the USA in 1978. There were also many more meetings and conferences with themes related to death and dying.

Parkes published research-based work on widows in 1970 and on the psychology of grief in 1972, building on the contribution of Bowlby. Shneidman (1973) and Becker (1973) continued to develop thanatology. Lofland (1976) and Fulton and Bendiksen (1976) continued the developing contribution from sociology, as did Kastenbaum and Aisenberg from psychology (1972). Even at this stage there were historical works on the emerging movement, notably Stoddard (1978) on hospice.

1980–90: Expansion of ideas but concern about impact

In this period there was an expansion into the areas of ethical and legal concerns. In the US standards and certification for death education and counselling were established and journals (*Omega* and *Death Studies*) flourished. There was, though, a recognition that all this scholarship was not making inroads on aspects of countervailing power, both within the professions and public opinion. For example medical education, hospital procedures and practices and a culture in which medicine was expected to endeavour to save lives were all proceeding in a direction other than that consistent with the scholarship of death and dying (see Benoliel 1988a, 1988b).

1990s revival of death and continuing bonds

Benoliel finishes her periodization in 1990 but we are fortunately well served with review work, at least as regards the British situation where British sociology engaged with death and Walter (1993) summarized its achievement. Walter was a contributor to Clark's volume that, in itself, represented a new emergence of an interest in death and dying in British sociology (Clark 1993). That volume included papers presented at what became a regular Symposium on Death, Dying and Bereavement. *Mortality*, the first European journal of death studies, began in 1996. A specific concern with the 'continuing bonds' thesis of Walter, Klass, Silverman and Nickman emerged in 1996 and continued at least to the end of the decade with Walter's *On Bereavement* (1999), which located the continuing bonds position in a wider consideration of the culture of grief.

Theory, research, models of practice

In this section two interrelated aspects of the response to bereavement will be examined. First, the development of a theoretical system, including the adaptation of psychoanalytic understandings and the development of 'stage' theories. Second, the accumulation of research evidence about patterns of bereavement.

Theoretical systems: Psychoanalysis, attachment theory and stage/task theories

Psychoanalysis

Freud saw grief as something that would free the ego from attachment to the deceased and, in so doing, allow new attachments to be formed. Silverman and Klass (1996) claim that this is a formulation that Freud arrived at via the selective use of the data available to him. In effect they argue that there was a difference between Freud's theories and his own experience of grief. Silverman and Klass (1996: 7) read into those of Freud's letters that describe his own bereavement experiences a realization that he could not cut old attachments and form new ones. In privileging this reading Silverman and Klass elevate the letters to the status of 'truth' apparently on the grounds that they encompass the subjective. In effect they are suggesting that what we say we feel is more truthful than what we say we think, and that their interpretation of the life should subvert the truth claims of the work.

Foucault's opposition to the idea of consistency, of there being an oeuvre, and his opposition to a primacy of human consciousness is relevant here (Smart 1985: 38). Rather than seek to demote one sort of idea because it appears inconsistent with what Silverman and Klass see as the higher truth of subjective experience, spoken autobiographically, Foucault would have us ask why one reading has been privileged and whose interests does this reading serve (Foucault 1977)?

There are two main approaches to understanding grief and bereavement that continue the Freudian tradition. The first, and particularly pertinent for a UK psychoanalytic tradition that looks to Melanie Klein, is projective identification; that is, the attribution to others of things properly belonging to the self (Hinshelwood 1994: 83). The second is attachment theory, which is considered below.

Klass and Silverman, and other critics of the Freudian prescription of cutting the bond with the deceased so that new attachments can be formed, underemphasize the sense of the positive associated with the Freudian model. This includes the process of overcoming denial of the loss and hence enriching the self. To summarize, simply to talk about letting go and moving on, which is the way the critics of Freud précis his position, does not do justice to the idea of resolution presented by the Freud and then developed by others from within the psychoanalytic school.

Steiner identified Freud in *Mourning and Melancholia* (1917) as describing: 'The process of mourning in beautiful detail, and emphasise that in the work of mourning it is the reality of the loss which has so painfully to be faced. In the process every memory connected with the bereaved is gone over and reality testing applied to it until gradually the full force of the loss is appreciated' (Steiner 1993: 34).

This does not mean cutting off in the way Silverman and Klass seem to assume. It is the use of the word 'reality' that is problematic here. It does not, when used in the Freudian sense, mean cutting yourself off and getting on with things. Rather it means recognizing which aspects of yourself you had located in the now dead person, taking these back into yourself and so being able to both know better what is you and to know what attributes really belong with the dead person:

> As reality is applied to each of the memories of the lost object what has to be faced is the painful recognition of what belongs to the object and what belongs to the self. It is through the detailed work of mourning that these differentiations are made and in the process the lost object is seen more realistically and the previously disowned parts of the self are gradually acknowledged as belonging to the self.
>
> (Steiner 1996: 1077)

Steiner (1993: 35–6) offers the example of Melanie Klein's writings as illustrative of this post-Freudian position. In 1940 she published an article, which included a case summary of Mrs A, whose son had died. Mrs A's early reactions were of feeling numb and closed up, wishing to deny the reality of her loss. Subsequently a dream allowed her to both see her true feelings but also to disentangle this loss from the death in childhood of her own brother. A further dream helped her understand how her son's death had made her fearful of her own. But she realised she could, and would, go on living and this meant that she could accept the event of the death free of the entanglements of her own fears and fantasies (Klein 1940). Hence, what one is freed of is not the person who has died but the projective identification we have lodged in them, that is the parts of our self we have allowed them to act out for us. We have to re-own those parts so we can properly relate to the person who has died.

If we go back to Silverman and Klass's suggestion that Freud as a person experienced things that as a psychoanalytic writer he could not allow into his paradigm, Grosskurth's (1986) comments on the case study of Mrs A are instructive. Melanie Klein wrote the paper, which was published in 1940, shortly after she had lost her own son in a mountaineering accident. It is clear that the Mrs A of the paper was, in fact, herself. As with Freud, Klein saw as the fundamental cause of melancholia (or depression) the loss of a love object. 'Both in children and adults suffering from depression, I have discovered the dread of harbouring dying or dead objects (especially the parents) inside one and an identification of the ego with objects in this condition' (Klein 1935: 266). But if one can be more in touch with external reality then it is possible to relate to the other as apart from the self in a way that allows feelings like relief and hope (see Weatherill 1998: 44).

Psychoanalysis uses language in a special way. We have to approach psychoanalysis on its own linguistic terms – 'reality' and 'loss' are not used in the way they are used in general communication and to respond as if they are makes psychoanalysis appear to be advocating a crude 'forget the dead person and get on with life' approach, which it is not.

Attachment theory

The attachment theory of grief, developed by John Bowlby, was central to his attempts to revise psychoanalytic theory and has been hugely influential in developing understanding of grief and loss. Bowlby, working both in the Tavistock Institute in London and as a consultant to the World Health Organization on the needs of homeless children, based much of his work on the observation of children. This was a different approach to the Freudian or Kleinian perspectives, which engaged with psychic trauma in the internal world. Much of his theory developed from observation of children's sep-aration, in stressful circumstances, from their mothers. James Robertson had observed children in short- and long-term residential nurseries and in hospital children's wards. His resulting stage theory saw children responding with protest, despair and then denial (also called detachment) (see, for example, Robertson 1958). Bowlby's attachment theory replicated these stages and linked them with the central problems of psychoanalytic theory. That is, protest can be linked to separation anxiety, despair to grief and mourning and detachment to defence (Bowlby 1973: 27). Essentially Bowlby's theory of bereavement is an extension of his theory of separation anxiety. He saw the psychological response to the trauma of separation as something biologically programmed, just as we physiologically respond to trauma. For example:

> Following Darwin, Bowlby sees the facial expressions and crying of the bereaved as a resultant of the tendency to scream in the hope of awakening the attention of the negligent care-giver. . . . This is then an evolutionary view (not the teleological view of Freud in which the survivor detaches memories and hopes from dead).
>
> (Holmes 1993: 91)

Bowlby categorizes four phases of mourning: numbness; yearning, searching and anger; disorganization and despair; and, reorganization. These stages are seen as occurring successively and, as such, they suggest a possible blueprint for those who wish to offer help to the bereaved. A model of the 'work of grief' was developing.

Bowlby sought to separate healthy mourning from features indicative of pathology. His work on mourning was prompted by reading Marris's 1958 study of how widows responded to the loss of their husband and then realizing that these responses were similar to those he and Robertson has reported in young children separated from their mother:

> This led me to a systematic study of the literature on mourning, especially the mourning of healthy adults. The sequence of events that commonly occur, it became clear, was very different from what clinical theorists had been assuming . . . The clearer the picture of mourning responses in adults became, the clearer became their similarities to the responses observed in childhood.
>
> (Bowlby 1988: 32)

The mistakes of the previous theorists, he identified, included their belief that mourning in mentally healthy individuals does not last more than six months and that anger, disbelief and a tendency to search for the lost person in the hope of reunion are not, in themselves, indicative of pathology but can be components of healthy mourning. Bowlby's assumptions and beliefs were subsequently supported by research undertaken from the Tavistock Clinic in London by Colin Murray Parkes (1972) and by other research studies (Kliman 1965; Maddison and Walker 1967; Furman 1974; Raphael 1982).

By 1979 Bowlby was considering whether the term mourning should be replaced by grieving (Bowlby 1979: 91). In part this was an attempt to create some distance from the specific analytic understanding of mourning – to overcome some of the confusion created when analytic terms were transposed into popular usage, as described above. In part the shift in terminology was also designed to emphasize the internal world of grief as opposed to the social manifestation of mourning.

The capacity for healthy grieving, according to Bowlby, was shaped by childhood experience. Specifically, it was shaped by the extent to which attachment behaviour had been regarded sympathetically as opposed to it being something to be grown out of as quickly as possible. Indeed the experience of a positive attachment experience allows the necessary first expressions of feelings. Bowlby believed that one should encourage the bereaved, in Shakespeare's words, to 'give sorrow words'.[1] In the process it is:

> Both unnecessary and unhelpful to cast ourselves in the role of a [representative of reality] ... our role should be that of companion and supporter, prepared to explore in our discussions all the hopes and wishes and dim unlikely possibilities that he still cherishes, together with all the reproaches and the disappointments that inflict him ... Yearning for the impossible, intemperate anger, impotent weeping, horror at the prospect of loneliness, pitiful pleading for sympathy and support – these are the feelings that a bereaved person needs to express, and sometimes first to discover, if he is to make progress.
>
> (Bowlby 1979: 94–6)

Colin Murray Parkes, who found himself arriving at the same understandings as Bowlby's *vis-à-vis* grief, augmented the impact of attachment theory by contributing research study data. He reported from three studies, now known as the Bethlem, the London and the Harvard studies. The first involved four male and 17 female bereaved patients at the Bethlem Royal and Maudsley Hospitals in London (Parkes 1965). The second was of 22 London widows under the age of 65 (Parkes 1970). A third study involved US collaborators and presented data on 41 widows and 19 widowers, all under the age of 45 (Glick *et al.* 1974; Parkes and Weiss 1983). These studies, in turn, offered insight into non-typical and typical forms of reaction to bereavement and explored why some people come through bereavement unscathed while others exhibit physical or mental illness.

Parkes's research data, alongside clinical material and observation, led him to identify grief as:

> a process and not a state. Grief is not a set of symptoms which start after a loss and then gradually fade away. It involves a succession of clinical pictures which blend into and replace one another ... numbness, the first phase, gives way to pining, and pining to disorganisation and despair, and it is only after the stage of disorganisation that recovery occurs. Hence, at any particular time a person may show one of four quite different clinical pictures.
>
> (Parkes 1986: 27)

Parkes has continued to refine his understanding and approach. He has revisited questions about those factors that precipitate breakdown after bereavement. He has engaged with the impact of different types of loss, for example traumatic bereavement. He has looked at cultural difference (Parkes *et al.* 1996); and has explored in more detail considerations as to the changes in one's assumptive world and social self (Parkes 1996: Ch 7). In so doing he has addressed a number of the areas of criticism that have been directed at his approach.

Parkes argues that the concepts of 'anticipatory grief' and 'grief work' have been misunderstood in much the same way as have his phases of grief. 'Critics such as Wortman and Silver (1989) have elaborated these misunderstandings into an attack on the supposed 'Myths of coping with Loss', ignoring the fact that few authorities at work in the field believe in the 'myths' as stated by them' (Parkes 1996: xiii).

Nonetheless, as Walter has identified, there remains an identifiable 'clinical lore', which many working with the bereaved look to, and which all too readily takes Parkes's nuanced reading and transmutes it into a fixed sequence through which every bereaved person must pass in order to recover from bereavement (Walter 1999: 161–2). While this (mis) reading of Parkes should not detract from his contribution it does suggest the omnipresence of the modernist project that transmutes tentative, qualified hypothesis into systems of interventions applicable to all.

It is of particular interest here, as we consider aspects of the intellectual history of responses to bereavement in the context of prevailing social systems of thought, that we look at the sense of misunderstanding and controversy which Parkes identifies in more detail. Attachment theory has been widely translated into popular beliefs about the importance of bonding with one's child and planning for separation. Likewise, in relation to grief, there are popular understandings gleaned from attachment theorists. These include the need to express emotion ('not to bottle things up') and the sense that one will move on, and past, the initial stages of reaction (you will 'put this behind you' as 'time becomes the great healer'). In the transition from the esoteric world of attachment theory into public understanding, the nuanced position argued by Parkes and others gets incorporated into the dominant paradigm. Hence the essentially reflexive and indicative ideas of Parkes and others become universal and prescriptive. The critics, including Wortman and Silver, appear then to be criticizing one of two things, the reading of the followers rather than the words of the founders or a sense of the theories predisposition to be misinterpreted in a particular way. In either case their objections have to be considered as part of the same modernist world view that shaped the theories and determined the form in which they moved out from their founders.

Stage and task approaches

In the late 1960s and early 1970s there were a number of stage theories of dying and bereavement (Littlewood 1993: 71–2). They were, in the main, acontextual and all risked easy translation into prescriptive devices.

These stage theories included Averill (1968) who identified shock, despair and recovery as the stages of grief. Kübler-Ross's analysis (1969) relates not to the grief that occurs after a death but to the adjustment of people as they contemplate their own death. However, the five progressive stages of denial, anger, bargaining, depression and finally acceptance have been applied to bereavement.

Parkes (1972) identified numbness, pining, depression and recovery as the relevant stages that followed the loss of a loved person. Grief work, in Parkes's approach, has three components:

1 A preoccupation with thoughts of the lost person, which derives from the urge to search for that person.
2 Painful repetitious recollection of the loss experience. This 'worry work' must occur if the loss is not fully accepted as irrevocable.
3 The attempt to make sense of the loss and either fit it into one's prevailing assumptive world or modify that world accordingly (Parkes 1986: 95)

Worden (1982) recommended to the 'mental health practitioner' that we think in terms of tasks of mourning rather than stages or phases. There were four such tasks:

1 To accept the reality of the loss.
2 To work through the pain of grief.
3 To adjust to an environment in which the deceased is missing.
4 To emotionally relocate the deceased and move on with life.

Others have advocated a concern with process rather than task. Rando (1993) sees the shortcoming of a task-based approach as being the reliance on end points, rather than process measures, that is, an ongoing attempt to understand and assess the 'grief work' being engaged in by a bereaved person and their therapist. Her work is oriented to the 'treatment' of problematic mourning as well as to help understand healthy mourning. There are six processes in Rando's account:

1 Recognize the loss.
2 React to the separation.
3 Recollect and re-experience the deceased and the relationship.
4 Relinquish the old attachments to the deceased and the old assumptive world.
5 Readjust and move adaptively into the new world without forgetting the old.
6 Reinvest.

For Rando each of these processes must be undertaken for healthy mourning. But they need not be experienced in the sequential way the listing above suggests. The processes are 'interrelated and tend to build on one another, (although) a number of them may occur simultaneously . . . Mourners may move back and forth among the processes, with such movement illustrating the non-linear and fluctuating course of mourning' (Rando 1993: 44).

Kübler-Ross and Parkes in particular came to have a key place in shifting the discourse of bereavement into the nexus of service development that we see alongside the model building we are describing here. The development of bereavement care is the subject of Chapter 6 but here we can note Kübler-Ross's impact on both nurse and doctor education (see Field 1984; 1986) and the impact Parkes had on bereavement care. Walter argues that his 'understanding of the psychology of grief provides the knowledge base for the British bereavement counselling movement' (Walter 1993: 283). It is the shift from insight into prescription that accompanied the work of Kübler-Ross and Parkes that is of most interest to the argument being developed here. Likewise, in the context of what became the institutionalization of innovation, we will see in Chapter 6 a corresponding observable shift 'from poetics to practice' (see James 1994). It is a process also observed in relation to hospice care and described, in Weberian terms, by James and Field (1991) as the routinization of charisma. (See also Walters's formulation of 'clinical lore' (1999: 106–8).)

The end result of the interplay of theory and practice is a problematic summarized in Samarel (1995) in relation to Kübler-Ross. It serves as a general warning about stage theories.

The stage theory is descriptive in nature but has been treated as prescriptive. That is, some health care professionals have abused the theory by attempting to force patients to move from one stage to the next according to an imposed schedule. Moreover, the prescriptive view of the dying process interprets the final stage of acceptance as the universally desired outcome for all dying individuals. It is interesting that this expectation exists despite Kübler-Ross's repeated assertions that progression through the various stages is not necessarily linear and may not be rushed and that not all people experience all stages.

(Samarel 1995: 94–5)

There are other reservations about stage and task approaches, not least the implication that there is an ending, a time when these are done with. Corr *et al.* (1997) warn of the conceptual and linguistic pitfalls of such approaches:

to recover from one's grief seems to suggest grief is a bad situation like an illness or disease. It also seems to imply that once one is recovered or 'healed' one is essentially unchanged by the experience. Alternatively, recovery, completion and resolution seem to suggest a fixed endpoint for mourning. If such a fixed endpoint did exist, once it was reached one would then be over and done with mourning . . . Finally adaptation seems mainly to imply that one has made the best of a bad situation, without necessarily incorporating the changes or the development of new ways of functioning that are essential in productive mourning and that may lead to personal growth.

(Corr *et al.* 1997: 239)

Stroebe and Schut (1995) offer another process model, this time a 'dual process' one. It appears not to succumb to the pitfalls identified by Corr *et al.* The emphasis is on coping and on dynamic processes oscillating between loss-oriented and restoration-oriented concerns. The balance of emphasis can, and will, change over time and the model allows for differing cultural emphases. That is, some cultures may emphasize loss over restoration. The model incorporates a sense that restoration means not a return to the pre-death way of living but to a new way of living with the loss.

That way of living can be described using either the language of the emotions or the findings of research:

when mourning has been completed, the mourner comes to feel the inner presence of the loved one, no longer an idealised hero or a maligned villain, but a presence with human dimensions. Lost irreversibly in objective time, the person is present in a new form within one's mind and heart, tenderly present in inner time without the pain and bitterness of death. And once the loved one has been accepted in this way he or she can never again be forcefully removed.

(Cantor 1978: 66–67 quoted in Corr *et al.* 1997: 241)

Research into bereaved families seven to nine years after the death of a child (McClowry *et al.* 1987) identified three strategies used to deal with the 'empty space' in their lives:

1 getting over it – putting their grief behind them;
2 filling the emptiness – usually by 'keeping busy';
3 keeping the connection – often done by cherishing vivid memories and stories about the deceased child.

There is a sense of a developing new orthodoxy that elevates the third of McClowry's strategies. This will be considered in more detail here and in Chapter 6. We have to recognize that this new orthodoxy will shape both popular applications and professional practice, so producing a discursive form that exercises influence over the messy world of ambiguity and oscillation that is the bereavement experience. Just as a prevailing orthodoxy of 'getting over it' shaped the encounter between the bereaved person and those offering help to him or her, so too will a belief in the efficacy of 'keeping the connection'. When these orthodoxies are considered in terms of their discursive power, it does not matter that one approach appears more emotionally acceptable than another. Indeed liberality, warmth or tolerance may be more difficult to step outside of than a more rigid sense of the proper.

Littlewood wonders if the best that can be hoped for is that:

> people who have been bereaved may begin to consider new ritual ex-
> pressions of grief appropriate to themselves and to their immediate
> mourning group. It can be hoped too that people outside of those
> groups will welcome this change rather than try to deny it or associate
> it with rituals of the past.
>
> (Littlewood 1993: 82)

It is these possibilities for devising one's own narrative of grief that suggest the potential of postmodernism and this will be explored below.

Continuing bonds

I have introduced above the criticisms made by Klass *et al. vis-à-vis* Freud's
formulations and have suggested that a new model for understanding bereavement is emerging, one that emphasizes the maintenance of continuing
bonds as opposed to disengagement. This new model is presented in Klass
et al.'s *Continuing Bonds* (1996) and Walter's (1996) 'new model of grief'.
This model has antecedents. Even in recent literature we can see the work
of Corr and colleagues and Stroebe and colleagues exploring some similar
areas. But the scope of Klass *et al.* and Walter's thesis (and the synergy
created by the proximity of their publications) mean that we are seeing an
attempt to not only critique established belief but replace it with a new
formulation. A paragraph early in Klass *et al.* underlines the far reaching
nature of the project they are engaged in:

> The implication of our new understanding of grief goes further than
> the fact that people maintain a relationship to the deceased or absent
> birth parent. It requires that we look at the way we see relationships in
> general in our society. We need to bring into our professional dialogue
> the reality of how people experience and live their lives, rather than
> finding ways of verifying preconceived theories of how people should
> live.
>
> (Klass *et al.* 1996: xix)

Klass and colleagues are seeking to acknowledge, and build on, two
interrelated factors.

1 An emerging consensus among bereavement scholars that our understanding of the grief process needs to be expanded.
2 A recognition in their own practice, prompted in part by working with
  people from different cultures or people who have experienced different
  sorts of losses (for example adopted children experiencing the loss of
  their birth parents), that existing models were inadequate.

In pursuing the consequences of these observations they are also addressing the broad context of cultural belief and practice. Specifically, they are
asking if the dominant understanding of people's reactions to bereavement
is based on the cultural values of modernity, rather than on any substantial
data relating to what people actually do. Finally, they are suggesting that
the new model is supported by a research paradigm that utilizes reflexivity
and narrative. Klass *et al.* begin from their professional practice experience.

> It appeared that what we were observing was not a stage of disengage-
> ment, which we were educated to expect, but rather, we were observ-
> ing people altering and then continuing their relationship to the lost or
> dead person. Remaining connected seemed to facilitate both adults'
> and children's ability to cope with the loss and the accompanying
> changes in their lives. These 'connections' provided solace, comfort
> and support, and eased the transition from the past to the future.
>
> (Klass *et al.* 1996: xviii)

Walter arrives at a similar point, although his starting point is his reflections on his personal experience of the death of friends and family. In a
review of Klass *et al.* (1996), Walter states:

> The fashionable idea that the purpose of grief is to detach from the
> deceased and move on is based neither on research nor clinical experi-
> ence, but on the western cultural value of autonomy. The studies
> reported in this volume present overwhelming evidence that, though
> some bereaved people do indeed cut their bonds, many do not. They
> continue to relate to the dead, sustaining an ongoing bond that is not
> static . . . but is continually evolving.
>
> (Walter 1997: 173)

Klass *et al.* are arguing that models based on disengagement chose to
exclude experiences which were inconsistent with the view that for successful mourning to take place the bereaved person should disengage from the
deceased and let go of the past. It was not that such experiences were absent,
rather they did not fit into the prevailing orthodoxy and were dispensed with.
This is the Procrustes approach discussed earlier in this chapter. Experience
is distorted to fit models rather than models being questioned in the light of
experience. It is in ways such as these that self-referring systems of belief
and practice are created (see Lipstadt 1994: 27). There is a danger, of course,
that the approaches of Klass *et al.* and Walter, which, in their turn, emphasize that a 'healthy resolution of grief enables one to maintain a continuing
bond with the deceased' and 'the purpose of grief is . . . the construction of
a durable biography that enables the living to integrate the memory of the
dead into their ongoing lives', will become a new orthodoxy. In a Procrustean
fashion, those people who present evidence of the benefits of disengagement
could find themselves at risk of exclusion.[2] There is also a danger that new

models will eventually be encompassed within the system building, generalizing metanarratives characteristic of the modernity that recent theorists set out to eschew when they speak of moving from the narrative of grief to 'how people experience and live their lives'.

Nonetheless, the new model does involve a reflexivity that allows Klass *et al.* to recognize the potential contradiction inherent in seeking to offer an approach that sidesteps the modernism which restricted previous models whilst still offering an alternative overriding theory. They suggest, however, that this contradiction is resolvable on both methodological and epistemological levels. Their approach is built on the reports of qualitative research, the voices of those experiencing grief or, in Walter's model, the use of biography. It is not based on a positivist science looking for connections, seeking to build logical systems and dispensing with different views. Walter sees it as an approach consistent with late modern society where its members must continually recreate their own identity.

Reflexivity allows the development of small narratives and contingent meanings, a characteristic of postmodernity. These are posted in opposition not only to metanarratives, which offer a standard way of explaining/understanding, but also to an idea of meaning and truth (as opposed to truths). Nonetheless such an approach itself has to be critiqued and deconstructed in the same way as modernist models are critiqued. For example, to claim the legitimacy of personal experience legitimizes asking about the assumptions the writer brings to bear. (We have seen above how, for example, Klass and Silverman attribute greater truth to 'personal writing' than to academic works by the same person.) In so doing they incur criticism of the kind Nabokov invokes in his autobiography:

> An observer makes a detailed picture of the whole universe but when he has finished realizes that it still lacks something: his own self. So he puts himself in it too. But again a 'self' remains outside, and so forth, in an endless sequence of projections.
>
> (Nabokov 1999: 254)

Nabokov, here, is not too far from Nagel with his bat or even Baudrillard arguing that you cannot be an onlooker when you consider death. Further, to espouse a hierarchy of truth with personal experience at its top does not remove this truth from the realm of discourse. My 'personal' can be just as oppressive for you as my 'science'.

The Walter/Klass *et al.* position does, nonetheless, move the discourse of bereavement in the direction that Stroebe *et al.* had already suggested when they argued for an expansion of self-reflecting dialogue and for an expansion of a sense of personal responsibility for one's assumptions and practices. Further, Stroebe *et al.* present the 'self', in this context, as a social artefact:

> One becomes aware that assumptions of health and adjustments are by-products of cultural and historical processes. Similarly, one realises

that theories of personal deficit harbour implicit systems of value, favouring certain ideals over others. More generally, theories and therapeutic practices favour certain forms of cultural patterns over others. For good or ill they move the society towards or away from certain ends.

(Stroebe *et al.* 1996: 43)

The Walter/Klass *et al.* position offers a considerable challenge to an academic orthodoxy and is likely to supplant established views because it accords with bereavement practitioners' experience (see Simons's chapter in this volume) and because it also accords with a more diffuse (late) modernity that engages with intimacy and emotion in a different way (Giddens 1992).

Consistent with this late modernity we can see within these, and other approaches, a concern to create distance from grand narratives. Klass *et al.*, for example, say 'We should not impose any requirements for what healthy grief looks like' (1996: 353). Stroebe, with Hansson and Stroebe (1993), argues for the advantages of presenting a multiplicity of perspectives concerning bereavement:

Take for, example, the finding that widowers have higher mortality rates than widows, when compared with same sex, non-bereavement controls. To explain this pattern, a psychologist would look for cognitive and behavioural response differences between the sexes, and would find them. A sociologist might analyse patterns of sex roles or male–female support systems, and find differences. A psychophysiologist might study sex hormones and identify their modulatory effect on immune effector cells. To limit explanations to those of a single discipline would preclude a full understanding of the phenomenon of bereavement

(Stroebe *et al.* 1993: 458–9)

Others would go further and suggest that just multiplying disciplinary approaches does not go far enough. It is the assumption of logic particular to disciplinarity itself that we need to question. In his novel *see under: love* David Grossman argues that logic is not good at giving us an insight into people:

The role and mission of logic in our works is to divide things into categories and connect them to each other . . . But things in themselves . . . are totally lacking in logic! And so are people . . . A mixed leaven of passion and fear, a fine world, and what is logic? Only the divider and connector between them.

(Grossman 1989: 294)

Measuring and comparing bereavements

In Part II of this book we examine the way theory has been translated into practice guides and the way organizational structures have developed. Guides and organizations can be identified as an aspect of the developing discourse of bereavement. In the present section we comment on another stage in the discursive formation – the sense that the phenomena of bereavement are measurable, and that they are amenable to being graded according to severity. The very subject, one would guess, would cause consternation to Grossman as it would to others worried about the reductionism of a Procrustes-type science. Once we begin to examine the development of scales in this area we need to concern ourselves with the way people might use them to allocate scarce resources or to dismiss the needs of some who do not seem to have severe enough problems. The concern is that the elevation of one sort of evidence, supported by one sort of researcher in whose interests its promotion lies, shapes the encounter those in need have with those able to respond to need, and shapes it in a way consistent with a top-down construction of knowledge and truth,

Hence, a criticism of studies based on scales, samples, factor analysis, Likert scales, reliability coefficients and the like can be made on the grounds of the distortion their discursive power brings to bear on the field. Or, it could be argued, that they are simply reductionist and mechanistic, seeking to bring some sort of 'scientific' measure to a domain not amenable to measurement, to a domain that has to be engaged with in its totality and not diminished or trivialized by categorization and sub-division. But attempts at measurement and comparison are also potentially flawed in their detail. An introduction to some measures is presented below, as are some of these detailed criticisms.

There are a variety of instruments designed to measure aspects of bereavement. They have different emphases, or seek to help the exploration of bereavement in different populations. They are summarized in Burnett et al. (1997) and Middleton (1998). They include the Texas Inventory of Grief (Faschingbauer et al. 1977); the Grief Experience Inventory (Sanders et al. 1979); and the Expanded Texas Inventory of Grief (Zisook and DeVaul 1984). There are scales for particular groups, the Widowhood Questionnaire (Zisook and Schuchter 1985) and a scale for the elderly devised by Lund et al. (1985). There are scales with multiple dimensions (Jacobs et al. 1987); and scales focused on grief, the Grief Resolution Index of Remondet and Hansson (1987), the Grief Reaction Measure (Vargas et al. 1989); and the Bereavement Phenomenology Questionnaire (see Byrne and Raphael 1994).

Many of these scales have been criticized in terms of their validity, the methodology being subject to doubts in terms of a lack of normative data from representative community samples, a lack of cross-sectional research and an absence of prospective studies. For example:

Despite oft-quoted observations inferring that bereavement reactions for parents of young children were more severe than for spouses, or that bereaved spouses had more intense reactions than adult children who had lost a parent, studies using the same protocol to compare the bereavement reactions of spouses, widows and children longitudinally are sparse

(Middleton 1998: 3; see also Sanders 1980 and
Owen et al. 1982)

Other criticisms include a concern with meaning. For example, how we can be sure that words such as normal grief and pathological grief are understood in some sort of shared way (Jacobs and Kim 1990).

A further feature of a 'measurement culture' is a sense, present in some of the literature, that one can compare bereavements. Hence we have research findings that show that the bereavement reactions of parents whose young children die were more severe than for adults who lose a spouse (Videka-Sherman 1982), or that bereaved spouses can have more intense reactions than adult children who had lost a parent (Owen <i>et al.</i> 1982). There is also research, Kastenbaum (1985) and Lieberman (1989) for example, which comments that the impact of a death may be greater for survivors in later life than at any other junction of the life course. In his introduction to a special edition of the journal <i>Omega</i> devoted to a consideration of kinship bereavement in later life, de Vries (1997) cites the potential for a more complicated post-bereavement adjustment when two lives have been intertwined for many years. He also argues that later life bereavement may 'befall individuals whose resources to cope with such stress may be already compromised or diminished through the repeated charges on health and well being of a long life' (de Vries 1997: 2).

While most literature on bereavement in later life focuses on spousal loss and, in particular, widowhood, de Vries sums up some of the potential variation we must appreciate:

> For example, the death of a spouse signals a change in the present and daily conditions of one's life and in one's social relations. The death of a sibling alludes to one's own mortality and threatened history. The death of a parent similarly occasions a permanent break with connections to the past as middle aged orphaned grievers enter the Omega generation. The death of a child severs connections to the future and represents a violation of the natural order of the universe. The death of a grandchild and the concomitant generational extension exacerbates these reactions.

(de Vries 1997: 3)

There are also types of loss that present complications when viewed through the lens of conventional models of bereavement. Death in disasters or war are examples (see Eyre's chapter in this volume). There are also bereavements which are, in Doka's phrase, disenfranchized (Doka 1989).

Those partners of gay men dying with AIDS who were excluded in the final stages of life as the family of origin closed ranks, who were excluded from funeral arrangements and whose loss and grief was not acknowledged are notable examples.

The recognition of difference in terms of the bereavement experience does not imply the necessity for comparison. To order phenomena, to rank and compare under an overarching scheme is quintessentially modernist. The need to leave such approaches behind is one of the themes of this chapter.

Modernity and the discipline of the therapeutic

Thus far I have argued that the way we understand and respond to grief and bereavement contributes to, and is shaped by, the prevailing discourse. Modernity provides the framework within which many disciplines engage with death. Specifically, an aspiration to understand by developing a metanarrative that offers a framework for answering everything and an approach that breaks things down into manageable (controllable) sections and arranges them sequentially are defining characteristics of modernity.

We have looked at how modernity shaped psychoanalytic and attachment theories. In turn these theories generated the discipline of the therapeutic as a key aspect of modernity. That discipline's potential to impact on how we see ourselves was highlighted in the 1960s when Rieff identified 'self knowledge again made social as the principle of control upon which the emergent culture may yet be able to make itself stable' (Rieff 1966: 20). More than 30 years later we can see Rieff's theory as to *The Triumph of the Therapeutic* producing not only a 'know thyself' society but also one where, 'We are, I fear, getting to know one another. Reticence, secrecy, concealment of self have been transformed into social problems; once they were aspects of civility . . .' (Rieff 1966: 20). Now, apropos Foucault, we can see that such civility (or silence) is not the opposite of discourse but another version of it, as is the invocation to self-knowledge and social intimacy. Likewise the denial of death (Becker 1973), or its revival (Walter 1994), or the sense that one should get over loss through moving on, or foster continuing bonds with the dead, are not moves from darkness to enlightenment but rather reflect on the nexus of the individual, society and the prevailing form of disciplinary power. That is, we should not understand changing ways of understanding bereavement and grief in some Hegelian way as moving towards perfectibility through the conflict of opposing views and the arrival at a new and higher synthesis. It is just that we have a different view now, supported by different sorts of evidence. Soon another will come along to supplant it.

Modernity and sequential time

The quintessential modernist construct is that of time – metanarrative and sequential organizing epitomized. The ability to have popularly accepted the idea of present work for future gain, and the compartmentalization of the day into defined work/non-work sections was essential to the triumph of the industrial revolution and, in particular, the factory system. That the gain could be on earth or in heaven was at the heart of Protestantism, as one lived one's life with an eye to the future judgement that would be brought to bear on it. This can be contrasted with the cyclical and less differentiated agrarian community that preceded the industrial/modern.

Models of bereavement and grief, described above, all draw on models of sequential time and time-defined lives. But, it may be argued that bereavement fractures the sequential experience of time and that any model of grief and mourning that relies on a straightforward passage of time construct is inappropriate. Myerhoff offers the idea of 'simultaneity' where 'a sense of oneness with all that has been one's history is achieved' (Myerhoff 1982: 110). At this point the sequential arrangement of events across time is temporarily undone. As applied to mourning such an approach critiques Freud in much the same way as does the Klass *et al.* critique presented in *Continuing Bonds*.

> Freud . . . suggests that the completion of the mourning process requires that those left behind develop a new reality which no longer includes what has been lost. But . . . it must be added that full recovery from mourning may restore what has been lost, maintaining it through incorporation into the present. Full recollection and retention may be as vital to recovery and wellbeing as forfeiting memories.
>
> (Myerhoff 1982: 110)

However, it is not just the Freudian view that can be critiqued if one abandons the idea of time-defined lives and time-framed experiences. Any approach that includes stage theories, any sense of letting go, or of continuing bonds, is also constrained by linear time assumptions.

In effect the modernist understanding of time, like the modernist constructions of order and control, does not survive the impact of extreme experiences like bereavement. The modern exists as a layer on top of other ways of making sense of experience; for example, fate, faith and so on. Once fissures appear in the veneer of the modern we are allowed glimpses of the underlying residual belief systems, many of which are pre-modern. The coming together of the dying person or the bereaved, within this complex of beliefs, and the professional trying to cling to the structures of the modern creates the sorts of dissonance that can make for problematic encounters with bereavement services.

There are many examples in literature of ways we move beyond the contingency of linear time. Ralph Waldo Emerson wrote that 'Sorrow makes us all children again'. Psychoanalyst Adam Phillips (1999) has observed that nobody grows up in relation to death. That is, we are always the same age in relation to it. He is suggesting that we can travel one of two routes; either accept that we live in nature and that one of its basic conditions is that we might die at any time, or live our lives without an awareness of our mortality. It is not then how old we are but how we engage with the physicality of our existence that defines our relationship to death. Novelist Jim Crace argues that death reminds us that we are not future leaning but essentially live our lives retrospectively. In his story *Being Dead*, the narrative begins with the deaths of his central characters and then looks back on their lives – an interlude between the formlessness of how they began and the formlessness of what they will become (Crace 1999). But it is not just in relation to our personal histories that linear time is displaced; there is also the domain of the social and its history.

Rethinking historicity and the science of the indefinite

In a challenging book about the historicity of both AIDS and nuclear terror, Havers (1996) brings a different sort of language to the Freudian discourse on mourning and melancholia. He describes Freud's world of mourning as, 'a process by which the dead are rendered radically other by means of a process of dissociation or separation' (Havers 1996: 57). They are objectified as an abject object in the work of mourning, which historicizes the dead. In so doing the wounded ego is restored to an integration it seeks. If that wounded ego is not restored and there remains a (narcissistic) identification of the ego with the abandoned object (Freud 1917: 246); then melancholia results. (This condition, Havers suggests, is represented by the vampires and ghosts in our literature.)

However, Havers goes on to argue that this construction misses out the sociality that is 'the very existentiality of historicity' (Havers 1996: 60). It is in, and through, our exposure to death that we can appreciate the contingency of our intersubjectivities, of our relationship with our friends and with our 'cultural consolations'. If we relegate the dead 'other' to a historicism that we separate ourselves from, we do not see mourning as central to the cultural world of society and to our own sociality. While Havers's subject is mourning we can see that if we can redirect his concerns towards grief and bereavement we can re-emphasize the social and the relational, rather than that which is located in the internal world.

That interface between the social and the internal worlds is negotiated via the medium of language, which constructs, and gives expression to, concepts of the self and the emotions. The emotional self is a dynamic project existing at the intersection of the past, the present, the personal and the social. Some of it exists at an unconscious level. But, while language constructs and gives expression to this self, there is also a sense that the emotional experience has an embodied dimension (Lupton 1998). Seale (1998) uses the experience of dying to illuminate embodiment in social life and presents an 'imagined community' in which dying and bereaved people can live and where they can draw on various cultural scripts as well as their own narrative biography.

Against logic, for the sociality of our existence

Irigaray has argued 'the West has been slow to develop a science that can measure and model patterns of the indefinite and of fluidity' (see Battersby 1993: 35). 'We need to think individuality differently; allowing the potentiality of otherness to exist within it, as well as alongside it; we need to theorise agency in terms of patterns of potentiality and flow' (Battersby 1993: 38).

Thinking about individuality and agency in new ways allows us to move beyond modernity. One route is to look to the small narratives and contingent meanings that characterize the postmodern (see Mannion and Small 1999). The death of someone close to us takes us, as individuals, to a place that exists at the brink of the crisis of modernity. We are not in control, we do not understand. Our sense of self, our relations with others, even the way we experience time is challenged. Those whom we meet at this place can stay with us or they can try and pull us back. The modernist discourse of grief and bereavement risks the charge of hubris because it offers a route map to impose a meaning that is from there not here, that is theirs not yours. That many of those we encounter at this point do not seek to impose their meaning is a tribute to their recognition of the poetics of loss rather than the logic of theories of loss. They accept that they do not understand your loss but do appreciate the sociality of all our lives and deaths.

Notes

1 This is the Shakespearian injunction to 'Give sorrow words: the grief that does not speak whispers the o'er-fraught heart, and bids it break' (Malcolm in *Macbeth* Act IV Scene 3). The resonance of these often quoted lines is diminished somewhat when we realise it is Malcolm responding to the news of the death of Macduff's family and servants. He then advises the bereft Macduff to 'Be comforted: Lets make us medicines of our great revenge, to cure this deadly grief'. 'Dispute it like a man . . . Be this the whetstone of your sword: let grief convert to anger; blunt not the heart, enrage it'. Macduff is inclined to remember that which

had been precious to him but his first regret is that Macbeth, the instigator of the murder, has no children of his own that Macduff might murder. Jenny Hockey, in her chapter in this volume, discusses grief and rage in the contemporary anthropologist Rosaldo following the accidental death of his wife, and in the society he was studying, the Llongots of northern Luzon in the Philippines. They combined grief, rage and head hunting in a manner they saw as self-evident. Macduff, I suspect, would have been more at home in this company than acting as an icon for the more restrained intellectuality of the grief counsellors who invoke the advice given to him as a model of good practice.

2 We are venturing into theories of knowledge formation and change here. Lipstadt (1994) sees the danger in those who advocate extreme views shifting the locus of discourse simply via the noise they make and the attention they generate. A rather different view of the ways orthodoxies are challenged, and new ones emerge, is the Kuhnian idea of shifting paradigms (1962). For Kuhn paradigms are universally recognized scientific achievements that, for a time, provide model problems and solutions to a community of practitioners. 'A paradigm is what members of a scientific community share, and, conversely, a scientific community consists of men who share a paradigm' (Kuhn 1962: 176). However anomalies or 'violations of expectations' occur that cannot be made to conform to the paradigm and a crisis may be induced. If these anomalies or violations persist and expand then a scientific revolution, a shift of paradigm occurs.

References

Anthony, S. (1940) *The Child's Discovery of Death*. New York: Harcourt.

Averill, J.R. (1968) Grief: Its nature and significance. *Psychological Bulletin*, 70: 721–48.

Battersby, C. (1993) Her body/her boundaries, in A. Benjamin (ed.) The Body. *Journal of Philosophy and the Visual Arts*: 31–9.

Baudrillard, J. (1990) *Cool Memories*. London: Verso.

Becker, E. (1973) *The Denial of Death*. New York: The Free Press.

Benoliel, J.Q. (1988a) Institutional dying: a convergence of cultural values, technology and social organisation, in H. Wass, F.M. Berardo and R.A. Neimeyer (eds) *Dying: Facing the Facts*, 2nd edn. New York: Hemisphere Publishing.

Benoliel, J.Q. (1988b) Health care delivery: not conducive to teaching palliative care. *Journal of Palliative Care*, 4: 41–2.

Benoliel, J.Q. (1994) Death and dying as a field of inquiry, in I.B. Corless, B.B. Germino and M. Pittman (eds) *Dying, Death and Bereavement*. Boston, MA: Jones and Bartlett.

Bierstedt, R. (1978) Sociological thought in the eighteenth century, in T. Bottomore and R. Nisbet (eds) *A History of Sociological Analysis*. London: Heinemann.

Bowlby, J. (1961) Process of mourning. *International Journal of Psychoanalysis*, 42: 317–40.

Bowlby, J. (1973) *Loss: Sadness and Depression*. New York: Basic Books.

Bowlby, J. (1979) *The Making and Breaking of Affectional Bonds*. London: Tavistock.

Bowlby, J. (1988) *A Secure Base*. London: Routledge.

Burnett, P., Middleton, W., Raphael, B. and Martinek, N. (1997) Measuring core bereavement phenomena. *Psychological Medicine*, 27: 49–57.

Byrne, G.J.A. and Raphael, B. (1994) A longitudinal study of bereavement phenomena in recently widowed elderly men. *Psychological Medicine*, 24: 411–21.

Cantor, R.C. (1978) *And a Time to Live: Towards Emotional Well-being During Crises of Cancer*. New York: Harper and Row.

Clark, D. (1993) *The Sociology of Death*. Oxford: Blackwell.

Clark, D. (1998) Originating a movement: Cicely Saunders and the development of St Christopher's Hospice, 1957–67. *Mortality*, 3(1): 43–63.

Clark, D. (1999) 'Total pain', disciplinary power and the body in the work of Cicely Saunders, 1958–67. *Social Science and Medicine*, 49(6): 727–36.

Corr, C.A., Nabe, C.M. and Corr, D. (1997) *Death and Dying, Life and Living*, 2nd edn. Pacific Grove, CA: Brooks/Cole.

Crace, J. (1999) *Being Dead*. London: Viking.

Doka, K. (ed.) (1989) *Disenfranchised Grief*. Lexington, MA: Lexington Books.

Durkheim, E. ([1912] 1965) *The Elementary Forms of the Religious Life*. New York: Free Press.

Eliot, R.D. (1933) A step towards the social psychology of bereavement. *Journal of Abnormal and Social Psychology*, 27: 114–15.

Faschingbauer, T.R., Devaul, R.A. and Zisook, S. (1977) Development of the Texas Inventory of Grief. *American Journal of Psychiatry*, 134: 696–8.

Feifel, H. (ed.) (1959) *The Meaning of Death*. New York: McGraw-Hill.

Field, D. (1984) Formal instruction in UK medical schools about death and dying. *Medical Education*, 18: 429–34.

Field, D. (1986) Formal teaching about death and dying in UK nursing schools. *Nurse Education Today*, 6: 270–6.

Foucault, M. (1977) *The Archaeology of Knowledge*. London: Tavistock

Frazer, J.G. ([1890] 1963) *The Golden Bough*. New York: Macmillan.

Freud, S. (1917) Mourning and melancholia, in J. Strachey (ed.) *The Standard Edition of the Complete Psychological Works of Sigmund Freud*, Vol. 14. London: Hogarth Press and Institute of Psycho-Analysis.

Fulton, R. and Bendiksen, R. (eds) (1965) *Death and Identity*. Bowie, MD: Charles Press.

Fulton, R. and Bendiksen, R. (eds) (1965) *Death and Identity*, 2nd edn. Borrie, MD: Charles Press.

Furman, E. (1974) *A Child's Parent Dies*. New Haven: Yale University Press.

Giddens, A. (1992) *The Transformation of Intimacy*. Cambridge: Polity Press.

Glaser, B. and Strauss, A. (1965) *Awareness of Dying*. Chicago, IL: Aldine.

Glaser, B. and Strauss, A. (1968) *A Time for Dying*. Chicago, IL: Aldine.

Glick, I., Parkes, C.M. and Weiss, R.S. (1974) *The First Year of Bereavement*. London: Wiley Interscience.

Gorer, G. (1955) The pornography of death. *Encounter*, October.

Gorer, G. (1965) *Death, Grief and Mourning in Contemporary Britain*. London: Cresset.

Grosskurth, P. (1986) *Melanie Klein*. London: Hodder and Stoughton.

Grossman, D. (1989) *See Under: Love*. London: Picador.

Havers, W. (1996) *The Body of this Death*. Stanford: Stanford University Press.

Hertz, R. ([1907] 1960) *Death and the Right Hand*. New York: Free Press.

Hinshelwood, R.D. (1994) *Clinical Klein*. London: Free Association Books.

Hinton, J.M. (1967) *Dying*. Harmondsworth: Penguin.

Holmes, J. (1993) *John Bowlby and Attachment Theory*. London: Routledge.

Jacobs, S. and Kim, K. (1990) Psychiatric complications of bereavement. *Psychiatric Annals*, 20: 314–7.

Jacobs, S.C., Kosten, T.R., Kasl, S.V. *et al.* (1987) Attachment theory and multiple dimensions of grief. *Omega*, 18: 41–52.

James, N. (1994) From vision to system: the maturing of the hospice movement, in R. Lee and D. Morgan (eds) *Death Rites. Law and Ethics at the End of Life*. London: Routledge, pp. 102–30.

James, N. and Field, D. (1991) The routinization of hospice. *Social Science and Medicine*, 34: 1363–75.

Kastenbaum, R. (1985) Dying and death: a life-span approach, in J.E. Birren and K.W. Schaie (eds) *Handbook of the Psychology of Ageing*, 2nd edn. New York: Van Nostrand.

Kastenbaum, R. and Aisenberg, R.B. (1972) *The Psychology of Death*. New York: Springer.

Klass, D., Silverman, P.R. and Nickman, S.L. (1996) *Continuing Bonds, New Understandings of Grief*. Washington, DC: Taylor & Francis.

Klein, M. (1935) A contribution to the psychogenesis of manic depressive states. Reprinted in *Love, Guilt and Reparation and Other Works 1921–45*. London: Hogarth Press.

Klein, M. (1940) Mourning and its relation to manic-depressive states. *International Journal of Psycho-Analysis*, 21: 125–53.

Kliman, G. (1965) *Psychological Emergencies of Childhood*. New York: Grune and Stratton.

Kübler-Ross, E. (1969) *On Death and Dying*. New York: Macmillan.

Kuhn, T.S. (1962) *The Structure of Scientific Revolutions*. Chicago, IL: University of Chicago Press.

Lieberman, M.A. (1989) All family losses are not equal. *Journal of Family Psychology*, 2: 368–72.

Lieberman, M.A. and Borman, L.E. (eds) (1979) *Self-help groups for coping with crisis*. Washington, DC: Jossey-Bass.

Lindemann, E. (1944) Symptomatology and management of acute grief. *American Journal of Psychiatry*, 101: 141–8.

Lipstadt, D. (1994) *Denying the Holocaust*. New York: Plume.

Littlewood, J. (1993) The denial of death and rites of passage in contemporary societies, in D. Clark (ed.) *The Sociology of Death*. Oxford: Blackwell.

Lofland, L. (ed.) (1976) *Towards a Sociology of Death and Dying*. Beverley Hills, CA: Sage.

Lofland, L.H. (1985) The social shaping of emotion: the case of grief. *Symbolic Interaction*, 8(2): 171–90.

Lund, D.A., Diamond, M.E., Caserta, M.S. *et al.* (1985) Identifying elderly with coping difficulties after two years of bereavement. *Omega*, 16: 213–24.

Lupton, D. (1998) *The Emotional Self*. London: Sage.

McClowry, S.G., Davies, E.B., May, A., Kulenkamp, E.J. and Martinson, I.M. (1987) The empty space phenomenon: the process of grief in the bereaved family. *Death Studies*, 11: 361–74.

Maddison, D. and Walker, W.L. (1967) Factors affecting the outcome of conjugal bereavement. *British Journal of Psychiatry*, 113: 1057–67.

Mannion, R. and Small, N. (1999) Postmodern Health Economics. *Health Care Analysis*, 7: 255–72.

Marris, P. (1958) *Widows and their Families*. London: Routledge and Kegan Paul.

Marris, P. (1974) *Loss and Change*. London: Routledge and Kegan Paul.

Middleton, W. (1998) Different losses: different grief. *Grief Matters*, April: 3–6.

Miles, M.S. and Demi, A.S. (1994) Historical and contemporary theories of grief, in I.B. Corless, B.B. Germino and M. Pittman (eds) *Dying, Death and Bereavement*. Boston, MA: Jones and Bartlett.

Myerhoff, B. (1982) Life history among the elderly: performance, visibility and remembering, in J. Ruby (ed.) *A Crack in the Mirror: Reflexive Perspectives on Anthropology*. Philadelphia, PA: University of Pennsylvania Press.

Nabokov, V. (1999) *Speak, Memory*. London: Everyman.

Nagel, T. (1987) *What Does it all Mean?: A Very Short Introduction to Philosophy*. Oxford: Oxford University Press.

Owen, G., Fulton, R. and Markusen, E (1982) Death at a distance: a study of family survivors. *Omega*, 13: 191–225.

Parkes, C.M. (1965) Bereavement and mental illness. *British Journal of Medical Psychology*, 38: 1.

Parkes, C.M. (1970) The first year of bereavement: a longitudinal study of reaction of London widows to the death of their husbands. *Psychiatry*, 33: 444.

Parkes, C.M. (1972) *Bereavement: Studies of Grief in Adult Life*. London: Tavistock.

Parkes, C.M. (1986) *Bereavement: Studies of Griet in Adult Life*, 2nd edn. Harmondsnorth: Penguin.

Parkes, C.M. and Weiss, R. (1983) *Recovery from Bereavement*. New York: Basic Books.

Parkes, C.M., Laungani, P. and Young, W. (1997) *Cross-cultural Aspects of Death and Bereavement*. London: Routledge.

Phillips, A. (1999) *Darwin's Worms*. London: Faber.

Quint, J. (1969) *The Nurse and the Dying Patient*. New York: Macmillan.

Rando, T.A. (1993) *Treatment of Complicated Mourning*. Champaign, IL: Research Press.

Raphael, B. (1982) The young child and the death of a parent, in C.M. Parkes and J. Stevenson-Hinde (eds) *The Place of Attachment in Human Behaviour*. London: Tavistock.

Raphael, B. (1983) *The Anatomy of Bereavement*. New York: Basic Books.

Remondet, J.H. and Hansson, R.O. (1987) Assessing widow's grief: a short index. *Journal of Gerontological Nursing*, 13: 31–4.

Rieff, P. (1966) *The Triumph of the Therapeutic*. Harmondsworth: Penguin.

Robertson, J. (1958) *Young Children in Hospital*. London: Tavistock Publications.

Rushdie, S. (1999) *The Ground Beneath her Feet*. London: Jonathan Cape.

Samarel, N. (1995) The dying process, in H. Wass and R.A. Neimeyer (eds) *Dying: Facing the Facts*, 3rd edn. Washington, DC: Taylor & Francis.

Sanders, C.M. (1980) A comparison of adult bereavement in the death of a spouse, child and parent. *Omega*, 10: 303–22.

Sanders, C.M., Mauger, P.A. and Strong, P.N. (1979) *A Manual for the Grief Experience Inventory*. Tampa, FL: Loss and Bereavement Resource Centre, University of Florida.

Saunders, C. (1969) The moment of truth: care of the dying person, in L. Pearson (ed.) *Death and Dying*. Cleveland, OH: Western Reserve University.

Seale, C. (1998) *Constructing Death*. Cambridge: Cambridge University Press.

Shneidman, E. (1973) *The Deaths of Man*. New York: Quadrangle.

Silverman, P.R. and Klass, D. (1996) Introduction: what's the problem?, in D. Klass, P.R. Silverman and S.L. Nickman (eds) *Continuing Bonds. New Understandings of Grief*. Bristol, PA: Taylor & Francis.

Smart, B. (1985) *Michel Foucault*. London: Tavistock.

Steiner, J. (1993) *Psychic Retreats*. London: Routledge.

Steiner, J. (1996) The aim of psychoanalysis in theory and practice. *International Journal of Psycho-Analysis*, 77(6): 1073–83.

Stoddard, S. (1978) *The Hospice Movement: A Better Way of Caring for the Dying*. New York: Random House.

Stroebe, M., Hansson, R.O. and Stroebe, W. (1993) Contemporary themes and controversies in bereavement research, in M. Stroebe, W. Stroebe and R.O. Hansson (eds) *Handbook of Bereavement*. Cambridge: Cambridge University Press.

Stroebe, M., Gergen, M., Gergen, K. and Stroebe, W. (1996) Broken hearts or broken bonds?, in D. Klass, P.R. Silverman and S.L. Nickman (eds) *Continuing Bonds, New Understandings of Grief*. Washington, DC: Taylor & Francis.

Stroebe, M. and Schut, H. (1995) The dual process model of coping with loss. Paper presented at the meeting of the International Work Group on Death, Dying and Bereavement, Oxford, 29 June.

Torrie, M. (1970) *Begin Again: A Book for Women Alone*. London: Dent.

Tylor, E.B. ([1871] 1958) *Primitive Culture*. New York: Harper.

Van Gennep, A. ([1909] 1960) *The Rites of Passage*. Chicago, IL: University of Chicago Press.

Vargas, L.A., Loya, R. and Hodde-Vargas, J. (1989) Exploring the multidimensional aspects if grief reactions. *American Journal of Psychiatry*, 146: 1484–8.

Videka-Sherman, L. (1982) Coping with the death of a child: a study over time. *American Journal of Orthopsychiatry*, 52: 688–99.

de Vries, B. (1997) Kinship bereavement in later life. *Omega*, 35(1): 1–7.

Walter, T. (1993) Sociologists never die: British sociology and death, in D. Clark (ed.) *The Sociology of Death*. Oxford: Blackwell.

Walter, T. (1994) *The Revival of Death*. London: Routledge.

Walter, T. (1996) A new model of grief: bereavement and biography. *Mortality*, 1(1): 7–25.

Walter, T. (1997) Letting go and keeping hold: a reply to Stroebe. *Mortality*, 2(2): 263–6.

Walter, T. (1999) *On Bereavement*. Buckingham: Open University Press.

Wass, H. and Neimeyer, R.A. (1995) *Dying. Facing the Facts*. Washington, DC: Taylor & Francis.

Weatherill, R. (1998) *The Sovereignty of Death*. London: Rebus Press.

Worcester, A. (1935) *Care of the Aged, the Dying and the Dead*. Springfield, IL: Charles C. Thomas.

Worden, J.W. (1982) *Grief Counselling and Grief Therapy: A Handbook for the Mental Health Practitioner*. New York: Springer.

Wortman, C.B. and Silver, R.C. (1989) The myths of coping with loss. *Journal of Consulting and Clinical Psychology*, 57(3): 349–57.

Zisook, S. and DeVaul, R.A. (1984) Measuring acute grief. *Psychological Medicine*, 2: 169–76.

Zisook, S. and Schuter, S.R. (1985) Time course of spousal bereavement. *General Hospital Psychiatry*, 7: 95–100.

2 Is grief an illness? Issues of theory in relation to cultural diversity and the grieving process

CAROLINE CURRER

Introduction

In this chapter, I focus upon the process of grieving. Sociological interest in death and bereavement is relatively recent (Clark 1993; Walter 1994, 1996, 1999; Seale 1998) although there is an established body of research relating to processes of dying (following early work such as Glaser and Strauss 1965, 1968; Sudnow 1967). In relation to grieving, Tony Walter's 'new model of grief' (1996), which forms part of what he describes as a current revolution in this field, offers a sociological counterbalance to the individual psychological focus which has dominated both theory and practice. Walter has himself discussed the reasons for both sociological neglect (1993) and for the dominance of an individualistic view of grieving in the neo-modern period (1994). This position is now beginning to change, with substantial contributions from Seale (1998) and Walter (1999).

My interest here is in looking at whether understandings from studies of concepts of health and illness (e.g. Pill and Stott 1982; Cornwell 1984; Currer and Stacey 1986) might be applicable to the study of grief and mourning. A paper by Gunaratnam (1997) concerning service responses to issues of cultural diversity in palliative care has strong parallels with work of a decade earlier (Pearson 1986) in relation to broader issues of health education. This encourages me to think that a model that came out of research into the health concepts of a particular ethnic group (Currer 1986) might also yield insights in relation to understanding mourning and grieving behaviour. This model was one that addressed the concerns that Guneratnam now expresses in relation to cultural issues in palliative care, albeit in a different context.

Such questions inevitably raise the question of whether grief should be considered, in sociological terms, to be an illness. This has been a matter of debate within psychology (Engel 1961; Parkes 1972: 8; Parkes *et al*. 1997: 213). Practice issues such as the training, location and referral practices of bereavement counsellors can be seen to reflect differing approaches to this issue. It is my hope that the attempt to apply models developed within the sociology of health and illness may raise questions about the ways in which grieving is, or is not, similar to other states of emotional distress.

My argument falls into two main sections. First, I will offer an overview of the ways in which cultural difference and ethnicity have been dealt with in the literature concerning grieving. A selection of classic texts will be considered, as well as work that does focus upon issues of cultural difference, and the recent models proposed by Stroebe and Schut (1998) and Walter (1996). The second section starts from an established body of work within the sociology of health and illness – the study of concepts of health. After summarizing some major themes within this literature, I will look at links that might be made with the work on grief. The questions I raise in conclusion concern the extent to which such approaches might offer a useful way of considering grieving. The question in my title is not so much '*is* grief an illness?' as 'is it fruitful for sociologists to use models that have been applied to illness conditions to the issue of grieving?' I argue that it is.

The grieving process: universal or culturally variable?

> As I read the literature [*on conceptualizing grieving*] I found the conventional Western psychological wisdom unchallenged by non-Western practices: though these were cited in order to criticize the Western way of dying, they were never used to criticize Western psychological models of grief.
>
> (Walter 1996: 9–10)

The conventional wisdom

This statement by Walter is a fair summary of the position, although it does conceal a variety of approaches to questions of cultural variation. I shall refer briefly to those of three leading writers in this field, whose work forms the basis of teaching in nursing, bereavement counselling and social care: Worden (1991), Raphael (1984) and Parkes (1972), Glick, Weiss and Parkes (1974), Parkes, Laungani and Young (1997).

William Worden, Professor of Psychology at Harvard Medical School, whose 'tasks of mourning' have become a popular basis for bereavement counselling, is sufficiently disinterested in issues of cultural difference that neither culture nor ethnicity is referenced in his work. Only one paper, published in 1962, is referred to in the single paragraph given to this topic in the 1991 edition of his 'handbook for the mental health practitioner'

(Worden 1991: 9). This influential text is therefore essentially blind to cultural difference.

Beverley Raphael's *Anatomy of Bereavement* (1984), also subtitled a 'handbook for the caring professions', takes cultural issues and difference more seriously, but sidesteps the issue of whether these might offer a challenge to conventional wisdom by listing 'transcultural aspects' as the first of six 'explanatory models of bereavement,' thus separating these 'aspects' from psychodynamic aspects, attachment theory and cognitive and stress models, amongst others. After reviewing in this subsection a number of relevant studies, she concludes that 'while the rituals of different cultures and societies do not explain bereavement, they show its universality and also reflect the recognition of some of its basic processes' (Raphael 1984: 65). In common with other authors (e.g. Firth 1993), Raphael also notes that 'many of the ceremonies and rituals of other cultures fit better with the emotional needs of the bereaved than do those of modern Western society' (1984: 65).

Psychiatrist Colin Murray Parkes is one of the most influential writers in this field. Parkes' approach derives from that of John Bowlby (1973), owing much to attachment theory. Much of his early research was, however, in partnership with sociologists. His work takes cultural variations seriously. Even in 1974, we find his co-authored study considering the question of cultural relativity, concluding that 'cultural emphases can produce somewhat different expressions of grief, even though the experience of grief is nearly universal' (Glick *et al.* 1974: 11). The authors do, however, note a significant difference revealed by research on mourning in Japan: this concerns the 'sense of presence', which bereaved persons experience more frequently in that culture. This observation is a first indication of a more sustained contemporary critique of theoretical understandings (Wortman and Silver 1989).

More recently, Parkes is one of the co-editors of a volume looking particularly at issues of cultural variation (Parkes *et al.* 1997). Here we find the co-editors, including Parkes, uncomfortably aware that their exploration of these issues sits awkwardly with the psychological enterprise (1997: 6–7), but committed to opening up these issues in order to facilitate the delivery by practitioners of culturally sensitive responses. Although they argue that the search for meaning takes place within a cultural context that is deeply influential, the authors maintain that 'there may still be fundamental consistencies, themes and truths that appear in one culture after another' (Parkes *et al.* 1997: 6). They back off dangerous ground by preferring 'to leave open the underlying nature of these phenomena' (p. 6).

As Field, Hockey and Small comment about work in this vein: 'explanations are sought within the experiencing individual rather than in the social contexts and social relationships within which these experiences occur' (1997: 24), although these contexts may be seen to influence greatly the ways in which experiences are *expressed*. In summary, then, bereavement has been considered by most leading authors to be 'a universal rather than culturally variable experience' (Field *et al.* 1997: 9).

Other voices, and the nature of theoretical challenges

Classic understandings of grieving have, then, been largely unthreatened by discordant notes derived from cross-cultural research. Yet from the late 1970s onwards, there has been in Britain considerable work which carefully documents the customs and practices of those from minority ethnic groups (e.g. Henley 1979, 1987; Green 1991, 1992). Although having some value when used with care, such 'factfiles' essentially reflect a 'culturalist' approach (Pearson 1986) to the health care needs of minority ethnic groups. A recent article by Gunaratnam (1997) offers a clear and thorough theoretical critique of this approach, showing how it 'can present barriers to the achievement of a genuine, anti-racist multi-culturalism' (p. 169). As she points out, the purpose of such work is *not* to challenge the professional discourse, and it is clear that it does not do so. Within such an approach, professional wisdoms are taken as universal and given; it is only the service user whose behaviour is influenced by cultural norms. Hence no challenge is present at the level of theory. I shall return to this issue because of the parallels with my own work in the 1980s (Currer 1990).

There have, nonetheless, been a number of reviews that might have offered such theoretical challenge. For example, an article on 'cross-cultural aspects of bereavement' written by Eisenbruch in 1984, places mourning practices firmly in a historical and cross-cultural context, noting that:

> . . . the schemata devised by Western thanatologists describe the normative stages of the grief process of Westerners. Yet more than three-quarters of the world's population are non-Western. The indiscriminate application of Western models of grief to other ethnic and cultural groups is an example of Kleinman's (1977) 'category fallacy'.
>
> (Eisenbruch 1984: 324)

As early as 1976, anthropologist Paul Rosenblatt and colleagues compared the anthropological accounts of grief and mourning in 78 different societies (Rosenblatt *et al.* 1976). Amongst other things, this demonstrated that the suppression of emotion common at a funeral in the West is atypical when compared with a range of responses. Nearly 20 years later, in 1993, Rosenblatt comments:

> New anthropological studies of dying, death and grief suggest there is no one grief theory or one psychology of ego defenses that applies to everyone . . . Western cultural concepts such as 'dying' and grief originated in the context of its culture. It now seems that realities differ

so greatly from culture to culture that it is misleading and ethnocentric to assume that Western concepts apply generally.

(Rosenblatt 1993: 13)

In a paper published in 1997, he goes further:

There are no emotions or emotional expressions that are universally present at death. . . . What emotions are felt, how they are expressed and how they are understood are matters of culture. Moreover, the distinctions many Westerners draw between feeling and thought is also a matter of culture . . . Many Westerners think of grieving as an individual action and much of grief therapy is individually focused . . . it is important to remember that the concept of 'help' comes out of Euro-American cultures.

(Rosenblatt 1997: 35; 43; 46)

It is interesting that these two papers are published in different collections, neither of which is committed to radical critique. The first (by Irish, Lundquist and Nelson 1993) is one cited by Gunaratnam as being constructed around a culturalist theme (Gunaratnam 1997), whilst the second is in the collection co-edited by Parkes (1997), to which I have already referred. Again, the overall aim seems not to be to offer a robust critique of dominant theory, nor a radical alternative, despite the apparently unequivocal position taken in the above quotations. In general, then, it is fair to conclude that although there has been work which has explored issues of cultural difference, it has taken a long time for this to be brought together into a sustained critique of established, culture-blind models.

New models, Walter and Stroebe

As Walter has argued, bereavement research 'is currently in a revolutionary phase' (1997: 173). One of the new approaches that has been proposed, by psychologist Margaret Stroebe and her colleague Henk Schut, claims to be a specific response to the questions raised by cultural difference. They write:

. . . a study of patterns of grieving across cultures shows very different ways of reacting to loss and Western concepts of 'normal' reactions or 'healthy' ways of coping emerge as ethnocentric constructions. These cultural differences led us to look again at the traditional understanding of the grieving process and to propose a different model of effective coping which takes cultural variation into account.

(Stroebe and Schut 1998)

This is promising, but turns out to stop short of a real critique, representing instead a broadening of conventional understandings to accommodate grief responses that have been reported cross-culturally. The writers conclude:

There seems to be a universal reaction of grieving (emotional disturbance) after the loss of a significant other, but ... grief is also
affected by the imposition of cultural meaning and can vary in duration according to cultural prescriptions. A societal belief system may,
in extreme cases, be powerful enough to obliterate any overt indications of emotional disturbance. In these cases, it may be possible to
identify physiological changes which would indicate grieving.

(Stroebe and Schut 1998: 9)

Stroebe and Schut's 'dual process model' proposes that there are, within
the experience of grieving, two processes (or orientations), one toward the
loss and the other toward restoration. The balance between these orientations
is seen to vary between individuals, with factors such as gender and culture
identified as important influences upon the expression of grief. This model
therefore makes room for cultural variation. Even here, however, the meaning of life and death appears to be peripheral to the process, rather than at
its centre.

By contrast, Walter's model (1996) is social rather than individual, and
relates grieving to sociological theory. Following Giddens (1991), he locates
his understanding of 'bereavement as biography' firmly within neo-modern
culture in which the social construction of identity is seen as an ongoing
project. Similarly, Seale (1998) is careful to limit his observations to anglophone societies. As sociologists, these authors acknowledge the importance
of culture and context by being specific about the source and relevance of
their propositions: they are not looking to delineate universal processes.

I now consider whether a different sociological framework might also
usefully be applied to the analysis of grief and grieving behaviours. Analysis
of concepts of health and of their impact upon illness behaviour has long
taken account of cultural variation (Currer and Stacey 1986). Like Stroebe's
model, the framework that draws on this body of work offers a way of
understanding an individual and their particular responses, which is of use
to the practitioner. Yet it is rooted in an approach that takes professional
understandings to be themselves culturally contingent (Stacey 1986: 10).

Concepts of health and illness: some parallels with the work on grieving

Classic description of grief reactions owes much to the work of Lindemann,
whose 1944 study described the expressed distress of 101 Americans following a tragic fire in a night club in which over five hundred people lost
their lives (Lindemann 1944). In 1973, Joan Ablon commented upon the
responses of members of a Samoan community to a similar disaster (Ablon
1973). She contrasted their reactions with those described by Lindemann,

drawing attention to a 'stoicism' which characterized the responses of the Samoan people, and to factors such as religious beliefs, community support and social powerlessness, which might account for such differences. In my own research into the experiences of Pathan women in Britain, and their concepts of mental well- and ill-being (Currer 1986), I found parallels to the stoicism described by Ablon. I also found the same three factors to be of importance in determining both the *experience* of distress and behavioural responses to this.

The link between religious beliefs and response both to illness and death is hardly surprising; it fits a lay expectation that grieving is (in part, at least) about the meaning we attribute to life and death. It is perhaps only surprising that some theoreticians insist upon the universality of the emotional processes of grief, in the face of apparently contradictory beliefs about the implications of dying (total extinction or the gateway to something better, for example). The presence or lack of social support has also been found in most studies to be influential in bereavement (see Riches and Dawson 1999 for a recent example).

The link between emotional response and social position is perhaps more surprising, but here again there are strong parallels between research into grieving, and research on concepts of health and illness. Thus, Antonovsky (1987) links an individual's sense of having the resources to manage life's demands with the sense of coherence and of control that are two key dimensions within the construct 'health'. D'Houtaud's large-scale French study (see d'Houtaud and Field 1986) identified social position as a key factor influencing the way in which health and illness are understood. Pill and Stott (1982) studied women living in Wales and also found a connection between concepts of health and factors such as home ownership and level of schooling.

Is social position important in relation to grief and grieving? There is evidence that it is. Ruth Bright (1996) links grief with powerlessness. Margaret Stroebe and colleagues from Utrecht found in a longitudinal control study of widowed people (Stroebe and Stroebe 1989) that 'internal control beliefs' (the idea that you have some influence over events) were significant in predicting the outcome of grieving in the case of sudden death. At the level of society, Peter Marris (1991) suggests that vulnerability to loss (and therefore to situations giving rise to grief) is socially structured, with those who are powerless likely to experience more grief than those with more control and power. A link is therefore established both between actual powerlessness (or lowly social position) and grief, and between a person's perception of their power to control events and grief. Here again then, we find important parallels between work on grieving and work on concepts of health and illness.

My study of Pathan mothers (1986) looked at concepts of mental well- and ill-being. At the time there was much discussion of 'why Asian mothers do/do not attend antenatal care' and of ways to convey to them advice concerning childcare. Such debates were part of a culturalist agenda which, like that described by Guneratnam in relation to palliative care (1997), assumed that giving more information to health professionals about the cultural practices of minority groups would be a means of ensuring that services were culturally sensitive and appropriate. In common with Gunaratnam, I noted the way in which concepts (of pregnancy in my paper, of dying in hers) might reflect the collective religious position or the particular experience of the individual. Cornwell (1984) described these different understandings (which might both be honestly expressed by an individual but to different audiences) as 'public' and 'private' concepts. In relation to death and dying, as in relation to pregnancy, we can see the dangers of taking a religious position as either fixed or overriding. In both situations, it is clear that people vary in the extent to which they are, as individuals, aware of religious practices, or to which they follow them, even when they identify with an overall religious group.

One of the outcomes of my own study was a model that seemed to be useful in understanding the link between concepts of health and illness, and illness behaviours, including help-seeking. I concluded that three factors influenced the actions of the women whose views I studied. First, their *concepts* or understandings of health and illness. Work on concepts of health, illness and disease has shown that concepts are not merely cultural constructs: social position, gender and age as well as cultural and religious beliefs can all be shown to influence them (Currer and Stacey 1986). Second, I found that material circumstances (*options*) exerted a powerful influence upon behaviour. For my sample of Pathan women, this might be the availability of a car or telephone. Such material circumstances of minority ethnic groups are frequently ignored within a culturalist approach (Currer 1990). Last, but significantly, I found that women's actions were not completely determined either by cultural or material factors. Other life events (such as a forthcoming visit to Pakistan) made some help-seeking a priority, even when it did not fit well with the way in which women understood the issue, and when it was not easy to achieve. Such prioritization is of course a common feature of help-seeking behaviour, described originally by Zola (1972). I called it *interests*.

By going further and suggesting that the actions of health professionals are also influenced by these three factors, biomedical concepts of health and illness are placed firmly within the same framework as lay concepts. Professional understandings too are culturally and structurally contingent. Moreover, health workers, like their patients, are influenced in what they do both by the resources at their disposal and by prioritization, usually but not always geared to the interests of service or management demands.

The last, but very significant aspect of this model is that the meeting between patient and health worker does not exist in a vacuum: it takes place within a social context shaped by racism and other relations of power. No such context is assumed or allowed for by educators who think that more or better information alone will make for services that are truly accessible for those from minority ethnic groups.

Such a model answers many of the criticisms rightly leveled by Guneratnam at the culturalist approach. But is it applicable to the study of grief and grieving? Might it offer a way of thinking about grieving behaviours (including the seeking of counselling or other solace) following bereavement? Clearly, the ways in which the grieving individual understands death (concepts) are a critical determinant both of their experience of loss and of their behavioural responses to it. This includes religious understandings at both an overall cultural level and the individual's own modifications of these. It also includes the meaning of this particular death, which may affect the social status of the bereaved ('I am no longer a wife, sister . . .'). Options for grieving (in terms both of facilities and of material resources) affect mourning practices. Laungani (1997) and Jonker (1997) have each described variations in mourning practices amongst immigrant communities, and material resources are an important determinant of funeral arrangements for all groups, now as in the past (Clark 1993). They also determine the options that individuals have or do not have to engage in activities that foster restoration, as outlined in the 'dual process model' of Stroebe and Schut (1998). At first sight, decisions about whether to seek help, either of a formal kind, or from friends and neighbours, may be said to be a feature of societies that are characterized by individualism, rather than those in which overt mourning practices and customs are culturally prescribed. Nevertheless, choices remain. My study was of a group whose choices were powerfully limited both by culture and gender, but I found that it was still not an accurate representation of the women's position to describe their actions as completely determined. This may also be so in relation to responses to bereavement.

Conclusion

Suggestions concerning the ways in which this particular framework might apply to situations of bereavement are offered to stimulate discussion, debate, and possibly research. Consideration of the ways in which issues of cultural variation have been dealt with in the literature concerning bereavement suggests, however, that there are strong parallels with work relating to concepts of health and illness. To date, links do not appear to have been made between these areas of study. Exploration of such links might produce new insights, throwing light on the extent to which grief and grieving are – or are not – a special case.

References

Ablon, J. (1973) Reactions of Samoan burn patients and families to severe burns. *Social Science and Medicine*, 7: 167–78.
Antonovsky, A. (1987) *Unravelling the Mystery of Health*. London: Jossey-Bass.
Bowlby, J. (1973) *Loss, Sadness, and Depression*. New York: Basic Books.
Bright, R. (1996) *Grief and Powerlessness: Helping People Regain Control of Their Lives*. London: Jessica Kingsley.
Clark, D. (ed.) (1993) *The Sociology of Death*. Oxford: Blackwell.
Cornwell, J. (1984) *Hard Earned Lives*. London: Tavistock.
Currer, C. (1986) Concepts of mental well- and ill-being: the case of Pathan mothers in Britain, in C. Currer and M. Stacey (eds) *Concepts of Health, Illness and Disease: A Comparative Perspective*. Leamington Spa: Berg.
Currer, C. (1990) Racism in the study of ethnic minorities. Paper presented on course on research appraisal, by Tower Hamlets Primary Health Care Unit in conjunction with the Centre for the study of Primary Care.
Currer, C. and Stacey, M. (eds) (1986) *Concepts of Health, Illness and Disease: A Comparative Perspective*. Leamington Spa: Berg.
D'Houtaud, A. and Field, M. (1986) New research on the image of health, in C. Currer and M. Stacey (eds) *Concepts of Health, Illness and Disease: A Comparative Perspective*. Leamington Spa: Berg.
Eisenbruch, M. (1984) Cross-cultural aspects of bereavement II: ethnic and cultural variations in the development of bereavement practices. *Culture, Medicine and Psychiatry*, 8: 315–47.
Engel, G.L. (1961) Is grief a disease? A challenge for medical research. *Psychosomatic Medicine*, 23: 18–22.
Field, D., Hockey, J. and Small, N. (1997) Making sense of difference: death, gender and ethnicity in modern Britain, in D. Field, J. Hockey and N. Small (eds) *Death, Gender and Ethnicity*. London: Routledge.
Firth, S. (1993) Cultural issues in terminal care, in D. Clark (ed.) *The Future for Palliative Care*. Buckingham: Open University Press.
Giddens, A. (1991) *Modernity and Self-identity*. Oxford: Polity.
Glaser, B.G. and Strauss, A. (1965) *Awareness of Dying*. Chicago: Aldine.
Glaser, B.G. and Strauss, A. (1968) *Time for Dying*. Chicago: Aldine.
Glick, I., Weiss, R. and Parkes, C.M. (1974) *The First Year of Bereavement* London: John Wiley.
Green, J. (1991) *Death with Dignity: Meeting the Spiritual Needs of Patients in a Multi-cultural Society*, Vol. 1. London: Macmillan Magazines.
Green, J. (1992) *Death with dignity: Meeting the Spiritual Needs of Patients in a Multi-cultural Society*, Vol. 2. London: Macmillan Magazines.
Gunaratnam, Y. (1997) Culture is not enough: a critique of multi-culturalism in palliative care, in D. Field, J. Hockey and N. Small (eds) *Death, Gender and Ethnicity*. London: Routledge.
Henley, A. (1979) *Asian Patients in Hospital and at Home*. London: Kings Fund.
Henley, A. (1987) *Caring in a Multiracial Society*. London: Bloomsbury Health Authority.
Irish, D., Lundquist, K. and Nelson, V. (eds) (1993) *Ethnic Variations in Dying, Death and Grief: Diversity in Universality*. Washington: Taylor & Francis.

Jonker, G. (1997) The many facets of Islam: death, dying and disposal between orthodox rule and historical convention, in C.M. Parkes, P. Laungani and B. Young (eds) *Death and Bereavement across Cultures*. London: Routledge.

Kleinman, A. (1977) Depression, somatisation and the 'new cross-cultural psychiatry.' *Social Science and Medicine*, 11: 3–10.

Laungani, P. (1997) Death in a Hindu family, in C.M. Parkes, P. Laungani and B. Young (eds) *Death and Bereavement across Cultures*. London: Routledge.

Lindemann, E. (1944) Symptomatology and management of acute grief. *American Journal of Psychiatry*, 101: 141–8.

Marris, P. (1991) The social construction of uncertainty, in C.M. Parkes, J. Stevenson-Huide and P. Marris (eds) *Attachment Across the Life Cycle*. London: Routledge.

Parkes, C.M. (1972) *Bereavement, Studies of Grief in Adult Life*. London: Tavistock.

Parkes, C.M., Laungani, P. and Young, B. (eds) (1997) *Death and Bereavement Across Cultures*. London: Routledge.

Pearson, M. (1986) Racist notions of ethnicity and culture in health education, in S. Rodmell and A. Watt (eds) *The Politics of Health Education*. London: Routledge, Kegan and Paul.

Pill, R. and Stott, N. (1982) Concepts of illness causation and responsibility: some preliminary data from a sample of working class mothers. *Social Science and Medicine*, 16: 43–52.

Raphael, B. (1984) *The Anatomy of Bereavement: A Handbook for the Caring Professions*. London: Hutchinson.

Riches, G. and Dawson, P. (1999) *An Intimate Loneliness*. Buckingham: Open University Press.

Rosenblatt, P., Walsh, R., and Jackson, D. (1976) *Grief and Mourning in Cross-cultural Perspective*. Washington DC: HRAF Press.

Rosenblatt, P. (1993) Cross-cultural variation in the experience, expression and understanding of grief, in D. Irish, K. Lundquist and V. Nelson (eds) *Ethnic Variations in Dying, Death and Grief: Diversity in Universality*. Washington: Taylor & Francis.

Rosenblatt, P. (1997) Grief in small-scale societies, in C.M. Parkes, P. Laungani, and B. Young, B. (eds) *Death and Bereavement Across Cultures*. London: Routledge.

Seale, C. (1998) *Constructing Death*. Cambridge: Cambridge University Press.

Stacey, M. (1986) Concepts of health and illness and the division of labour in health care, in C. Currer and M. Stacey (eds) *Concepts of Health, Illness and Disease*. Leamington Spa: Berg.

Stroebe, M. and Schut, H. (1998) Culture and grief. *Bereavement Care*, 17(1): 7–11.

Stroebe, W. and Stroebe, M. (1989) *Bereavement and Health*. Cambridge: Cambridge University Press.

Sudnow, D. (1967) *Passing On: The Social Organisation of Dying*. New Jersey: Prentice Hall.

Walter, T. (1993) Sociologists never die: British sociology and death, in D. Clark (ed.) *The Sociology of Death*. Oxford: Blackwell.

Walter, T. (1994) *The Revival of Death*. London: Routledge.

Walter, T. (1996) A new model of grief: bereavement and biography. *Mortality*, 1(1): 7–25.

Walter, T. (1997) Letting go and keeping hold: a reply to Stroebe. *Mortality*, 2(3): 263–6.

Walter, T. (1999) *On Bereavement*. Buckingham: Open University Press.

Worden, W. (1991) *Grief Counselling and Grief Therapy* (2nd edn). London: Routledge.

Wortman, C.B. and Silver, R.C. (1989) The myths of coping with loss. *Journal of Counselling and Clinical Psychology*, 57: 349–57.

Zola, I.K. (1972) Studying the decision to see a doctor. *Advances in Psychosomatic Medicine*, 8: 216.

Four siblings' perspectives on parent death: a family focus

MIRIAM S. MOSS AND SIDNEY Z. MOSS

Introduction

The meaning of the death of a family member is embedded in the ongoing social construction of the family. Family meanings are created and maintained through interactions, and these meanings may contribute to family identity and stability. Routines and rituals add to a sense of shared ideology and continuity. In this chapter we seek to enrich our understanding of bereavement by taking on a family perspective, thus expanding the traditional dyadic view, which focuses on one survivor and the deceased.

Most of the literature on family response to the death of a close member has come from a clinical base (Bowlby and Parkes 1970; Gelcer 1986; Rosen 1990; Detmer and Lamberti 1991; Walsh and McGoldrick 1991; Silverman *et al.* 1992; Patterson and Garwick 1994; Kissane and Bloch 1994; Shapiro 1994; Davies *et al.* 1995; Gilbert 1996; Nadeau 1998).

This chapter examines family themes that emerge from the narratives and dialogues with adult siblings in one family. Specifically we explore how the family is perceived *vis à vis* the elderly mother's death, the impact of this loss on the sense of family and on the individual's role within the family. We believe that this family perspective should be integrated into research and clinical work in bereavement.

The death of an old person over age 65 is a modal death, comprising 72 per cent of all deaths in the United States. It is expected and is accepted as a natural flow of life: the old are replaced by the younger generations. Although the death of an elderly parent is seen as a normative experience in the family, it is steeped in significance for surviving children (Moss and Moss 1997).

What limited research has been done on the impact of elderly parental death, focuses almost exclusively on one individual child's experience whether examined by researchers (Bass and Bowman 1990; Douglas 1990; Scharlach 1991; Scharlach and Fredericksen 1993; Umberson and Chen 1994; Pruchno *et al.* 1995; Moss and Moss 1997; Smith 1998) or by clinicians (Birtchnell 1970; Malinak *et al.* 1979; Horowitz *et al.* 1981).

There are few research studies involving multiple siblings around family deaths. Exceptions to this include Nadeau's (1998) examination of family bereavement around a range of family deaths and several more focused studies of family bereavement, such as young families' reactions to parent death (Worden 1996), family impact of cancer deaths of young children (Davies *et al.* 1995), deaths resulting from farm accidents (Rosenblatt 1993) and one family's bereavement around father's death (Fitzsimmons 1994).

Several foci have emerged from the broader (non-bereavement) literature on adult siblings: first, identification and solidarity with family including shared sense of history, responsibility, loyalty, and concern with continuity; second, inter-sibling processes including modelling, protectiveness, tolerance, and rivalry; and third, patterns of parent–child ties including affect, behaviours, and perceptions (such as favouritism) (Bank and Kahn 1982; Bedford 1992; Connidis 1992; Cicirelli 1995; Gold 1996). Each will be woven into our discussion.

After introducing the family and the four siblings who are central to the analysis, we examine three interwoven themes and explore the impact of the death on the family. Finally, we outline a paradox implicit in this family's bereavement.

Method

Members of one family were interviewed as an offshoot of a major qualitative study of the impact of the death of 107 elderly widowed mothers on a non-clinical, community sample of surviving middle-aged daughters. In order to broaden our perspective we wanted to interview multiple siblings in a single family. Ellen, an initial participant, who came from a large family, agreed to contact her siblings who would be amenable to being interviewed.

Each of four siblings participated alone in an audiotaped qualitative interview, which lasted about two hours. The interviews were designed to elicit a wide range of feelings and attitudes about the bereavement experience. Conversational in style, the interview explored the meaning of significant topics raised by the informants. Analysis followed standard qualitative analytic methods (Miles and Huberman 1984; Crabtree and Miller 1992; Luborsky 1994; Manning and Cullum-Swan 1994). Interview tapes were transcribed with commentary, and themes were explored through multiple rounds of coding.

Ethical issues of respondent confidentiality are complex when multiple family members are the focus of research (Rosenblatt 1995). At no time did we share what one sibling said with another. In order to maintain the integrity of the family while maximizing confidentiality we have modified characteristics of individuals and the family structure.

This is a Catholic, urban, middle-class family with both Irish and Italian roots. The mother, a housewife, died at age 90. The father was a factory worker who died at age 81, ten years earlier. They had a total of 11 children: one died at birth, four sons died in adulthood, and three sons and three daughters were living at the time of the study. After the father's death, the mother continued to live with her handicapped son George, who died several years before her. In spite of her increasing frailty and loss of short-term memory, the mother continued to live alone in the family home where each of the children had been raised. When intensive parent care became necessary for the final two years of her life, each of the children agreed to be responsible to stay with mother a full 24-hour day each week. This routine caregiving became a central family ritual.

Each of the four siblings lives in the same metropolitan area, several in the same neighbourhood as the mother. They are currently married, except Jim a widower, and each have three or more children. Jim is the oldest living sibling, 69, a retired policeman, widowed two years before his mother died. He felt as close to his mother-in-law as to his mother. Ellen, 56, retired from her office job several months before her mother died in order to spend more time with her. Her daughter, Jenny, died in an accident 15 years ago. John, 50, is a bookkeeper, the only one to have completed one year of college. He is the executor of his mother's estate. Mary, 47, the youngest sibling, is a legal secretary. She has cancer which is currently in remission. Two other siblings refused to be interviewed: one a sister, 65, and one a brother, Joe, 52, who was considered the least involved of the six siblings in caregiving and in family matters.

Family themes

Several family themes emerged from the interviews: continuity of family identity, equality and acceptance of diversity, and maintenance of the deceased within the family boundaries. We explore the ways in which the ties with the mother and with other deceased family members are maintained.

Continuity of family identity

A strong sense of family identity and closeness is pervasive. Each of the siblings has internalized an ethos of family solidarity, and the theme of 'we-ness' is central. This sense of identity was played out in recent years in the family ritual of lengthy shared caregiving, the most central activity at the end of the mother's life. 'I have to say in the last couple years when we began taking care of mom, that it was a bonding of the siblings . . . a rebonding of the siblings' (Ellen).

The joint caregiving formed the ground on which subsequent family decisions and activities were based: the shared 24-hour hospital bedside vigil during the final two weeks, each sibling's active participation in the funeral ceremony, the equal distribution of possessions, and the mutual decision to sell the family home and share the proceeds.

Additionally, the interviews were replete with frequent comparisons with other siblings (Nadeau 1998). Each tends to see the self and siblings as part of the family constellation and to refer to 'the family' as a whole in narratives of mother's death.

Equality and acceptance of diversity

The siblings emphasized the intertwined themes of equality and acceptance of diversity. The mother was seen as concerned with fairness and equality, and the siblings have taken that as a family legacy. Each of the siblings felt important, needed, and appreciated by their mother. Although, Steve who died ten years earlier was described as 'a jelly fish, with a chink in his character', Mother's love for him 'overcame her common sense. We all lived with that, no problem' (Jim).

Associated with the theme of equality is that of acceptance of diversity. In talking about caregiving, there was recognition of the unequal contributions of the siblings. 'I think some of us did more than others. I would say that Joe did the least, but I would think that was all that Joe had. He didn't have the same sensitivity as the rest of us' (Ellen).

Talk of favouritism recurred. Although there is evidence that there are most favourites and least favourites among siblings (Bedford 1992; Klagsbrun 1992), we found some equality of favouritism. Although we did not initiate the issue of favouritism, it proved to be important for each of the four siblings. George who was handicapped, was viewed as a quasi 'son' by each of the siblings, and a 'favourite'. Eddie, who was killed in the Second World War, was 'By all accounts, everyone's favourite' (Mary).

Ellen and John each perceive themselves as being seen as 'favourites' by the family. We asked Ellen: 'Did mom tell you you were her favourite?' She replied, 'No, everybody else used to tell me. I could do no wrong. Anything I said was gospel'. John said, 'I think some in the family would say that I'm the favourite, for whatever reason. And there's always a little animosity that goes with that. And it's kinda you wanted to be the favourite, now you're going to pay for it with this thing (being executor)'. Additionally, Ellen and John are careful to deny their special place, or to rationalize it by describing aspects of their lives that warrant it.

Favouritism is potentially divisive in that a favourite child may evoke envy and blame for being in that special position *vis à vis* mother. The favourite may be criticized more than the parent who designated the favourite (Bedford 1992). Favouritism may also be seen as unifying, when siblings deny its impact, and affirm sibling equality and parental fairness.

Maintenance of the deceased within family boundaries

Siblings stressed the continuity of the tie with the mother as well as with other deceased close kin. The meaningful relationships, which had been built up over the decades, persisted and were expected to continue into the future. In the realm of family, there seems to be only addition, not subtraction.

Tie with the deceased mother

The bond with the mother is maintained in multiple, interconnected ways: through possessions, continued interaction and reunion.

Possessions

Siblings described concrete and symbolically meaningful personal treasures that embodied the essence of mother.

Ellen's mother had used a tile to keep her teapot warm, now Ellen uses it 'almost every night ... and that's when my mom comes to dinner every night when I put it in the oven'. John has mother's little leprechaun figure representing his mother's cultural legacy: 'she was very Irish leaning'. Mary prizes her mother's holy things, such as her mother's crosses, which she now wears.

Continuing interaction

There is a sense of mother's presence, which affects the current lives of the siblings. She tends to be endowed with a life force that she had in previous years. According to Jim: 'we never had a problem since mom died, who wants what furniture and that kind of thing. Let's not have it now that the house is almost sold. So she's still keeping the family together'.

Mary refers to a broad range of contexts in which she talks to and thinks about her mother; each elicits different memories and feelings. When asked, 'Nowadays, do you find yourself thinking about your mother'? she replied:

Now? Oh, sure, maybe as often as daily ... If I am with my brothers and sisters we talk about her care. If I am with my girl friends ... remember the night your mother had that stick ... she never let you stay out late. If I am with my husband we talk about how she didn't like him . . . he wasn't Catholic and was a foreigner. Later he was very much a favourite. We talk about her when the kids are around to keep the memory alive . . .' (Referring to a recent CAT scan): 'The old girl was there. She said, "You'll be alright". I said, "Mom, mom, mom". She was just there . . . (I called over and over) "Mom where are you? I need you, I want you here" '.

Reunion

Each sibling referred to the overall family as comprised of both a segment of deceased members and a segment of living members, with highly permeable boundaries between the segments. Siblings often spoke about anticipated reunions with the dead, described their own brief reunions or visits with the dead, and easily referred to dead members having reunions with others who are dead. These reunions are active and family oriented. The deceased as well as the living maintain past roles, relationships and behaviours. Reunion is a strong affirmation of the continuity of family.

Even back when mother was alive, she and the family talked about her eventual reunion with her husband and deceased sons. John said, 'You could kid with her about that . . . going up to dad, he's waiting for you, Dad and George. And she has enough sons up there that she had a job.'

Ellen was asked, 'Do you in any way feel that you will meet your mother again sometime?' 'Absolutely! She'll be waiting there for me'. Jim shared this view: 'I think my mother's happier now than she was when she was here. She's with her husband and kids. I think she trusts that we're all okay . . . I believe we'll all be together again. I don't know in what form. In a sense I look forward to it. I think it'll be the greatest experience ever in my life or in anyone's life'.

Tie with other deceased family members

Overall, the mother's death was repeatedly referred to in the context of other family deaths. Each sibling had experienced highly significant deaths (Figure 3.1). Jim lost his wife and brother, Charles, whom he saw as a mentor; Ellen lost her daughter, Jenny; John lost the older brother Eddie whom he hardly knew, yet he continues to try to reconstruct Eddie's life; Mary lost a nephew (her oldest sister's son) to whom she felt as close as a sibling. Some family deaths are more private, some more shared. The process of bereavement is not uniform; some are mourned more than others (note: one brother, Steve, is not on the figure).

All siblings felt the deep loss of George, their handicapped brother, their 'son'. George's death evoked a sense of individual and collective mourning and reminiscing. 'I dealt more poorly with that [his death] than I did with

Figure 3.1   Significant family deaths

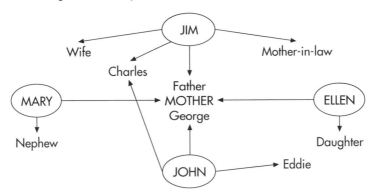

mom's death I think' (John). 'The most important death was my brother, George. I grieved very deeply for him. I still miss George. We still talk about him like he's still here' (Mary).

Jim spoke of his brother, Charles: 'I consider him to be the only friend I have had. I had many acquaintances, good pals. But never went to visit his grave. Never in 25 years'. (Interviewer: 'How come?') 'I don't know. I don't have to. I talk to him everyday in my mind . . . Not a day goes by that I don't think of him'.

John also felt a continuing bond with Charles who was his godfather. John was strongly tied to Eddie, who was killed in the Second World War when John was only in kindergarten.

> I think about Eddie a lot. He was 20 years, 3 months and 9 days. I still carry his little card. I always looked up to him because of the way everybody talked about him. On visiting the cemetery: 'I don't think of them [deceased family members] as being dead I think of them as being alive . . . My thoughts of them are that they are alive.

Ellen's attitude towards her mother's death was tied in with her loss of a daughter, only 14 years old:

> I think that I will always relate more of my mother's death experience to that of Jenny's . . . It's always there. I feel like my mom will be with me the same way that Jenny is with me . . . I don't really see a comparison. I think that Jenny's death was a tragedy, and mom's death was a natural evolution . . . a piece of me didn't die with my mom.

Jim's wife died two years before his mother. 'I was still bent out of shape by the loss of my wife so I may not be a fair judge for you . . .' (Interviewer: 'How would you compare the death of your mother to your wife's?') 'No comparison. I can't. My wife was me! Like a couple of arms fell off. My mother's? I loved her dearly . . . I just say, [to my wife] help me, give me some sign like this that you approve of what I've been doing. I do talk to my loved ones as if they are with me, and maybe they are'.

Impact of death on the family

Each sibling spoke of mother as central to the meaning of family, although each used different family metaphors (Rosenblatt 1994): 'the core' and 'the knot in the common thread' (Jim), 'focal point' (Ellen), 'the glue' (John), 'the supreme head' and 'bond that held us together' (Mary).

Further, each sibling identifies with different parts of the mother. An adult child's tie with mother is rooted in the past. Although the mother was central to the family, each sibling perceived a somewhat different mother:

> She was stubborn and I think I inherited that from my mother.
>
> (Jim)

> I'm told I look like her . . . Our views of some things are pretty much the same . . . My mother was not good with her hands, neither am I.
>
> (Ellen)

> I think I have a lot of her ways.
>
> (John)

> I know I raised my children the same way she raised me. Almost identically . . .
>
> (Mary)

Although each sibling described him or herself as deeply affected by the mother's death, each highlighted unique themes in describing her death:

> The tide runs out, you go . . . she had her shot.
>
> (Jim)

> She was just dying inch by inch it was a very unpleasant death, a painful death.
>
> (Ellen)

> It was a function of the heart . . . It was old and worn out.
>
> (John)

> I feel terrible. I would have liked to have been there [when she died].
>
> (Mary)

The brothers' emphasis on factual and mechanical themes and the sisters' emphasis on relationships and empathy are congruent with gender styles (Moss *et al.* 1996–1997; Martin and Doka 1998).

Although the siblings describe the process differently, each recognizes the threat or reality of weakening of family and sibling ties after the prolonged and intense closeness around caregiving. Each of the siblings acknowledged that changes in the family would occur after mother's death. They focus on family rather than individual dyads. Ross and Milgram (1982) have found that there tends to be more stability in family closeness than in closeness to individual siblings. As Mary said:

> [Without mother] you have to create a whole new relationship with the rest of the family if it's going to stay together. Because to me she was the bond that held us together. Now we have to hold each other if we want to. I don't even think we'll let Joe go even if he wants to. I can see us getting further apart, but Joe will never get so far that he won't be reachable. Never.

Ellen said, although there will be less interaction, 'we will still be bound'.

There is evidence that siblings' ties may be strengthened after a family death (Connidis 1992). Siblings in this family having already experienced the off-time deaths of their brothers may have developed an enhanced sense of closeness as the family dealt with those common tragedies. This closeness may have helped to form the base for their response to their mother's death. The death of the last parent has been found to have a great and overwhelmingly positive impact on sibling closeness in midlife (Gold 1996). In part the bonds are strengthened because children are no longer buffered by the older generation and share the increasing threat of mortality (Gold 1996). This threat of personal finitude for new members of the omega generation was expressed by both brothers.

Each of the four siblings saw the family as perceiving him or herself as central to the continuity of the family. Mary says, 'Before, I felt that my mother was the supreme head of the family, now I am'. John, who was executor and decision-maker, feels like 'the leader'. Ellen recognizes that she is 'now the matriarch'. Jim is uncertain about 'being the patriarch'. Rather than a central kin keeper, there seems to be a tendency for each child to feel that she or he is now central to the maintenance of the family.

Paradox in family bereavement

The siblings' reactions to the mother's death suggest a major paradox, which occurs in this family, and is likely to be present in many families who are bereaved. We suggest that families actively deal with the acceptance of the simultaneous reality of the presence as well as the absence of the deceased. Absence and presence of the deceased are simultaneous.

Mother in this family is accepted as dead, but she is still actively present in the family: she provides expectations, support, approval, protection, a model for behaviour, and is a viable image for the living. She and other deceased kin remain within family boundaries, and yet in some ways the living must close off and restructure in order to survive as a living family.

In order to consider a future reunion with mother one must feel separate from her, yet the deceased still seem to be within the family boundaries. Thus, the survivors simultaneously hold on to the mother, and let go of the mother. In accepting the finality of death they are recognizing the loss, while at the same time they maintain multiple aspects of the tie.

This is a very large family and it may have been especially strong in socializing the siblings for fairness, sharing, tolerance, and desire to belong and be needed (Bossard and Boll 1956). The dynamics, however, may be similar to smaller families, particularly where terminal care for a frail parent has been central to the sibling's interaction.

Conclusions

The themes that emerged in this family may be worth exploring for their presence or absence in other families that have experienced the death of a close member.

The four siblings in this chapter have described the unique experience of one large family in relation to the death of their elderly mother. We suggest that the themes which have emerged, while not generalizable to other families, do represent dimensions that are potentially significant for most bereaved families: a sense of family identity may be stronger or weaker; equality and acceptance of diversity may be more or less significant than divisiveness, rivalry and coalitions. Earlier family deaths may play a more or less significant role in the family's reaction to parent death. Although we have found in our broader research that the death of the first parent is salient for children experiencing the death of the last parent (Moss and Moss 1997), in this family the impact of the father's death was muted and tended to be peripheral to the siblings. The degree to which the deceased are integrated into the daily lives of the survivors is heightened in this family, particularly for the daughters.

Future research on the death of an elderly parent, as well as other family deaths, may benefit from examination of the themes discussed here. Bereaved individuals experience most deaths within a family context. Just as a focus on the individual can facilitate understanding of family losses, a concurrent focus on the family can maximize understanding of individual losses.

References

Bank, S.P. and Kahn, M.D. (1982) *The Sibling Bond*. New York: Basic Books.
Bass, D.M. and Bowman, K. (1990) The impact of an aged relative's death on the family, in K.F. Ferraro (ed.) *Gerontology: Perspectives and Issues*. New York: Springer.

Bedford, V.H. (1992) Memories of parental favouritism and the quality of parent–child ties in adulthood. *Journal of Gerontology: Social Sciences*, 47: S149–S155.

Birtchnell, J. (1970) Depression in relation to early and recent parent death. *British Journal of Psychiatry*, 116: 299–305.

Bossard, J.H.S. and Boll, E.S. (1956) *The Large Family System*. Westport, CT: Greenwood Press.

Bowlby, J. and Parkes, C.M. (1970) Separation and loss within the family, in E.J. Anthony and C. Koupernick (eds). *The Child in his Family*. New York: John Wiley.

Cicirelli, V. (1995) Sibling relationships in middle and old age, in G.H. Brody (ed.) *Sibling Relationships: Their Causes and Consequences*. Norwood, NJ: Ablex Publishing.

Connidis, I.A. (1992) Life transitions and the adult sibling tie: a qualitative study. *Journal of Marriage and the Family*, 54: 972–82.

Crabtree, B. and Miller, W. (1992) A template approach to text analysis: developing and using codebooks, in J. Morse (ed.) *Qualitative Health Research*. Newbury Park, CA: Sage.

Davies, B., Reimer, J.C., Brown, P. and Martens, N. (1995) *Fading Away: The Experience of Transition in Families with Terminal Illness*. Amityville, NY: Baywood.

Detmer, C.M. and Lamberti, J.M. (1991) Family grief. *Death Studies*, 15: 363–74.

Douglas, J.D. (1990) Patterns of change following parent death in midlife adults. *Omega*, 22: 123–37.

Fitzsimmons, E. (1994) One man's death: His family's ethnography. *Omega*, 30: 23–39.

Gelcer, E. (1986) Dealing with loss in the family context, *Journal of Family Issues*, 7: 315–35.

Gilbert, K.R. (1996) We've had the same loss, why don't we have the same grief? Loss and differential grief in families. *Death Studies*, 20: 268–83.

Gold, D.T. (1996) Continuities and discontinuities in sibling relationships across the life span, in V.L. Bengtson (ed.) *Adulthood and Ageing*. New York: Springer.

Horowitz, M.J., Krupnick, J., Kaltreider, N. *et al.* (1981) Initial psychological response to parental death. *Archives of General Psychiatry*, 38: 316–23.

Kissane, D.W. and Bloch, S. (1994) Family grief. *British Journal of Psychiatry*, 164: 728–40.

Klagsbrun, F. (1992) *Mixed Feelings*. New York: Bantam.

Luborsky, M. (1994) Identification and analysis of themes and patterns, in J. Gubrium and A. Sankar (eds). *Qualitative Methods in Old Age Research*. Newbury Park, CA: Sage.

Malinak, D., Hoyt, M. and Patterson, V. (1979) Reaction to the death of a parent in adult life. *American Journal of Psychiatry*, 136: 1152–6.

Manning, P. and Cullen-Swan, B. (1994) Narrative, content and semiotic analysis, in N. Denzin and Y. Lincoln (eds) *Handbook of Qualitative Research*. Thousand Oaks, CA: Sage.

Martin, T.I. and Doka, K.J. (1998) Revisiting masculine grief, in K.J. Doka and J.D. Davidson (eds) *Living with Grief*. Philadelphia, PA: Brunner Mazel.

Miles, M. and Huberman, A.M. (1984) *Qualitative Data Analysis: A Sourcebook of New Methods*. Beverly Hills, CA: Sage.

Moss, M.S and Moss, S.Z. (1997) Middle aged children's bereavement after the death of an elderly parent, in J.D. Morgan (ed.) *Readings in Thanatology*. Amityville, NY: Baywood.

Moss, S.Z., Rubinstein, R.L. and Moss, M.S. (1996–1997) Middle aged son's reaction to father's death. *Omega*, 34: 259–77.

Nadeau, J.W. (1998) *Families Making Sense of Death*. Thousand Oaks, CA: Sage.

Patterson, J.M. and Garwick, A.W. (1994) Levels of meaning in family stress theory. *Family Process*, 33: 287–304.

Pruchno, R.A., Moss, M.S., Burant, C.J. and Schinfeld, S. (1995) Death of an institutional parent: predictors of bereavement. *Omega*, 31: 99–119.

Rosen, E.J. (1990) *Families Facing Death*. Lexington, MA: Lexington.

Rosenblatt, P.C. (1993) Coping with losing a family member in a farm accident. Publication No. FO-6205B. St Paul, MN: Minnesota Extension Service.

Rosenblatt, P.C. (1994) *Metaphors of family systems theory*. New York: Guilford Press.

Rosenblatt, P.C. (1995) Ethics of qualitative interviewing with grieving families. *Death Studies*, 19: 139–55.

Ross, H.G. and Milgram, J.I. (1982) Important variable in adult sibling relationships: a qualitative study, in M.E. Lamb and B. Sutton-Smith (eds) *Sibling Relationships: Their nature and significance across the lifespan*. Hillsdale, NJ: Lawrence Erlbaum.

Scharlach, A.E. (1991) Factors associated with filial grief following the death of an elderly parent. *American Journal of Orthopsychiatry*, 6: 307–13.

Scharlach, A.E. and Fredericksen, K.I. (1993) Reactions to the death of a parent. *Omega*, 27: 307–17.

Shapiro, E.R. (1994) *Grief as a Family Process*. New York: Guilford Press.

Silverman, P.R., Nickman, S. and Worden, J.W. (1992) Detachment revisited: the child's construction of a dead parent. *American Journal of Orthopsychiatry*, 62(1): 494–503.

Smith, S.H. (1998) *African American Daughters and Elderly Mothers*. New York: Garland.

Umberson, D. and Chen, M.D. (1994) Effects of a parent's death on adult child relationships: salience and reaction to loss. *American Sociological Review*, 59: 152–68.

Walsh, F. and McGoldrick, M. (1991) *Living beyond loss: Death in the family*. New York: W.W. Norton.

Warner, W.L. (1975) *The Living and the Dead*. Westport, CT: Greenwood Press.

Worden, J.W. (1996) *Children and Grief*. New York: Guilford Press.

'Naturalizing' death among older adults in residential care

CAROL KOMAROMY AND JENNY HOCKEY

> Death is increasingly occurring within a narrow age range in later life
> (Bytheway 1995: 127)

In his account of ageism, Bytheway shows how many older people find themselves inhabiting a social category that is clearly differentiated from the social category, 'adult'. He identifies the 'them' and 'us' nature of discourses and practices that create social divisions between individuals, based purely on the passage of time. And, as indicated above, death is now distanced to that 'other' category of 'the elderly', just as it is to those foreign or historically remote 'others' who die in battles or epidemics.

This chapter crosses the divide between 'them' and 'us' to examine the experience of inhabiting the 'narrow age range in later life' within which death increasingly occurs. Our setting is care homes where 'we' look after 'them'. It argues that staff's exposure to frailty and death puts at risk the socially constructed boundary between those who distance themselves from death and those likely to die. Exposure to residents' pain, confusion and dying can disturb staffs' equanimity in relation to their own embodied ageing and that of close family members. Read from this perspective, their practices are implicitly geared to repairing this boundary. Death is continuously relocated to the site of old age where it takes on different, age-specific meanings – it is 'timely', a 'release' or a 'blessing'; dying residents are 'ready for it', willing to be 'taken', 'getting tired'. The following data show how care work produces the 'timely' deaths of 'the elderly' and, in the process, constrains the emotional lives of residents and their families.

The 1980s feminist literature on the concept of care highlighted its ambiguity as both labour and emotion (Finch and Groves 1983). In addition 'care' is gendered (Dalley 1988), women being required to care *for* the family members they cared *about*. However, those professionals who care for individuals who represent a future of deterioration and decay must manage the emotion of care with caution, conducting emotional labour not only with regard to themselves but also on behalf of residents, their families, other residents and colleagues (Hochschild 1983).

The good/ideal type death in care

While ageism secures the boundary between 'adulthood' and 'old age', additional socio-cultural processes then transform the deaths of older people. Here models of the good death play a key role (see Kellehear 1990; Bradbury 1996). Death among younger adults is unanticipated and therefore by definition 'bad'. The good deaths of elderly residents, however, are thought to occur in a controlled and timely manner. They are deaths that residents 'accept' and which occur without pain or distress. These deaths are therefore not meant to stimulate problematic emotion. Indeed, if we examine the policies of residential homes, the management of the 'naturally' occurring death of older people does not seem to merit much by way of special provision.

In a questionnaire survey (see Siddell *et al.* 1997) only one-third of the 412 homes that responded claimed to have a written policy on death and dying. A smaller sub-sample returned copies of their policies. Varying in length and detail, they mainly focused on physical care at the time of death – mouth care, pressure areas and the administration of fluids – but downplayed its emotional dimensions. In one example, it was not until Guideline 28 that a reference appeared:

> Don't ever be afraid to sit on a bed with a very sick person or even the dying. Hold her hand, be understanding and talk to her. It's not really difficult and they won't feel so alone.

If the need for emotional support was acknowledged, this was framed abstractly by comparison with the practices specified for physical care. For example:

> Provide physical, emotional and psychological comfort and support to the resident and his/her family, and with sensitivity endeavour to find out what their wishes are with regard to any further arrangements.

Within the sub-sample of 30 policies, only one acknowledged any emotional connection between staff and residents:

> To care for the dying the carer must be able to: First cope with their own fears about death, the resident's fear and those close to him/her.

The profile of the good/ideal type of death in residential care, although only implicit within policy documents, was nonetheless articulated in interviews.

First, staff believed that home was the best place to die as it provided a 'secure and comfortable' environment. Since the institution was represented by staff as the residents' 'home', it therefore became the optimum place for their death, something to which they had a right. Indeed this right was seen as universal since by definition the 'good' death took place in familiar surroundings where the individual's needs were understood. In the residential home, care staff were best placed in this respect, having cared for residents over an extended period.

Second, when staff were invited to talk about well-managed deaths, they highlighted the quality of a 'peaceful' death, something achieved when residents 'accepted' their deaths and were free of pain. 'Acceptance', they believed, was possible only when pain was alleviated.

Third, 'good' deaths were predictable, so allowing family to be emotionally prepared and physically present when the event took place. To die alone was to contravene the model of a good death.

Fourth, 'good' dying was neither protracted nor sudden, its shape constituting a straightforward trajectory from deterioration to death. Those that involved the ups and downs of deterioration and improvement challenged the ideal type. Contained, controlled and timely deaths were therefore the ideal product of homes in which older people came to accept the 'natural' ending of their lives.

Theory and practice

In tandem with a questionnaire survey, the study also involved observation, a method which revealed a tension between the good/ideal type death and what actually appeared to take place (Siddell et al. 1997). For example, although staff had talked about residents' right to die in their residential 'home', its rigid hierarchy could undermine any attempts at 'homeliness'. Indeed, institutional hierarchies became more prominent when a resident was dying, the head of home often establishing the rules and regulations that determined their care, particularly when care staff lacked nursing qualifications. Similarly, tension existed between 'home' as a site within which the individual has territorial control and 'home' as rule-bound institutional space where personal control is severely constrained. Nonetheless, hospital-type interventions at the death bed scene such as the administration of artificial hydration and drugs were often missing, their absence being explained in terms of the 'naturalness' of death in old age. Yet here again inconsistencies were evident. Though death was posited as a natural, 'homely' event, death bed scenes were constructed as dramatic events with key actors playing leading roles. Family attendance was privileged above that of friends, particularly if the friends were other residents. Care staff therefore undertook the physical care of dying residents while family kept a death bed vigil. These 'roles' were not negotiated, except in cases where a relative had previously contributed to a resident's physical care and might then continue to do so.

Direct observations also revealed that staging the model 'death bed scene' did not always occur. Staff did not have time to sit with residents. Instead they made regular visits and as a result were not always present at the death. Residents' 'acceptance' required freedom from pain, yet a dying woman was observed to scream each time she was moved. In general, caring for dying residents, although seen as important, was not done at the expense of living residents. One staff member said: 'When I'm with a dying resident, I worry about the others, and when I'm with them, I feel I'm neglecting the dying resident. I think we need enough staff to be able to do one thing or the other'.

Residents' models of death

During the study, residents were invited to talk about their thoughts on death. On these occasions it was not unusual for them to reflect on the losses they had experienced in their life. For many, the most prominent loss was associated with physical deterioration and reduced independent mobility. Hannah explained: 'I can't do much any more. I'm not really living. I can't go out'. Another resident, Mildred, said that her life was worthless because: 'I can't do anything'.

Staff's construction of death as 'natural' and therefore, in an ideal sense, 'acceptable' to residents contrasts with residents' resignation when faced with the absence of any better alternative. If they did not see themselves as 'really living' then death became 'acceptable' in a rather different sense to the one intended by staff. Alongside residents' perceptions of their lived experience as constituting something less than 'life', can be placed their responses to the losses of significant others.

Ada, for example, continued to grieve her stillborn baby and the subsequent deaths of her husband, sister and niece. They became an unbearable weight, which she often talked and cried about before her own death. Another woman described carrying grief over her two sons' deaths 'inside her'. 'I cannot let go of it', she said. For residents faced with a set of circumstances that they experienced as less than a 'life', in addition to bereavements which they perceived as 'untimely', a state of shock and incomprehension was not uncommon. Deaths in old age, which for younger adults might seem to be 'natural' and 'acceptable' because they were deferred, for older people themselves represented a disorienting prospect. Their bodies, familiar to them across 70 years or more, had become strange. Those significant others who should have been there at life's ending had predeceased them. Hannah, for example, was 89. She could not understand why she had not died at the age of 70. Although she had a sense of personal triumph over death by surviving two major illnesses, her two sons had meanwhile died and she remained alone, puzzling as to what she had been saved for.

As regards the manner of their deaths, residents clearly had models of what they hoped for – and dreaded. A retired priest and a nun said that they expected God's will to dictate the manner of their death, a reflection of a view of themselves as instruments of God. Their stories contrast with other accounts involving the will of God where there was evidence of varying degrees of influence and negotiation. Not only in a Catholic home, but in other settings too, residents called upon God's will to make their exit 'easy': 'I hope the Lord will make it easy for me'. 'There isn't anything I can do. I just have to accept it all. It's in God's hands'.

These residents saw God as the agent who could decide their fate. Others offered accounts of their own good works in an expression of hope that they could influence their own dying. Most were women who had nursed family members, For example: 'I want my end to be quick, when it comes. I nursed my husband for years after his stroke. I promised to look after him in sickness and in health'.

Many residents hoped for a short period of dying, with a peaceful death in sleep as an ideal. In contrast they offered accounts of the less than ideal deaths of fellow residents: 'She's only there and suffering you know, getting bedsores and that as a rule. It isn't a nice way of going is it? It isn't a nice way – best to go quick'.

A resident at another home echoed this sentiment: 'What sort of life is it for me if I can't go out? I just hope when it comes it is quick'.

As these data indicate, rather than an inevitable 'given' of old age, death is frequently a focus for speculation if not fear among people living in residential care. An earlier study (Hockey 1990) revealed residents' persistent references to their age, their closeness to death and the deaths of their contemporaries. They pointed out that they had removed jewellery so that funeral directors would not steal it from their bodies; they made references to death in gesture rather than words by lying with eyes closed and arms folded when morning tea was brought in; they asked staff to 'finish them off' by putting them in black plastic bags when they were sweeping up rubbish or pushing them under in the bath or giving them a lethal drug injection. They also worried that their illnesses might be fatal; that a wealth of birthday cards might mean this was to be their final year. And they grieved afresh for earlier losses, which gathered intensity when compounded by other losses. Examples were a miscarriage followed by a childless marriage, a source of enduring grief in widowhood; and the deaths of adult children.

Emotional labour: care staff

From this evidence it becomes clear that for many residents death is not anticipated as potentially 'good', 'natural' or 'acceptable'. Rather it is a focus for intense and problematic emotion, much of which is made evident in everyday interactions, whether directly or obliquely. Staff, however, in managing their daily encounters with residents' bodily deterioration, sought to uphold models of a good death. This involved taking responsibility for the multiplicity of emotions and values surrounding residents' deaths. Although they felt close to many of the residents, it was largely unacceptable for staff to express more than minimal grief after an individual's death. Not only would a show of emotion indicate a lack of professionalism, but also an apparent illogicality in regretting the death of someone whom had lived a very long life. This 'timeliness' of death among residents was shored up through comparisons with the deaths of staffs' younger friends and relatives. Data show them highlighting the difference in significance and drawing on an age-based contrast between residents who had 'had their life' and younger people deprived of the years to which they had a right.

As noted, this talk constitutes a kind of emotional labour (Hochschild 1983), here focused on staff's own potentially problematic feelings. They said the death of a close friend or relative sensitized them, for example to the needs of residents' family and friends.

A nurse in a nursing home for older people expressed it thus: 'Ever since my brother-in-law's death, which really affected me, I've seen things differently. I think I'm much more in touch with the families' feelings now'.

Some did disclose persistent grief after a resident's death, but qualified this as an unusual occurrence: 'We're not supposed to . . .' 'I don't know why that particular death . . .' 'I was the only one who really understood her . . .' 'They tell me I'll have to harden up . . .'

In this way they attributed an illegitimate status to their feelings.

Emotional labour: heads of homes

Self-management of emotion among staff was complemented by the emotional labour of heads of homes. They often set the tone for acceptable emotional demeanour and some cited staff who had failed in this respect and had to leave or seek counselling. Grief that continued to be expressed by staff after a few weeks or months would be seen in this light. If they grieved 'excessively', this risked overshadowing the feelings expressed by families – although it became more acceptable when families were labelled 'uncaring'. Here a head of home describes a staff member's response to the death of a resident she had known for ten years: 'I think they do recognize there is a time that is appropriate for people to go. Of course, when she was on her own she cried after that . . . They manage their sort of bereavement.'

Looked at more holistically, the emotional labour of both staff and heads of homes combines to create a cultural framework for the management of emotion (Menzies 1970; de Swaan 1990: 31–56). For example, staff's talk of residents' deaths commonly took the form of compensatory narratives. In these the quality of life was privileged over quantity, the deaths of older people being represented as easier to accept because an individual had had a 'good innings'. The study also invited staff to discuss particular deaths retrospectively and in these accounts particular deaths were often evaluated. For example, if the quality of dying constituted a good death, this could provide a fitting end to life. This was especially the case if the resident was felt to have come to terms with their death and so achieved a peaceful death. However, if the process of dying had been difficult, death could provide a release from suffering and as such be a 'blessing'. These retrospective reflections were well rehearsed and took on a rhetorical quality as repertoires of compensation (Potter and Wetherell 1987).

In producing the 'good' and therefore acceptable deaths of older people, staff were at pains both to provide an appropriate staging of the death bed and to forestall problematic emotional responses. Warning families and friends about an imminent death was seen as important by heads of homes, a duty of senior staff or the GP. As noted, family were privileged over friends at the death bed and access to the dying resident and information about their condition was provided according to this hierarchy of privilege. Although care staff supported friends and family on a practical and emotional level, precise information about a resident's condition was given only by the person in charge.

Despite this, some relatives spoke of unclear disclosures and unanswered questions about the resident's condition. The daughter of a resident in a small home described her meeting with her mother's GP: 'He came when Rita sent for him and he just said that she had pneumonia and he just said she is poorly, she is old. She wasn't eating at the time and I just wanted (begins to cry) and I just said to him, 'Could she have some veg?' and he said, 'Well it won't do any good'.

By aligning the concepts of 'poorly' and 'old', this GP conveyed the mother's status as dying, without saying so directly. More commonly heads of homes, rather than GPs, disclosed information. Yet they too tended to say that a resident was ill or 'poorly', rather than dying. The wife of a relatively young man who died in one home said: 'The Matron came up and . . . she said it was for the best. But they didn't discuss it – she didn't say, 'He is dying'. But I think it was – she implied that you know . . . I mean they were very caring and that, but as far as giving me any information it was very small'.

It would seem therefore that staff, and GPs, are at pains to diffuse potential emotional outbursts that might result from more direct language. Relatives, however, made their own judgements in this respect. A deceased resident's daughter said:

I think they are trained not to show their feelings really, because I don't know if it was that day or whether it was the day before, I can't just remember now, Asha (care assistant) was very quiet, she was really quiet was Asha and I said to her, 'What's the matter?' . . . and she said, 'Nothing' and I said, 'Come on just tell me what the matter is'. And she said, 'It is your mother'. And she got upset, she really got upset, and then she sort of, she said, 'We have got to be strong'.

She went on:

I think it is good. It seemed to me . . . that everybody did care. You know if they didn't show their feelings you would think they were a bit hard or whatever.

Where the family were absent at the time of death, it was the head of home who broke the news. Sometimes the way in which the news was to be imparted had been negotiated beforehand. The son of a deceased resident said:

Matron, she said, 'We will let you know but not in the middle of the night, because there's nothing you can do'. I said, 'Well no, thank you, that's a point'. No point them ringing me to tell me in the middle of the night mum had gone.

Many relatives were similarly clear that they did not want to be told in the night of a death, particularly if they themselves were old and lived alone.

Staff were also aware of relatives' difficulty in collecting a dead resident's belongings. Those who had established friendships with other residents might continue to visit them; in the case of voluntary homes they sometimes became involved in support work within the home. Mostly, though, the relationship with the home, however long, would end abruptly once personal items had been retrieved.

Conclusion

This chapter shows how a multi-faceted conception of 'naturalness' underpins the cultural practices through which heads of homes and their staff manage the social and emotional lives of those brought together at the leaky boundary between adulthood and old age (Yanagisako and Delaney 1995). Not only residents and their families but staff themselves are included here. As the data indicate, this often gives rise to contradictions. For example, since death in later life was considered to be 'natural', residents were thought to be reconciled to the proximity of their own deaths and those of fellow residents, a conception of naturalness based on age. However if residents' children pre-deceased them this was an 'unnatural death' and a legitimate focus for grief – even when these 'elderly' children were in their seventies. Here 'naturalness' is grounded in the principle of generation and not age. Just as death is expected to take the oldest before the youngest, so it is 'natural' for earlier generations to pre-decease later ones. However, people who live on into their nineties confound the synchrony of age and generation by remaining alive beyond the point at which the next generation are ready to die 'natural' deaths. When staff discussed relatives' responses, however, age-based 'naturalness' was put into abeyance. Instead, the 'natural' strength of feeling of the child for its parent is expected to persist into adult life, making the 'timely' death of an elderly parent a source of grief.

In summary, this chapter has presented data that underscore the emotional susceptibility of older people and their families to the constraints imposed by a care staff whose everyday working lives take place at the critical boundary between adult life and death in old age.

References

Bradbury, M. (1996) Representations of 'good' and 'bad' death among deathworkers and the bereaved, in G. Howarth and P. Jupp (eds) *Contemporary Issues in the Sociology of Death, Dying and Disposal*. Basingstoke: Macmillan.

Bytheway, B. (1995) *Ageism*. Buckingham: Open University Press.

Dalley, G. (1988) *Ideologies of Caring. Rethinking Community and Collectivism*. Basingstoke: Macmillan.

de Swaan, A. (1990) *The Management of Normality*. London: Routledge.

Finch, J. and Groves, D. (1983) *A Labour of Love: Women, Work and Caring*. London: Routledge and Kegan Paul.

Hochschild, A. (1983) *The Managed Heart: Commercialization of Human Feeling*. Berkeley, CA: University of California Press.

Hockey, J. (1990) *Experiences of Death. An Anthropological Account*. Edinburgh: Edinburgh University Press.

Kellehear, A. (1990) *Dying of Cancer: The Final Year of Life*. Chur, Switzerland: Harwood Academic.

Menzies, I. (1970) *The Functioning of Social Systems as a Defence against Anxiety* (Reprint of Tavistock Pamphlet 3). London: Tavistock Institute.

Potter, J. and Wetherell, M. (1987) *Discourse and Social Psychology: Beyond Attitude and Behaviour*. London: Sage.

Siddell, M., Katz, J. and Komaromy, C. (1997) *Death and Dying in Residential and Nursing Homes: Examining the Case for Palliative Care*. Milton Keynes: The Open University.

Yanagisako, S. and Delaney, C. (eds) (1995) *Naturalizing Power. Essays in Feminist Cultural Analysis*. New York: Routledge.

5

Just an old-fashioned love
song or a 'harlequin romance'?
Some experiences of
widowhood

JANE LITTLEWOOD

This chapter is concerned with the experiences of a number of widows who professed a deep and enduring love for their dead husbands. For many widows, this love was reciprocal, insomuch that they felt the 'presence' of their deceased spouse particularly in times of upset or trouble. For many women, their dead husbands effectively protected them from what they perceived to be a potentially hostile world. One is reminded of Harlequin who, according to Evans (1989), is 'a mischievous fellow supposed to be invisible to all eyes but those of his faithful Columbine. His function is to dance through the world and frustrate the knavish antics of the clown' (p. 525).

Widowhood: grounds for objection?

The information that informs this chapter was derived from two, related, sources. The first source was meetings with active members of the National Association of Widows (NAW) (Littlewood 1992a, 1993). NAW is an organization that befriends, advises and attempts to meet the needs of widows of all ages. The second source of information was a general questionnaire widely distributed to members of NAW. During the course of the initial meetings, three specific issues were raised: dissatisfaction with literature concerning grief and bereavement; bemusement associated with the notion of the resolution of grief; and a disinclination to relinquish a strong attachment to a dead husband. More specifically:

• A degree of cynicism concerning conventional explanations associated with the grieving process. In particular, it was suggested that such explanations made no 'sense' to many of the widows present. Furthermore, the majority of these widows were well aware that some of the more influential explanations had largely been based upon interpretations of the experiences of widows. This added considerably to their disenchantment with what they perceived to be the conventional literature associated with the area.

- Concerning issues associated with the resolution of grief, some members of NAW held the opinion that they had no intention of 'resolving' their grief. They reported holding highly positive feelings concerning their dead husbands. Furthermore, they remained convinced that there was nothing 'complicated' or 'pathological' about their reactions at all.
- Related to the above, were feelings associated with a strong and continuing attachment to their deceased spouses. Whilst this attachment appeared to take many different forms, almost all of the widows present expressed the view that, in many ways, they still felt married. However, an equally large majority of those present were unhappy with the social status of widowhood, which they found to be both stigmatizing and demeaning. Nevertheless, they expressed no wish to change their social status.

However, the perceptions of members who are particularly active in any organization may, or may not, reflect those of other members. Consequently, a postal questionnaire was devised. This questionnaire was subsequently sent to a broad spectrum of the membership of NAW (Littlewood and Walker 1995). Whilst many of the questions were based upon Gorer's (1965) seminal work, other questions focussed upon the following areas:

- Beliefs concerning the most effective ways of coping with widowhood and the most important ways that NAW contributed towards the widows' ability to cope with their experiences.
- Details of the ways in which widows felt that they maintained a relationship with their dead husband.

The questionnaire benefited from an unusually high response rate (in excess of 95 per cent) and, together with the observations of the more active members of NAW, forms the basis of an evaluation of the relationship between the knowledge and experience of these particular widows and the 'conventional wisdom' concerning widowhood.

'Conventional wisdom': Grounds for objection indeed?

Whilst conventional explanations of bereavement are many and varied (see, for example, Littlewood 1992b), several elements of these explanations would appear to be relevant to the concerns expressed by members of NAW. Specifically, issues relating to resolution, gender and the potential for complications to arise during the process of grieving have all been addressed by the relevant literature.

Resolution

A consistent theme of twentieth-century accounts of grief has been that of resolution. For example, Freud (1917) saw the process of mourning as one in which the libido is slowly removed from the lost object and eventually attached to a new one. Specifically:

> Each one of the memories and situations of expectancy which demonstrate the libido's attachment to the lost object is met by the verdict of reality that the object no longer exists. The ego is persuaded by the sum total of narcissistic satisfactions it derives from being alive to sever its attachment to the object.
>
> (Freud 1917: 255)

Whilst he acknowledged that this process tended to be achieved both slowly and painfully, for Freud, detachment from one object followed by re-attachment to another effectively paved the way to resolution.

Alternatively, the highly influential work of Parkes (1972), whilst adopting a different theoretical perspective, was also concerned with the issue of recovery/resolution. Parkes identified a complex range of reactions which he grouped into 'numbness', 'pining', 'depression' and 'recovery'. In a later work (Glick *et al.* 1974), recovery was equated with the possibility of re-marriage. In many ways it is variations of this particular understanding that have permeated contemporary popular culture. Obviously, for women who state very clearly that they have no intention of either 'resolving' their loss or giving up their attachment to their dead husband then such explanations are quite clearly a potential, if not an actual, source of discontent.

Gender

Another, if somewhat understated, theme of the later twentieth-century accounts of grief has been gender. In many ways, the experiences of widows have been central to the development of our contemporary understanding of bereavement. For example, the early work of both Marris (1958) and Parkes (1972) was concerned almost exclusively with widows. Marris (1986) subsequently used his previous work to develop a generic theory concerning loss and change. Widowhood was used as the example *'par excellence'* of the generic experience of, and adaptation to, change. Interestingly enough, resistance to change was central to his thesis. Parkes (in Glick *et al.* 1974) went on to compare the experiences of widows and widowers and concluded that the differences were few, apart from widowers expressing less overt emotion, feeling more 'like themselves' again a year after their bereavement and being more willing to contemplate remarriage earlier than widows. Furthermore, the work of Parkes has subsequently been utilized as a general theory and the original focus upon widows has effectively been lost. Whilst later works (for example, Mulkay 1993; Littlewood 1994; Cline 1995) have attempted to address the uniquely social, rather than the psychological, issues pertaining to widows, this body of work would appear to have done little or nothing to allay the mistrust in social theory held by a group of women who essentially wish to maintain a relationship with their dead spouse without considering themselves to be 'deviant' in any way.

Complicated grief

Descriptions of complicated grief are not uncommon in the literature pertaining to bereavement. These descriptions tend to be loosely gathered under three headings: delayed grief; absent or distorted grief; and chronic grief. Estimations concerning the occurrence of complications arising from the process of grief vary from the relatively rare (for example, Marris 1986) to approximately one in three (for example, Raphael 1984). Whilst delayed, distorted or absent grief would not appear to be relevant to the issues raised by members of NAW, chronic grief may offer a potential explanation concerning the position that this particular group of widows chose to adopt. In simple terms, chronic grief has been reported in connection with bereavements that are followed by the expected range of reactions and involve the bereaved person failing to resolve/recover from them. 'Mummification', a variant of chronic grief, has been identified by Gorer (1965). Mummification is a process in which the world of the bereaved individual appears to be frozen in time following the death. The person who is grieving often behaves as if the dead person will return at some future date. Gorer cites the example of Queen Victoria, following the death of Prince Albert, as a prime example of this type of grief. Marris (1986), in making a similar point, cites an example from literature, that of Miss Haversham: a woman who, consumed by bitterness, waited for the rest of her life by the ruins of what should have been her marriage feast. Literally, as well as figuratively, time stood still for Miss Haversham.

However, it could be argued that membership, active or otherwise, of an organization specifically concerned with widowhood might be contraindicative of a response similar to that of Miss Haversham. Specifically, these widows were not expressing the belief or hope that their husbands would literally return to them, neither did they seem to be trying to avoid the fact that the death had occurred. Rather, they were expressing the ability and the desire to conduct an ongoing relationship with a person they knew to be dead. The way in which Queen Victoria responded to the death of Prince Albert may be more informative in this respect. However, several authors have questioned the extent to which Queen Victoria was motivated by grief and grief alone. As Thompson (1990) indicates, Queen Victoria had her own strategies for dealing with her femininity at a time when the monarchy was not popular in all quarters. Victoria allowed, and contributed to, a construction of herself as a woman of 'a strongly feminine quality of maternal devotion and disinterested family loyalty which impressed itself on subjects of many nations and many races' (Thompson 1990: 125). Because of fears of republicanism, Queen Victoria deliberately accentuated the domestic and non-political nature of the Queen. Consequently, Victoria encouraged a construction of herself as a wife and a mother in order to appear 'less politically threatening to opponents of the monarchy ... and more amenable to constitutional control in the eyes of those who supported a limited monarchy' (Thompson 1990: 138).

As Homans, in her article 'To the Queen's Private Apartments: royal family portraiture and the construction of Victoria's sovereign obedience', states 'Victoria both functioned publicly as the nation's wife and was herself, in private, a wife, she both publicly impersonated a domestic woman and really was one. She did indeed appear to be a middle class woman' (Homans 1993: 5). Homans also indicates that when Victoria was widowed there were calls for her to abdicate. If she was no longer a wife in private how could she possibly be one in public? In short, the expression of Victoria's grief, so often cited as complicated, may well have been affected by her contribution towards a particular presentation of herself, a presentation that had become central to her national and international identity. Perhaps she simply could not afford to let Albert go? So, one explanation might be that she continued to behave as if her husband were still alive and available to accompany her when, and if, she believed this to be necessary (Littlewood forthcoming).

Whilst it may be possible that many of the NAW widows could be seen as adopting a position believed to be associated with a 'complicated' reaction to bereavement, it could equally well be argued that there may be extremely good reasons for adopting such a position. What is, perhaps, more difficult to explain is why a group of women would wish to identify with the social status of 'widow' when virtually all of them perceived it to be both detrimental and stigmatizing.

On stigma and invisibility – no grounds at all?

According to Cline (1995), most authors who have considered the position of widows have focussed upon the stigmatization and/or the sociocultural invisibility of widows. Cline identifies a web of factors which, historically, have identified widows as being 'unlucky' and 'impure'. For example, in an early work in this area, Cochrane (1936) identified a pattern of avoidance that widows were expected to observe in order to protect others from being 'touched' by death.

Even earlier, work on witchcraft would also appear to indicate that widows were often marginalized, stigmatized and eventually forced to 'disappear'.

Purkiss (1996) identifies the socio-economic pressures which effectively pushed widows into the margins of society. Without any other source of income many were forced to operate in the areas of helping other women to give birth, and/or to treat the sick and lay out the dead. If anything went wrong, as it often did, widows became prime suspects of witchcraft: they were often accused by the very women they had tried to help. In an earlier work Larner (1981) also noted, but did not comment upon, the fact that many of the victims of the witch-hunts in Scotland were widows.

Obviously, the extreme case of the maltreatment and stigmatization of widows is, arguably, that of suttee (or sati), a Hindu practice that encourages widows to be ceremoniously burned alive on the funeral pyres of their husbands. As Mayo indicates:

> That so hideous a fate as widowhood should befall a woman can be but for one cause – the enormity of her sins in a former reincarnation. From the moment of her husband's decease till the last hour of her own life, she must expiate those sins in shame and suffering and self-immolation, chained in every thought to the service of his soul. Be she a child of three, who knows nothing of the marriage that bound her, or be she a wife in fact, having lived with her husband, her case is the same.
>
> (Mayo, cited in Daly 1979: 119)

Alternatively, suttee immediately solves any problems concerning the widow's future fidelity and may also be associated with considerable economic gains for her in-laws.

In the contemporary situation Cline argues that widows are subjected to being perceived as leading what she calls 'leftover lives' (Cline 1995: 140). In pursuing a similar point, Mulkay (1993) attempts to trace the social value afforded to widows from the Victorian era to the present day. Mulkay concludes that the extent to which widows could represent their dead relatives, primarily their husbands, was the extent to which they were accorded any social worth whatsoever. According to Mulkay, greater longevity has left many elderly women living under the shadow of the 'leftover lives' that Cline so movingly describes.

The difficulties experienced by the state in accommodating widowhood have been documented by Lewis (1984). In her consideration of the position of women in England from 1870 to 1950 Lewis notes that widows were virtually ignored in the provisions associated with the 1884 Poor Law Amendment Act. However, she also notes that various circulars warned against giving outdoor relief to able-bodied widows who were either childless or had only one dependent child. According to Lewis, this situation was only partly ameliorated upon the granting of widows' pensions in 1925. Nevertheless, she notes that ambivalence concerning the socially 'appropriate' place of the able-bodied widow continued into the 1940s and 1950s: a woman without a husband was expected to either work or remarry.

Littlewood (1994) in looking at the post-Beveridge era makes a similar point, that on the one hand women were encouraged to give up paid employment upon marriage but on the other, were expected, upon early widowhood, to either remarry or re-enter the labour market. Presumably these were perceived to be relatively easy tasks.

However, despite a long history of stigmatization or social invisibility, Cline (1995) indicates that in the contemporary situation at least, a certain type of widowhood may be accorded a reasonable amount of respect. Specifically:

> Some years ago there was a salty series on British television about three women whose bank robber husbands all died in one raid leaving the feisty female trio to carry on the family business!
>
> The series was called 'Widows'. The drama offered women strong independent roles. It focused attention on bereaved women who had guts, gallantry, and a great support system. It was on prime-time television. It had large audiences.
>
> (Cline 1995: 140)

Perhaps guts, gallantry and a great support system are key elements in the largely unacknowledged survival strategies that have been adopted by widows both past and present to survive?

On death and bereavement: shaky ground?

The widows who responded to the questionnaire displayed the following characteristics:

• 85 per cent had been bereaved for more than one year.
• 77 per cent were aged between 41 and 60 years at the time of the death of their husband (husband's age at death between 46 and 65 years).
• The majority (60 per cent) had children over the age of 18 whilst only 7 per cent had no children at all.

As has been previously noted (Littlewood 1992b) both Parkes (1972) and Marris (1986) specifically excluded elderly widows from their studies so, in terms of age range, these widows were not 'unusual'. What was unusual, however, was the range of causes and the place of the relevant deaths. For example, almost half of the bereavements (45 per cent) were unanticipated and 25 per cent of deaths were caused by either suicide or accident. It is precisely these ways of dying which have been associated with the potential to complicate the process of grief (see, for example, Parkes 1972; Lazare 1979; Kalish 1985).

However, the majority of the experiences described by the widows (at least those experienced during the first year of bereavement) were essentially unremarkable in terms of their being indicative of the possibility of complications arising (see, for example, Worden 1982).

Some experiences of bereavement: normal ground?

Over half of the widows reported sleep disturbances, loss of appetite and a worsening of their general health. Furthermore, just under half of the sample thought that they either saw and/or heard their husband during the first year of their bereavement. However, the experiences described were not out of keeping with the previous literature in the area. For example:

'I've twice thought I've seen my husband in the street and both times ran to catch up with him only to discover it wasn't him. An awful feeling of despair overcame me both times.'

'Whilst driving a large vehicle which I had not driven whilst he was alive – he was beside me telling me what to do – when I resented this and turned towards him he told me to keep my eyes on the road. He was smiling – I was cross a) because he wasn't there and b) because if he wasn't alive why should I take any notice of him anyway?'

Also, the vast majority of widows (79 per cent) had experienced dreams about their husband but these dreams were essentially typical of those described by Parkes (1972); that is, an initial belief that all is well followed by a realization that the death had occurred:

'Very vivid, very upsetting usually. There had been a mistake, he was still alive . . . it was dreadful to realize that I had been dreaming'.

In fact, the importance of accepting that one's husband was dead was frequently expressed, for example:

'I know it sounds very cruel but I tell myself that my husband has died. He has not passed on or passed over, neither have I lost him. I won't insult my relationship by allowing myself or other people to suggest that he was a parcel I had lost or a glove I had mislaid.'

Why then, did almost all of the widows (79 per cent) feel the presence of their husband on several occasions (and in many instances on a reasonably regular basis) for a number of years following their bereavement?

The presence of the dead: paranormal ground?

As Parkes (1970) indicated, a strong desire to recover a dead person may, in some instances, be associated with a belief that the dead person is present in some way. The 'presences' felt by the widows were remarkably similar to each other. For example:

'It's embarrassing and impossible to convey but I feel him – I know he's there'.

'. . . kissing my neck and there are no obvious triggers to these events'.

'Not painful, not emotional. Usually I can smile to myself'.

'I feel very close to my husband, closer than to the person next to me, and I feel what he would like me to do in certain circumstances'.

Essentially, it was 'feelings' that were being described. The specific times when presences were felt also showed similarities between one widow and another:

'When I have a difficult decision to make he guides me'.

'A few weeks ago, I was feeling lonely and sad. He sat on the bed, giving me a cuddle'.

'I feel him very close at sad times, almost as if I can reach out and touch him and, at all times, I still feel his wife, as though he is still the one who offers security and special caring and love'.

In general terms, the presence of the husband is felt particularly strongly when a widow is feeling troubled or sad. In terms of location, the presence of one's husband would appear to be experienced in private and is associated with comfort and normality rather than distress. For example:

'I can have these experiences and still feel perfectly sane'.

As if to emphasize the point, four widows (a psychiatrist, two social workers and a teacher) all spontaneously noted their qualifications on the questionnaire. They were concerned that they should be considered 'normal' in every sense of the word. However, it is the very normality of the ways these observations are recorded that is of particular interest. Wooffitt (1992) in discussing the organization of factual discourses associated with the paranormal, the extraordinary and the traumatic notes that there is a distinct pattern that is followed when describing the recollection of such events. Wooffitt describes this as 'I was just doing X . . . when Y' (1992: viii). Specifically, 'the speakers formulate a recollection of what they were doing *just before* the onset of their first experience with the phenomenon' (Wooffitt 1992: 118). Wooffitt, having reviewed the general area, came to the conclusion that people usually recorded the mundane events they experienced immediately prior to reporting a paranormal event.

What is fascinating about the responses of these widows is that, in terms of 'seeing' or 'hearing' their dead husband, *all* of them responded in the way described by Wooffitt. However, when widows reported experiencing the presence of their husbands *none* of them did. As far as these women were concerned, they followed the rules associated with recording the normal rather than the paranormal. Could this be indicative, perhaps, of a terrible sense of social isolation?

Coping with widowhood: firmer ground?

In terms of coping with widowhood, the majority of widows, despite describing extremely painful experiences, reported a great deal of social support. For example, following their bereavement, 73 per cent received help from neighbours, 86 per cent received help from relatives and 69 per cent received help from friends. The vast majority (93 per cent) had interests outside of the home and all of them valued these activities. In terms of their association with NAW the widows were unanimous in their appreciation of being in touch with women whose experiences were similar to their own. For example:

> 'It's a means of meeting people in similar circumstances and being able to help each other'.

> 'The contact with people who knew exactly what I was talking about. A few days after my husband died, I received a letter from a young widow. Her husband had died two years previously and left her with three young children. She suggested I telephone her at bedtime, which I did. She was wonderful and told me about NAW. I felt that if I could help someone else in the way she helped me, I'd join NAW – I did'.

It might be suggested that, in Goffman's (1967) terms, these particular widows have access to both their 'own' (that is, women who had experienced a similar loss) and to their 'wise' (that is, people who understood, and were sympathetic to their situation). Theoretically, at least, this should go some way towards ameliorating the sense of social stigma which so many of them described. In any event, they were hardly describing any sense of social isolation.

The widows who contributed to this particular piece of research had several things in common:

- a disinclination to move towards a 'conventional' resolution of their bereavement;
- in many cases, the experience of a difficult bereavement;
- an ability to utilize several avenues of social support;
- a degree of cynicism regarding conventional explanations of bereavement.

However, it must be said that the majority of their experiences confirmed, rather than denied, the conventional psychological 'wisdom' in this area.

Rather, their disenchantment would appear to be directed towards the notion of 'moving on' and the social, rather than the psychological, marginalization of widows. It is perhaps paradoxical that a group of widows who would appear to be particularly well supported should voice such concerns:

> 'I am still coping with it, I refuse to be labelled. I am still a person, and I can speak.'

In terms of Cline's (1995) consideration of widows, these are not women who are leading 'leftover lives'. In terms of her consideration of the television series 'Widows', guts, gallantry and a great support system may not be quite enough. An ability to represent oneself would appear to help, at least in public, as would a 'harlequin romance'. In the final analysis the last words should go to a widow:

> 'I love him, I miss him, I need him sometimes. I have my family, I have my friends, I have my job. I know that he's dead but I can feel him with me and be completely sane. What's so bloody complicated about that?'.

References

Cline, S. (1995) *Lifting the Taboo: Women, Death and Dying*. London: Little, Brown.

Cochrane, A.L. (1936) 'A Little Widow is a dangerous thing'. *International Journal of PsychoAnalysis*, 17: 494.

Evans, I.H. (1989) *Brewer's Dictionary of Phrase and Fable*, 14th edn. London: Guild Publishing.

Freud, S. (1917) Mourning and melancholia, in J. Strachey (ed.) *The Standard Edition of the Complete Psychological Works of Sigmund Freud*, Vol. 14. London: Hogarth Press and Institute of Psycho-Analysis.

Glick, I.O., Weiss, R.S., and Parkes, C.M. (1974) *The First Year of Bereavement*. New York: Wiley.

Goffman, I. (1967) *Stigma: Notes on the Management of a Spoiled Identity*. Harmondsworth: Penguin.

Gorer, G. (1965) *Death, Grief and Mourning in Contemporary Britain*. London: Cresset Press.

Homans, M. (1993) To the Queen's private apartments: royal family portraiture and the construction of Victoria's sovereign obedience. *Victorian Studies*, 37 (1): 1–41.

Kalish, R.A. (1985) *Death, Grief and Caring Relationships*, 2nd edn. Pacific Grove, CA: Brooks/Cole.

Larner, C. (1981) *Enemies of God: The Witch-hunt in Scotland*. Oxford: Basil Blackwell.

Lazare, A. (1979) Unresolved grief, in A. Lazare (ed.) *Outpatient Psychiatry: Diagnosis and Treatment*. Baltimore: Williams and Wilkins.

Lewis, J. (1984) *Women in England 1870–1950*. Hemel Hempstead: Harvester Wheatsheaf.

Littlewood, J. (1992a) On *Falling in Love Backwards*, Discussion document. Birmingham, National Association of Widows.

Littlewood, J. (1992b) *Aspects of Grief: Bereavement in Adult Life*. London: Routledge.

Littlewood, J. (1993) 'A Little Widow is a dangerous thing: the amazing case of the women who simply refuse to disappear'. Key note speech of the Annual General Meeting of the National Association of Widows, Birmingham, July.

Littlewood, J. (1994) 'Widows' weeds and women's needs: the re-feminisation of death, dying and bereavement', in S. Wilkinson and C. Kitzinger *Women and Health: Feminist Perspectives*. London: Taylor & Francis.

Littlewood, J. and Walker, C. (1995) Responses to widowhood. Unpublished research report, Goldsmiths' College, London.

Littlewood, J. (forthcoming) *Misconstruing the Feminine: Social Change and Social Control*. London: Macmillan.

Marris, P. (1958) *Widows and their Families*. London: Routledge and Kegan Paul.

Marris, P. (1986) *Loss and Change* (2nd edn.). London: Routledge and Kegan Paul.

Mayo, K. (1979) 'Mother India', in M. Daly *Gyn./Ecology: The Metaphysics of Radical Feminism*. London: The Women's Press.

Mulkay, M. (1993) Social death in Britain, in D. Clark (ed.) *The Sociology of Death*. Oxford: Blackwell.

Parkes, C.M. (1970) Seeking and finding a lost object: evidence of recent studies of reactions to bereavement. *Social Science and Medicine*, 4: 187–201.

Parkes, C.M. (1972) *Bereavement*. New York: International Universities Press.

Purkiss, D. (1996) *The Witch in History: Early Modern and Twentieth-century Representations*. London: Routledge.

Raphael, B. (1984) *The Anatomy of Bereavement: A Handbook for the Caring Professions*. London: Hutchinson.

Thompson, D. (1990) *Queen Victoria, Gender and Power*. London: Virago.

Wooffitt, R. (1992) *Telling Tales of the Unexpected: The Organisation of Factual Discourse*. Hemel Hempstead: Harvester Wheatsheaf.

Worden, J.W. (1982) *Grief Counselling and Grief Therapy*. New York: Springer.

PART II

6

Discourse into practice:
the production of
bereavement care

NEIL SMALL AND JENNY HOCKEY

Introduction

In this chapter we build on the argument presented in Chapter 1, and developed in Chapters 2–5, where we sought to make sense of theoretical understandings of grief as discourse, understandable in the social context of a prevailing modernity. We now move on to a similar consideration of bereavement services, first looking at the way modernity elevates both the individual and the expression of feelings and then considering Foucault's insights into the exercise of power/knowledge. This provides a useful analytic framework for considering the ways that bereavement work has evolved since the late 1950s, not least in allowing us to draw on Foucault's conception of power to examine the social construction of an internal world of individualized emotion. We will then look at how theory has been translated into guides to practice and examine the evidence as to the impact of these ideas on the practice of care.

As with Part I of the book, the structure of Part II is such that this chapter is followed by focused considerations of bereavement care and examples of sites of practice. For example, the substantive chapters on bereavement counselling by Anderson and Árnason provide an anthropological interpretation of the beliefs and practices, which both underpin and are produced through a contemporary language of the emotions. The following three chapters by Katz, Simons and Heslop offer a focus on different aspects of child death.

As discussed in Chapter 1, theories of grief have been framed in terms of tasks or processes. The apparent prescriptiveness of such approaches is denied by their proponents who say, in effect, that theirs is not a route map but a frame to hold the picture of the experience of grief. In Part II of this book we go on to ask whether this more poetic, relativist model is actually translated into the literature and practice of grief counselling. Does the model become trapped in the cliché responses of the 'get on with your life', 'time is a great healer' variety? Does it manage to move us on from the protestant tinged notion of 'grief work' – the imperative to be busy, to get things done, to show some sort of success or positive, verifiable, outcome? Have theories of grief been translated into 'technique'-oriented grief work? Illich has argued that 'culture confronts pain, deviance and death by inter-preting them; medical civilisation turns them into problems which can be solved by their removal. Cultures are systems of meanings, cosmopolitan civilisations a system of techniques' (1975: 93). If we turn to Foucault's notion of surveillance via sites such as the clinic and the medical gaze, we find a similar set of concerns being articulated (1973). Using Foucault's account of how discursive power operates, we can therefore ask whether bereavement counselling constitutes a system of techniques or a set of inter-pretations – and whether it can be modified according to cultural preced-ents and individual preferences?

Grief, modernity and 'looking after yourself'

Lofland links grief, as currently understood, to a particular historical and anthropological phenomenon, modernity.

> The contemporary grief experience, with its intensity, with the exquisite range of its symptoms and with its considerable duration, would seem to be remarkably well-matched to the modern penchant for 'exploring and expressing one's deepest strivings, and to the modern temperament which 'seeks to give free play to inner feelings'. To the degree that this penchant and temperament is culturally and historically variable, that is, to the degree that there is cultural and historical variability in the self which grieves, then, surely, the grief itself must vary.
>
> (Lofland 1985: 180)

A prevailing modernity not only embraces the 'feelings' agenda but also, in the context of a prevalent neo-liberalism, calls on the individual to en-gage in self-examination, self-care and self-improvement (see Rose 1993). We are each being made an entrepreneur of our own health, including our psychological and spiritual health (Osborne 1997). In so doing we are inter-acting with expert views, even though we may find it hard to confid-ently locate authority in experts (Bunton 1997). In other words, we may be increasingly sceptical about the opinions of scientists, doctors and other professional experts, yet we still incorporate their views into our everyday practice, albeit mediated by others, by the media for example (de Swaan 1990). Even a narrow focus on self does not free the individual from the prevalent social constructions. The relationships and expectations that surround action may change, but any action that is defined in relation to them does not.

Walter uses the term 'policing' to describe this process, referring to the way in which society regulates emotion (1999: 120ff). Drawing on a Durkheimian perspective, he suggests that society not only shapes and curbs but also produces particular emotional behaviours. While Westerners popularly conceive of grief as an innate and natural emotion stimulated by loss, Walter supports the view that 'grieving' takes particular forms in particular places, depending on social norms. Indeed, without 'policing' of this kind individuals can find their reactions to loss disorienting.

This approach, to some extent, rides two horses simultaneously. In other words, it challenges the notion of a 'natural' response to loss, highlighting historical and cross-cultural variation in social requirements to grieve openly or not: 'tears . . .' argues Walter, 'are a product of a time and place' (1999: 134). Yet it suggests that without the guidance of social requirements an all too 'natural' response can arise, one which leaves the individual emotionally adrift and socially under-regulated, or, as Durkheim terms it, in a state of anomie. In other words, behind a focus on the social construction of emotion we find an essentialist model of innate emotionality. As Lupton says of this approach, 'Whilst it is generally acknowledged that social and cultural features may shape the expression of emotions in various ways, the belief is maintained that at the centre of the emotional self there is a set of basic emotions with which all humans are born' (1998: 10). Psychologists have introduced the notion of mediated emotions, that is innate feelings which are nonetheless shaped in response to the cognitive appraisal of both external and internal events. Nonetheless, as Lupton points out, there is a functionality to these explanations in that mediated emotional experience is often talked about as a 'coping response', which allows innate emotion to be managed. This emphasis on function finds parallels in Durkheim's account of emotion as 'collective effervescence', which shores up social solidarity. Walter's work on the culture of grief similarly foregrounds the question of function: 'Bereavement work, for example, may function to police grief or it may function to liberate clients from over-policing; the motives of bereavement workers may be entirely different' (1999: 126). Lupton takes issue with explanations of emotion as a coping resource, inherent within the individual, which functions at either a micro or macro level. Instead she espouses the 'strong' social constructionist model that identifies emotionality as an intersubjective experience, produced contingently in particular social situations. It is from this perspective that we look critically at bereavement guides, the practices associated with them and the academic commentaries and critiques of this sphere of thought and activity.

Following the 'strong' social constructionist line, we suggest that regardless of the model of grief, the notion of emotions as entities residing within the individual often goes unchallenged. Walter distinguishes between the expressive and private models of grief. He also supports the notion of a diversity of emotional experience, which, nonetheless, calls out for the 'life belt' of social regulation (1999). The question of whether or not the entities that we call 'emotions' actually exist is not, however, raised in his work. Yet when we do explore the view that emotions may not be entities in their own right, separable from bodily experience or their expression (Harre, cited in Lupton 1998: 16), debates as to how or indeed whether grief should be 'policed' take on a different status.

By pursuing a Foucauldian, post-structuralist line of argument we can see how the disciplines, which underpin bereavement counselling, act to produce their own subjects, the problematic 'emotions' that we know as grief. As Lupton says, 'It is through discourse on emotions, therefore, including "feeling rules", that the emotional self is shaped and reshaped as a continuous project of subjectivity' (1998: 26). This view clearly contrasts with the essentialist models that underpin the models of grief which debate whether or not the emotions produced within the bereaved person should be expressed. Emotions, the post-structuralists argue, pre-exist the individual, being available within discourse to be appropriated, actively, within the flux of social and personal circumstances. This is an approach that therefore foregrounds the agency of individuals, rather than subsuming them to macro-level social function. In addition it opens the path for a further critique of 'social order'-situated approaches.

In her ethnography of death ritual among the Inner Maniat women of Greece, Seremetakis champions Ariès's account of Western attitudes to death and dying (1991). His historical account emphasizes the continuity of death-related themes within a changing social landscape, his data supporting the view that death ritual needs to be seen as the deep structure of premodern social life, 'a zone of local resistance to centralising institutions' (Seremetakis 1991: 14). Rather than a Durkheimian view, which asks how society restores itself to a state of equilibrium when faced with the death of its members, Seremetakis asks us to give primacy to death rites themselves: 'Ariès's analysis moves from death to the social order rather than the reverse. The institutions of death function as a critical vantage point from which to view society' (Seremetakis 1991: 15). Emotional pain and its expression therefore constitute a site for challenge and, in her ethnographic context, socio-political resistance. When we move on to discuss mutual help groups we will revisit the question of whether or not the care of the bereaved is ever seen to legitimately involve externally focused political action (Walter 1999: 160). However, even when grief finds no external target, emotional volatility represents a powerful challenge to the emotional reserve of large sections of a British status quo (Walter 1999: 140), whether at the site of the family or the state. Here again we encounter the relevance of Foucault's arguments, which suggest that the modern state operates through a 'capillary', micro-politics of power which effectively produces docile bodies (1980). Lupton concludes her critical review of theories of the emotions by pointing out that although a post-structuralist view might seem to fly in the face of involuntary, embodied sensations such as fear or rage, bodily experience itself can be seen as a product of discourse. Individuals learn to filter, interpret and classify physical sensations such as tears, sweating, smiling and increased heart rate, drawing them into variable, historically and culturally specific association with 'emotion': 'the physicality of the emotions are interbound inextricably with sociocultural meanings and social relationships' (Lupton 1998: 33).

In exploring modernist requirements for self-monitoring in grief, we will therefore pay attention to the ways in which discourse and practice serve to produce their own subjects. Two examples of the power of expectations from the scholarship of death and grief illustrate this point. First, Kellehear has examined the 'good death' (1990), identifying socially defined sets of expectations and exchanges that individuals felt obliged to fulfil. If people did not act in accordance with these then they were not 'properly' preparing for their death. They were perceived to be denying, careless or maladjusted. Thus dying, like living, was and is steeped in social convention.

Second, we can look at 'anticipatory grief', a process whereby a person, it is claimed, rehearses the bereaved role and begins working through the profound changes that typically accompany loss. This has prompted a belief amongst many professionals that if such stages are not being exhibited then there should be 'the development of interventions during a terminal illness to facilitate "appropriate" grieving in anticipation of the impending loss' (Fulton et al. 1996: 1349). In a study of the way dying women negotiate their after-death identities, Exley (1999: 249–67) similarly demonstrates the challenges faced by a group of younger women (under 65 years of age) who felt that they should limit the distress felt by their families who would survive them. 'A good death' and 'anticipatory grief' are therefore terms that act as behaviour shaping and not just behaviour describing concepts, the former via self-regulation and the latter socially regulated.

Death, grief and bereavement have, of course, engaged people throughout history. It is the way they are shaped by modernity that makes them artefacts of one era, not their intrinsic importance. Some analyses cross eras:

Among disciplines focusing on death on a societal or cultural level, one research tradition has been to determine how social systems themselves break down death into distinctive dreads. For instance, one may investigate how religions mould death anxiety into fear of agonising hell or undesirable reincarnation as a means of obtaining moral obedience or how secularisation and the rise of contemporary medicine have shifted cultural death anxiety from fear of post-mortem judgement to fear of the dying process . . . how these anxieties are focused determines, at the individual level, the nature of the rituals people use to manage them; at the social level, the distribution of power, and at the cultural level, the nature of the death ethos.

(Kearl 1995: 3)

It is salutary to look to some of the oldest recorded meditations on death, and to the wisdom of the poets over the centuries and see the precursors to 'innovative' modern theorizing. For example, on the interface of external events, internal worlds and the positive impact of our sorrows the Stoic philosopher Epictetus spoke of how, although sorrows come from without, our reception of them is to some degree under our own command, enough to make it possible for us to first bear and then master them. He saw this as a process that would leave us with more insight into the human condition and more sympathy for others. Byron spoke of 'sorrow as knowledge' and saw grief as 'the instructor of the wise'. Seneca, in his Agamemnon wrote of the small comfort of sharing sorrows, 'Grief wounds more deeply in solitude; tears are less bitter when mingled with others tears' (see Grayling 1999).

These perspectives contrast with that alternative perception presented in Illich's view that 'medical civilization tends to turn pain into a technical problem and thereby deprive suffering of its inherent personal meaning' (1975: 93). Indeed he goes on to argue that 'Culture makes pain tolerable by integrating it into a meaningful system, cosmopolitan civilization detaches pain from any subjective or inter-subjective context in order to annihilate it' (1975: 93).

Foucault and the complexities of power

Neither Kellehear, in his work on the good death (1990), nor Fulton *et al.* in their work on anticipatory grief (1996) cite Foucault. But their studies nonetheless present scenarios consistent with Foucault's position in that they highlight the way models of what is appropriate behaviour are being constructed. These models limit and constrain modes of expression and belief, grief thus being 'policed' along the lines envisaged by Walter (1999: 126). Such constraints can be maintained even if the social group exercising power changes. 'Power is not a possession of particular social groups, but is relational, a strategy which is invested in and transmitted through all social groups' (Lupton 1997: 99). Thus a mode of subjectivity is constituted in social practice, individuals then acting reflexively in relation to it (see Fox 1997: 41). The good death and anticipatory grief are also examples of speculative lines of reasoning, which have been transformed into a professional orthodoxy via self-referential peer review.

Foucault shows how the modern rational systems that emerged from the Enlightenment are constituted by discursive practices, rather than the centralized and overt exercise of power. For example, the modern system of criminal justice moves the focus from the punishment of the physical body to a concern with mental states. However, the latter should not be assumed to be 'more liberal' than the former, rather it has a capillary power that reaches into every part of the social body. It is power sited 'within' each and every individual, rather than 'above' almost all of them (Foucault in Gordon 1980: 39). Such shifts in the nature of power and the practices through which it comes into being mark discontinuities of discourse and the ascendancy of a different form of power/knowledge. Knowledge, in this sense, becomes the site of strategies, struggles and conflicts for control (Harrison 1992: 85).

Characteristic of modern power are techniques of visibility, which combine both synoptic and individualizing effects. The synoptic effect is achieved through maximizing surveillance. Everything that happens becomes the appropriate subject of others' interest. Privacy, reserve, are not permitted; we are all to become transparent. Individualizing power emanates from subtle interrogation and moulding of the innermost thoughts of the person. The person is engaged in a process of self-surveillance that inserts a sense of what is deemed proper into their everyday actions (see Foucault 1979: 136–8; Foucault in Gordon 1980: 39). In this way some things become 'normal'. In their turn, the expert is constrained by the same devices and made into a 'docile body' that serves the prevalent power/knowledge discourse. It might appear that we can now talk about anything and everything, that all taboos have been confronted and overcome. But revelation does not equate with liberation in Foucault's world. Indeed revelation, in effect, just expands the domain of power.

Foucault's analysis of power also involves recognition of its complex levels. Specifically, he distinguishes between sovereign and disciplinary power. The former is power vested in a person or an identifiable group. It is based on sanctions and is negative. The latter is diffuse power, which creates its own identities and is positive. He also identifies bio-power which is oriented towards 'the subjugation of bodies and control of populations in general' (Clegg 1998: 32). In his presentation of bio-power, Foucault concentrates on sexuality but we might look, in this context, to its applicability to the emotional responses to death. We can also consider sovereign and disciplinary power as it relates to the discourse of grief and the practice of bereavement counselling.

An outpouring of talk, concern and writing . . . The effect . . . is the development of a whole new realm of discourse attending to the definition of what is 'normal' and what is not. Indeed Foucault focuses on the range of professional discourses that increasingly limit, define and normalise the 'vocabularies of motive' (Mills 1940) available in specific sites ('situated contexts' in Mill's terms) for making sensible and accountable what it is that people should do, can do and thus do. Bio-power normalises through discursive formations of psychiatry, medicine, social work and so on. The terms of the ways of constituting the normal becomes institutionalised and incorporated into every day life. Our own reflexive gaze takes over the disciplinary role as we take on accounts and vocabularies of meaning and motive that are available to us as certain other forms of account are marginalised or simply eased out of currency.

(Clegg 1998: 32)

Foucault, still talking of sex (1981), argued that silence was not the opposite of discourse but another facet of it. Armstrong (1997) invites us to consider how far such an analysis could be applied to Ariès's (1975) claim that discourse on death had been silenced for a hundred years between the mid-nineteenth and mid-twentieth century. In Armstrong's view, both the silence and the talk that broke the silence were constituted through discourse:

And rather than late twentieth century liberation the imposition of a new regime of truth? Yes, the new and massive discourse on death within medicine fitted almost exactly into the period of so-called silence. And the new requirement from the 1960s that the dying should mourn their own deaths fitted the point of so-called liberation.

(Armstrong 1997: 27; see also Armstrong 1987a)

For Foucault, subjects are constituted through discourse. There are rules of formation through which groups of statements achieve a unity as a science, a theory or a text. Over time these rules of formation shift and the history of thought reveals discontinuities, displacements and transformations. It is not structure, but the intersection of consciousness and the subject which must be understood (Foucault 1977: 16).

Translating theory into guides to practice

There is a wide literature on responding to grief and our intention here is neither to summarize nor to critically review it, but rather to see how it can be located alongside the theoretical understandings of grief and the research evidence about the nature of grief reactions. We will begin with work by two of the most cited authors, Worden and Parkes (both introduced in Chapter 1), and then move on to consider a small selection of books published in the UK during the 1990s that offer advice and practical guidance to those working with the bereaved.

Foucault's approach to expert knowledge is that it is both expansive and self-generating. Experts develop further expertise that only fellow experts can understand and implement. In the case of bereavement this knowledge colonizes areas of practice within a wide range of professions, as well as supporting a core of specialists. 'Bereavement counselling' is a key site, which is both produced by and produces this kind of knowledge. In practice, the term 'bereavement counselling' can encompass a confusing range of services, from befriending to psychotherapy (Raphael *et al.* 1993, cited in Payne *et al.*, 1999: 108); and within this range of services, a diversity of strategies are in use (Wilkes, cited in Payne *et al.* 1999: 108). As these authors note, the techniques and therapeutic models which bereavement counselling training can involve are similarly wide-ranging, a reflection of the broad range of theoretical approaches traced in Chapter 1 of this book. The generic use of the term bereavement counselling can therefore raise all sorts of competing and unfulfilled expectations. For example, there is an ongoing debate as to whether volunteers should be referred to as bereavement counsellors and, below, we go on to discuss changing views as to what bereavement care should provide.

This proliferation of forms of bereavement care represent part of the multiplicity of ways in which grief is 'policed'. Looked at from a Foucauldian perspective, we can see how these practices are implicated in the production of evermore precise and diverse forms of bereavement. A system of classification is therefore at work, based in the theories of grief outlined in Chapter 1. Arguably, it is through this framework that specific categories of 'need' continue to come into being. Via processes such as these, discourse therefore produces its own objects.

Core to much of this work is Worden's *Handbook for the Mental Health Practitioner*. It was first published in 1982 and a second edition was published in 1991. The second edition has been reprinted five times and in endorsements on the back cover is described as: 'practical, easy to read', 'down to earth . . . containing a wealth of information and advice', 'highly recommended for volunteer bereavement counsellors' and all health care professionals. It would 'greatly assist those dealing with those left behind'. Worden himself sums up his intention in this way:

> What I want to do in this book is to address those of you in these traditional professions who are already in a position to extend care to the bereaved and who have the knowledge and skills required to do effective intervention and, in some cases, preventative mental health work.
>
> (Worden 1991: 5)

He approvingly quotes Reilly.

> We do not necessarily need a whole new profession of . . . bereavement counsellors. We do need more thought, sensitivity, and activity concerning this issue on the part of the existing professional groups; that is, clergy, funeral directors, family therapists, nurses, social workers and physicians.
>
> (Reilly 1978: 49)

Worden's approach is linked to both psychoanalytic and attachment theory. For example, he is clear that to do grief therapy with more complex grief one needs a 'thorough knowledge of psychodynamics' (Worden 1991: 143). There are, however, needs that can be met by counselling and these are codified around four tasks: accepting the reality of the loss, working through to the pain of grief, adjusting to an environment in which the deceased is missing, and relocating emotionally in order to move on with life (Worden 1991: 10–18)). It is the counsellor's job to work with the bereaved person in pursuit of four goals related to these four tasks of grieving:

1 To increase the reality of the loss.
2 To help the 'counsellee' deal with both expressed and latent affect.
3 To help the counsellee overcome various impediments to readjustment after the loss.
4 To encourage the counsellees to say an appropriate goodbye and so to feel comfortable reinvesting back in life.

As Walter notes (1999: 198), bereavement counselling, like mutual self-help groups, encourages the client to tell the story of their loss, recounting not just who and what has been taken away, but also taking on board the full meaning and implications of that loss. This is achieved by creating a narrative, with the counsellor's help, which exists outside the bereaved person themselves and has a reality of its own (Hockey 1986: 334). The function of this story is to provide a stimulus for painful emotions, so bringing them up from the depths of the internal world to a 'surface' that is accessible to both client and counsellor. Once expressed, emotion can be 'worked through' satisfactorily. Anderson's chapter (this volume) explores this thesis in more detail using an analysis of the spatial metaphors through which counsellor and clients operate.

The story-telling format through which the first task of grief work may be accomplished is shared by the mutual help group. However, in that setting its function is different. As Walter (1999: 198) notes, the experiences and emotions of the bereaved person are validated in both settings but psychodynamically trained counsellors have a specific agenda that is both ideological and organizational. Not only is narrative work a task through which the goal of resolving grief may be accomplished, but the completion of that task has practical implications; for example, bereavement counselling services being put under pressure to limit their resources. Given that a 'need' for counselling has been produced, services have to ensure the passage of bereaved people out of, as well as into, their care. Further, as Walter notes (1999: 199), those services receiving NHS funding are under pressure to demonstrate their effectiveness. Grief resolution thereby acquires economic as well as social and emotional implications. By contrast, as we see below, mutual help groups are often longstanding, members being incorporated on the basis of shared losses and shared needs for one another. Story telling is therefore the contribution through which membership of the mutual help 'community' is secured.

In contrast with the sociality and long-term membership, which can characterize mutual help groups, bereavement counselling is oriented towards the re-creation of the autonomous individual who, with time, can free themselves from a now painful connection with someone who has died. This grieving process can be differentiated from mourning in that it is increasingly the bereaved person's internal world, rather than an external social environment, which constitutes the site for activity and change.

We can look to Cruse, an organization offering bereavement care, as an example (Árnason's chapter in this volume provides background and more detail.) In contrast with the social, economic and spiritual goals of early Cruse counselling, psychological models and psychodynamic tasks have come to predominate within its training and practice. Rather than the advice over pensions, health and the education of children, which comprised the Fact Sheets offered to widows by Margaret Torrie, the founder of Cruse, the organization's overall goal is to help the survivor complete any unfinished business with the deceased and say a final farewell.

The debate is not, however, closed. Payne *et al.* (1999) note settings in which bereavement care is understood as the provision of support rather than counselling. Then its goal is preventive. To offer counselling to a bereaved person is to risk pathologizing their experience of loss. To some extent the site in which care is being offered shapes the way it is understood: hospices often pro-actively offering support; organizations such as Cruse – Bereavement Care re-actively offering counselling. In the latter case, the bereaved person themself has categorized their experiences as intractable unless expert help is drawn on. However, we need to recognize the wider social context within which the individual will be reflecting on their emotions and we must bear in mind the 'feelings' agenda discussed above, with its requirements for self-examination, self-care and self-improvement.

Payne *et al.* (1999) also discuss stress and coping theories of bereavement, pointing out that according to this view social support is the crucial mediating factor that differentiates distressing but manageable grieving from stressful, intractable grief. They conclude that,

> stress and coping theory suggests that in general bereaved people are unlikely to need sophisticated therapy but rather support that compensates for the inadequacy of informal networks. Such support may be provided by volunteers or by people who have experienced bereavement themselves and wish to help others in similar situations.
>
> (Payne *et al.* 1999: 92)

With reference to the question as to who will take on the role of grief counsellor, Worden cites Parkes's (1980) identification of three types of person:

1 Professional services by doctors, nurses, psychologists or social workers done on either a group or individual basis.
2 Counselling provided by trained volunteers (supported by professionals).
3 Self-help groups in which bereaved people offer help to other bereaved people, with or without the support of professionals.

If different sorts of needs can be met by different sorts of services, identifying accurately who needs what becomes central. Specifically, the allocation or choice of appropriate services requires a system of knowledge through which factors likely to produce a higher risk of psychiatric morbidity following bereavement can be identified and classified. Raphael (1977) identified four variables in the widowed and widowers that were predictive of 'not doing well' one or two years after the spouse's death:

1 A lack of support in the bereaveds' social network.
2 Moderate levels of support plus a traumatic death.
3 Previous ambivalent marital relations, traumatic death or unmet needs.
4 The presence of a concurrent life crisis.

These models of the processes of grief and the identification of attendant risk factors translate, for Worden, into a set of ten principles and procedures for counselling. Here we see the hybrid nature of Worden's approach. A conceptual framework that looks to psychodynamics and attachment theory translates into practice guidelines that appear to draw on cognitive behavioural theories to help people identify and express their feelings, to accept that they can live without the deceased and to facilitate emotional relocation, to remind the survivor of the normality of contradictory grief emotions and cognitions and to encourage constructive coping styles.

For example, guidelines for a counsellor seeking to address 'Principle One: Help the Survivor Actualize the Loss' include 'help survivors talk about the loss'. This might be done by asking questions like, 'Where did the death occur? How did it happen?' Visiting the graveside is suggested. If they do not go to the churchyard or cemetery, ask them what their fantasy is about going. The aim here is to offer a counter to the predictable, 'common sense' approach of families who might see talking of the death as a torture for the bereaved. Contrary to this prevailing view, the counsellor assumes that one must first accept the reality of the loss before moving on to deal with its emotional impact. This point is exemplified in a study of the management of dying and bereavement, which involved taking on the role of a Cruse counsellor (Hockey 1990). Fieldnotes that record work with Mrs Robson, a widow in her late sixties, exemplify the discursive practices which Worden promotes:

> I tried to get her to talk about Frank (her dead husband). He's never from her thoughts, she said. She's been twice to the grave but been 'told' (by her sister-in-law) not to go again as she gets so upset. She

says she's frightened of crying as she gets so very upset – hysterical. She has to stem that sort of crying in front of others and at home she finds the drugs make it hard to cry. I offered to take her to the grave and she accepted gladly . . . She says that when she saw (Frank's) name in the In Memoriam columns at the anniversary in October, and indeed on the gravestone, she could hardly believe it. She's not putting it in the paper again. This suggests that perhaps she hasn't fully experienced her loss.

This particular 'client' lived in an isolated mining village and spoke frequently of suicide. As her 'counsellor' I tried to enlist the support of other agencies, particularly the local church, the community psychiatric nurse and the local health centre. The clergy who I visited after offering to accompany Mrs Robson to Frank's grave were politely dismissive, suggesting that she was manipulative and that someone should call her bluff about committing suicide. Fieldnotes from the visit continue as follows:

I felt very angry with them (the vicar and the curate) – and at the world of the 'caring' generally. Clients seem divided either into those who won't admit to problems and must be made to face them – or those who loudly admit to problems and are labelled 'manipulative'.

Meanwhile, in the more prosaic world of guides to practice, Worden offers the counsellor suggestions as to useful techniques, for example using 'evocative language' – 'your son died' as against 'you lost your son' – using the present tense to speak of the deceased, writing, drawing, role playing, developing a memory book and cognitive restructuring. The latter he describes as drawing on:

The underlying assumption that our thoughts influence our feelings . . . By helping the client to identify these thoughts and reality test them for accuracy or over generalization, the counsellor can help to lessen the dysphoric feelings triggered by certain irrational thoughts such as, 'No one will ever love me again', a thought that is certainly not provable in the present.

(Worden 1991: 53)

Turning to Parkes we can see a similar hybrid structure in which attachment theory is a starting point but, in this case, the client-centred school of Carl Rogers (1951) offers guidance when one moves from seeking to understand process to planning to intervene via counselling. As Árnason's chapter describes in more detail, the aim in this counselling is to establish a supportive relationship, help the bereaved identify and express their feelings, reassure them of the normality of common grief experiences, assist with problem solving and provide continuing and reliable support (Parkes et al. 1996: 140). The intent of the counsellor should be to work towards a position where the client is achieving greater and greater autonomy and hence can control the situation they are in, changing those problematic things that they can. For example, to help people feel less isolated and hopeless, the counsellor uses 'active listening'.

It means listening with our ears to what is being said and to the tone of voice, listening with our minds to understand the message contained in the words, listening with our eyes to what is being conveyed through the clients' posture, bearing and gestures, and listening with our hearts to the human being we are trying to understand. Listening in this way enables clients to feel that we are really there with them and value who they are. Receiving attention from another person is the first need that all of us share from the first moment of our life.

(Parkes *et al.* 1996: 60)

In addition to the intervention strategies that Worden and Parkes have developed, others have taken their work and modified or developed it. For example, in their guide for anyone who, in the course of their work or daily lives, might have to cope with the grief of others, Lendrum and Syme (1992) draw on attachment theory and the work of Parkes. (In their book's index Bowlby is listed with 11 entries, Parkes with nine and Robertson with two. The next highest for any name is four.) The list of people who they identify as likely to be exposed to the needs of bereaved people, and who they identify as the audience for their guide, includes teachers, nurses, police officers, doctors, personnel officers, and even neighbours and friends. Assuming we are all neighbours that means every one of us. While it is understandable that authors should seek to identify as wide a constituency for their work as they can, this all-embracing definition of who needs to know how, in their terms, to cope with the grief of others is indicative of Foucault's description of expansive and self-generating expert knowledge colonizing more and more areas of life (see above). Lendrum and Syme highlight the importance of active listening and reflecting experience and feelings with empathy (1992). Their aim is to allow those who are grieving to be less frightened and less condemning of the feelings they experience as part of grief. In this context, the counselling relationship can be both affirming and illuminating as the bereaved will express their loss and reveal feelings otherwise kept out of full awareness. This approach combines the work of Bowlby and Parkes on the nature of attachment and the impact of its rupture, with the understanding of the therapeutic relationship discussed by Truax and Carkhuff (1967) for whom there were three key factors: complete and unconditional acceptance, empathic understanding and genuineness.

When we look to theoretical models beyond Worden and Parkes we find additional hybrid constructions. For example, Spall and Callis look to Parkes and Worden in their use of the concepts of phases and tasks, but they find in Strobe and Strobe's words the best summary of what is required in working with the bereaved. That is, 'to encourage grief work . . . being able to talk over the loss, to be able to identify and express feelings of grief, helps the bereaved to come to terms with the death and to ultimately make a better adjustment' (Stroebe and Stroebe 1987, quoted in Spall and Callis 1997: 75).

Spall and Callis also emphasize that loss in areas other than bereavement should be taken into account and included in the model. In their view, those working with the bereaved should relate their own experience of loss to the understandings they gain from theory and their own practice. This is a point reiterated in Árnason's account of Cruse – Bereavement Care's training programme (this volume). The 'guide to effective caring' that Spall and Callis offer draws on Rogerian client-centred therapy, with its emphasis on acceptance, unconditional positive regard, congruence (the counsellor has to be 'real' with the client; that is, not pretending to be or to feel differently from that which they are trying to project) and empathy (Spall and Callis 1997: 150).

In her book for nurses, Penson (1990) uses Worden's and Parkes's idea of stages but she is also concerned to look at bereavement as transition (see Hopson and Scally 1989). Her emphasis is on identifying and responding to needs. In this she looks to the psychologist Maslow's identification of survival and growth needs (Maslow 1968). Some needs are for security, for physical health and fitness, for help in coping, to achieve, to be involved with others, to be self-indulgent at times. Others are concerned with the need for love and self-esteem. There are cognitive needs, to make sense of the world. There are aesthetic needs, to appreciate the good and the beautiful. Engaging with a needs-oriented approach of this kind makes possible attempts to conceptualize bereavement as, at least in part, the uncovering of a path to self-knowledge and self-actualization.

If responses to bereavement have been dominated by attachment theory and client-centred practice, there are approaches that reveal a different focus. Sutcliffe et al. (1998), in a volume including contributions from the UK and US, offer a systemic approach that concentrates on the family. Rather than a strictly psychological focus on the internal world of the individual, approaches of this kind engage with links between grief and mourning.

By and large the mental health field has failed to appreciate the impact of loss on the family as an interactional system. The extensive literature on bereavement has focused on individual mourning processes (Kübler-Ross 1969; Parkes 1972; Bowlby 1979; Worden 1982) and attended narrowly to grief reactions in the loss of a significant dyadic relationship. A systemic perspective is required to appreciate the chain of influences that reverberates throughout the family network of relationships with any significant loss (Walsh and McGoldrick 1998: 3). In Chapter 2 of this volume Currer develops this point in some detail.

Systemic approaches, for example those developed by Minuchin (1974), rest on three axioms:

1 An individual's psychic life is not entirely an internal process.
2 Change in the family structure contribute to changes in the behaviour and the inner psychic processes of the members of that system.
3 Therapist and family join to form a new therapeutic system.

Tuffnell *et al.* (1998) summarize the ways in which this approach differs from psychoanalytic/attachment theory models or cognitive models:

These approaches utilize a linear theory of causality and the aim of therapy is to achieve 'insight', in other words to transform the way the client feels about events. By contrast, the theory of change within the structural approach is not insight-oriented. Rather, the aim is to create a process of change within the system by means of re-patterning the interactions between the people present in the room.

(Tufnell *et al.* 1998: 90)

This re-patterning may both allow expression of feelings and encourage more effective functioning.

However, even though the theoretical approach is different, the resulting implications for practice are the same. It is the family, rather than the individual, who is still presented with 'tasks'. Thus they are to achieve a:

1 shared acknowledgement of the reality of death and shared experience of the loss;
2 reorganization of the family system and reinvestment in other relationships and life pursuits.

There is therefore something familiar in this remedy, even though its base assumptions are different.

This brief, and selective, review of (predominately) British guides to practitioners gives some insight into the nature of the discourse of bereavement and bereavement care. We have identified a theoretical sub-stratum that looks to an insight-oriented intra-psychic discipline and then, superimposed on it, a level guiding operational practice that is, at the very least, ego-orientated and in the main is structured around behavioural precepts. This hybrid construction makes it difficult to identify how the sense of meaning and the rationale for intervention can relate each to the other, and how either can relate to the action and outcome that follows. One can claim that the theory is sound, or that the practice works, but the shift from theory to practice involves leaping an epistemological break.

Having identified some of the theories and models of practice, we can now turn to look at the organizational context in which bereavement care is offered. Much of the growth in theory and practice of bereavement care has taken place in, or alongside, the modern hospice movement and we comment on recent reports of practice there. We also comment on the fact that it appears that much of the mainstream training offered to those professionals who might encounter the bereaved has not engaged substantially with the bereavement scholarship discussed above. Finally, we look at the proliferation of specialist, often voluntary sector, organizations operating in the field of bereavement care.

Reports of practice in bereavement services in hospice care are offered by Oliviere *et al.* (1998: 121–43). Experience in these settings, it is argued, shows that some 'emotional first aid' must be offered to help families and individuals begin the process of mourning. Bereavement support can strengthen the bereaved person's coping mechanisms, whilst bereavement counselling offers to help the person look at the changes they do, and will, need to make. According to Monroe (quoted in Oliviere 1998: 141), the role for a palliative care bereavement service should include:

1 normalizing grief,
2 promoting healthy grieving,
3 providing support to those in special need and those at risk,
4 providing or referring for more specialist help those who are stuck or whose grieving is complicated.

We have, then, some sort of gradation of need and response: first aid to initiate grieving, support, encouraging change for those evidencing healthy grieving, and recognizing the special needs and heightened risk of complicated cases. This identification of a diversity of needs is embodied in the range of services offered by some hospices, which can range from telephone support to memorializing activities.

The place given to bereavement in generic training – doctors, nurses, social workers, counsellors, psychotherapists, the police and so on – is limited. Social work, for example, does not make bereavement training a requirement in its Diploma in Social Work courses, although individual courses may decide to include it (Eaton 1998: 25). We have a scenario in which there is proliferation within the specialism of bereavement care but a marginalization from the mainstream. This carries the danger of the discourse of bereavement becoming self-referential and over specialized.

Alongside these specialist services must be placed the activities of another kind of expert, those individuals who have experienced particular forms of bereavement. Given the professionalization of many aspects of the care of dying, dead and bereaved people, the changing demographic profile and increased longevity, all of which characterized the twentieth century, firsthand experience of death is far less common than during previous centuries. Individuals who are the surviving member of twins, who have been bereaved of a child, bereaved through murder, or been bereaved as a result of a partner's stigmatizing illness in young adulthood may not only find that their experiences are not shared widely among family, friends, neighbours and colleagues; they also find that their experience has given them access to highly specialized knowledge. It is both out of their experience of a form of social exclusion, coupled with a commitment to the authenticity of personal experience as a source of knowledge (see discussion of readings of Freud's letters in Chapter 1), that mutual help groups are founded. Riches and Dawson's (2000) work on parental and sibling bereavement provides extensive documentation of experiences which exemplify the kinds of difficulties faced by individuals and families who have been bereaved in ways that are statistically uncommon and conceptually 'unthinkable'.

Walter identifies four focuses for mutual self-help groups (1999: 187): (1) a common event such as war or disaster; (2) a common form of bereavement such as the death of a child (see Chapters 10 and 11); (3) a form of bereavement, which is felt to warrant legal or political action such as the Snowdrop anti-gun campaign that followed the shooting of schoolchildren in Dunblane (see Chapter 9); and (4) a professionally identified focus, which leads a paid worker to initiate such a group.

In many respects, mutual help groups, whilst sharing the goal of bereavement care more generally – that is, the management of suffering – represent a kind of counter-culture. Walter describes them as subcultures in the sense that they represent communities of feeling (Riches and Dawson 1996). In relation to the subtitle of Walter's recent work *The Culture of Grief* (1999), there are also at least three ways in which mutual self-help groups could be described as counter-cultures or cultures of resistance. First, as Littlewood demonstrated in Chapter 5, they are frequently the site for models of grief that run counter to the culture associated with modernist process models of grief, which make resolution or closure their goal. As Walter notes, they can be a haven from these kinds of expectations (1999: 123). In the mutual self-help group, the maintenance of continuing bonds is a primary activity. The Compassionate Friends, as Riches and Dawson demonstrate (2000), is a setting in which the social identity of dead children is sustained and shared, birthdays and other lifecourse events being noted despite the absence of the dead child's embodied presence. Second, in groups where the death is seen to occur as a result of negligence, legal or political action may be core to the group's activities. As Howarth's chapter (Chapter 17) indicates, even for individuals who are not members of such groups, legal contexts such as the coroner's court are important settings within which less widely recognized aspects of mourning take place. Third, the validation of emotional expression at mutual help groups is an unusual and in many respects counter-cultural social activity. It challenges the prevailing norms that grief should be private, manifested either in the home or in the cloistered setting of a one-to-one encounter with a professional counsellor.

Evidence that mutual self-help groups of this kind represent resistance to modernist models of grief can be found in organizations such as Cruse

– Bereavement Care. This organization has long offered social groups as a way of complementing their one-to-one counselling work. Such groups were conceived of as 'half-way houses' that provided a safe setting for individuals *en route* for a final re-entry into the wider society. It was therefore a source of frustration for workers to discover that some bereaved people were not 'moving on', but rather, were becoming 'dependent' on such settings. More recently this organization has established Friendship Groups, which have a purely social agenda and which represent some kind of recognition of the ongoing social and emotional importance of a 'community of feeling' to many people who have been bereaved.

The organizational development associated with bereavement has seen not just a proliferation of groups but also a narrowing of focus. Again, many such groups reflect the privileging of highly specific personal experience as a knowledge source. In the UK there are groups that pursue research, such as the Bereavement Research Forum; groups that offer care to specific sections of the community, for example, the Jewish Bereavement Counselling Service and the Lesbian and Gay Bereavement Project; groups that focus on specific kinds of loss, such as Child Death Helpline (see Chapter 10), Cruse – Bereavement Care (Chapter 7), Compassionate Friends; and finally there are national coordinating organizations, such as the National Association of Bereavement Services. Wass and Balk (1995) identify 50 organizations in the USA which can act as a resource in relation to death and dying. Humphrey and Zimpfer (1996) list 23 organizations in the UK and US, some with international links, that offer a resource on dying, death and grieving. Parkes *et al.* (1996) list 11 such organizations in Great Britain, four in Australia, seven in America and two international organizations. In addition, there are nine organizations in Europe and America that can help respond to disasters (see Chapter 18). Many of these organizations can also act as referrers to other even more specialized or local organizations. Wass and Balk, Humphrey and Zimper and Parkes offer only partial listings. Indeed it is difficult to generate a comprehensive list. Groups and organizations come and go, some have a specific local catchment, for others it is not always immediately clear what their remit is. The organizations listed by Parkes *et al.* (1996) include educational organizations and organizations and groups offering help for specific sorts of loss. This latter category includes a number of groups responding to the death of children, for example:

- CLIMB, Inc, Centre for Loss in Multiple Birth (an international network)
- The Foundation for the Study of Infant Deaths (cot death research and support) (UK)
- National Sudden Infant Death Syndrome (SIDS) Foundation (US)
- Parents of Murdered Children (US)
- SANDS (Stillbirth and Neonatal Death Society)(UK)

- Rainbows for All God's Children (4000 affiliated groups internationally), for children and adults grieving a death, divorce or painful transition
- Share: international support group for parents who have lost a child, particularly through miscarriage, stillbirth or new-born death

For a fuller list of both groups relating to child death and to other sorts of death see Wass and Balk (1995: 454–6), Humphrey and Zimpfer (1996: 188–90) and Parkes *et al.* (1996: 193–7). The range and focus of such groups rapidly changes and the development of information technology, most notably the potential of the internet, raises new possibilities and in particular allows the maintenance of world-wide networks for support (for a discussion of the internet and self-help groups, see Small and Rhodes 2000).

The list of groups offered above is by no means an exhaustive list; it is not meant to be. Rather, we present it to identify three features of this proliferation of groups. First, the intrusion of interventionism into more and more areas of life; or the 'policing' of grief as Walter (1999) terms it. It is as if we have to respond to a theoretical insight with an intervention. Early work, including Freud's and Lieberman's, was meant to offer intimations into what might be happening and not necessarily invitations to do something about it. Second, the list gives some indication of the increasing spread of specialisms. Mutual help groups are developed for ever more narrowly specified clienteles. Consequently they elevate details of one's life circumstances over the experience of death. Third, the presence of these groups is both indicative of, and causally related to, the development of a popular culture about grief and counselling. Indeed the two can be conflated. A social movement of bereavement counselling has a life of its own, one that arguably is being pushed further than the evidence justifies. The risk is not only that one moves too far from evidence of what works but also that an omnipresence of counselling risks disempowering people, taking away their own means of coping. 'If the professionals move in does the neighbourhood move out?' There is a danger that we create a situation where you get offered counselling in all settings, indeed 'you are lucky if you can escape it' (Raphael 1998).

In light of this kind of proliferation, one might imagine that there remain few if any experiences of loss that have not attracted 'care' in some form, whether institutionalized, voluntary or lay. There are, nonetheless, examples of unrecognized bereavement and loss that prompt us to ask how much the expansion of scholarship and service has actually impacted on the society in which we live. Indeed, we need to ask whether the expansion of 'care' appears significant only to those working within its confines. Abrams (1995) has described the impact of the death of parents on school-age children and young adults. She gives an account of the trauma of the death of her father when she was age 18 years old and of her stepfather when she was 20 years old. She wrote a book because of the extent of the impact of these deaths on all aspects of her life and how: 'There was nothing available that spoke to me about my particular loss or helped me to deal with my particular grief. Reading about widows, widowers and single parents helped a little, but not much: their situation was not my situation' (Abrams 1995: xi).

The publication of her book prompted many to send her letters:

> The recurring themes of the letters mirrored precisely my own experience: the acute loneliness; the lack of understanding from other people, even close friends; the insensitivity of teachers and employers; the pressure to 'get over it' . . . What really surprised me about the letters was the age range of people writing them. While the book was intended primarily for readers in their teens and early twenties, it was actually being read by people aged anything from fourteen to eighty. These letters were proof, if any were needed, that the death of a parent is not something that becomes easier with age, nor is it a loss that fades with time: on the contrary, a parent's death stays with you and shapes you for the rest of your life; it becomes a condition of your existence, like having blue eyes or black hair.
>
> (Abrams 1995: xii)

While many of her correspondents were recounting stories from decades past, for example the 40-year-old woman who recalled being made to sit an 'O' level school exam the same morning as her father died, this absence of either information, support or understanding was still being recounted by people bereaved in the early 1990s. All the work that had been done, all the books and articles, all the groups, had not impacted on these people.

The value of research on bereavement

If the measurement and categorization of emotion feels at odds with death as represented in religious or poetic language, that is not to say that research *per se* is of little use. One example of a link between research and policy lies in Rutter's finding that among the bereaved children in his sample symptoms did not show up until several years after the death (Rutter 1996). Worden and Silverman (1996) confirmed this result and highlighted the complex nature of change in school-age children during the period that follows parental death. So far, data has been reported up to two years after death and more longitudinal study may show further impacts. While there are initial behavioural and emotional responses to the death, most of these attenuated by the end of the first year. However, in a significant minority of children, when compared with a matched group who had not been bereaved, there were differences in school performance, general behavioural conduct, overall self-esteem and sense of personal empowerment some two years later.

Worden and Silverman identify how these children will be badly served if bereavement care stops at the end of the 'conventional' period, for example, in the US, hospice programmes traditionally work with families for one year following the death. Children may need to be followed up for longer.

Other areas of well presented research evidence include Parkes's examination of the impact of trained volunteers (1981), Vachon on staff support (1979) and on widow to widow help (Vachon *et al.* 1980), Kissane on the impact of families (Kissane *et al.* 1996a, 1996b), Silverman and Worden on grief in children (1992; see also Silverman *et al.* 1992). We also have research data on the incidence of 'chronic, complicated' and 'traumatic' grief (Raphael and Middleton 1987). In addition there is a considerable sociology of grief, as discussed in Chapter 1, as well as anthropological accounts of, for example, the world of dying children (Bluebond-Langner 1978). In these examples the methodological sophistication is commensurate with the highest standards of these disciplines.

Research into the benefits of bereavement counselling has drawn on a variety of different methodologies. Nevertheless, there remain few demonstrable links between the accumulated research evidence and the personal sense, professed in good faith in the main no doubt, by the therapists that their work 'makes a difference' and the high levels of satisfaction displayed by recipients of counselling and psychotherapy (see Dineen 1999 for a critical survey of the evidence as to the impact of what she calls the 'psychology industry'). We have then a mismatch between a 'scientific evidence' paradigm and a 'personal experience' paradigm. We cannot assume that a confrontation of this sort will result in any real change to either.

As we discussed in Part I of this volume, developing theories of grief and bereavement must be located within the context of other social changes. These can act in ways that are antipathetic to the assumptions of good practice currently being developed and disseminated. Benoliel, for example, makes a still relevant warning about the direction of change in medical education and hospital procedures and its lack of harmonization with the scholarship of death and dying (see Chapter 1) (Benoliel 1988a, 1998b). There are, nonetheless, success stories. The Hospice Movement has now become world-wide, not only offering care itself but also acting as a beacon of good practice in the overall care of the sick and dying and of their families. Cruse – Bereavement Care is the largest bereavement care organization in the world, with 185 branches in the UK and, in 1998, offering support to more than 100,000 people. Further, there have been inroads into the prevailing orthodoxy of practice. For example, as Field and James point out: 'The care for parents bereaved by a still birth has been improved by the recognition that parents have difficulty in coming to terms with their loss without seeing the body, and so parents are now allowed to see and hold their dead infant' (Field and James 1997: 185; see Roberts and Oakley 1990). It is also likely that what bereaved people do, and how they talk about what they feel, is influenced by popularization of prevailing theories of grief (Hawkins 1990).

Conclusion

This chapter has drawn on post-structuralist theory to illuminate the historically and culturally specific nature of many of the practices recognized under the generic title 'bereavement care'. It has questioned approaches that either explicitly or implicitly treat grief as a universal and innate human response to loss which is responded to in different ways, depending on its time, place and circumstances. Instead we have sought to lay the whole notion of 'emotionality' open for questioning, so adopting a perspective from which to think as openly and creatively as possible about the experience of loss and how it has, and might be responded to.

Critiques of professionalized systems of care, from Illich (1975) onwards, have suggested that the emergence of experts can occur only in tandem with the disempowering of lay populations. Foucault is one theorist among many who seeks to expose the structures of welfare as a system of power (Gordon 1980). It would seem, therefore, that the losses associated with bereavement can be compounded by the subordination of the individual to the discursive practices of experts. However, as the examples presented in this volume indicate, this view fails to account for either the rejection of 'expert' models of grief by bereaved people or their innovative mourning practices. Indeed, the question of whether or not Foucault's models of power adequately account for resistance has been a focus for considerable debate (Lupton 1997: 102; Armstrong 1987b).

What the examples we present here suggest is that loss can incorporate forms of empowerment. While there is an extensive history to the notion that the individual who embraces the pain of loss can ultimately be strengthened, contemporary theories and practices associated with bereavement give little space to Seremetakis's account of grief as 'an idiom of resistance' (1991: 5). Yet, as our discussion of mutual help groups shows, loss can stimulate what Seremetakis calls 'affective enclaves' or 'communities of pain and healing', which 'correspond to Bauman's [1977, cited in Seremetakis 1991] notion of performance spaces as disruptive and disjunctive and as alternative social structures within or at the margins of social structure' (1991: 5).

One of the most dramatic examples of the formation of alternative social structures occurred immediately after the death of Diana, Princess of Wales, in 1997 when the monarch and members of her household yielded to public pressure to change the arrangements for Diana's funeral and to express their grief more publicly. The funeral itself was appropriated by Diana's brother, Earl Spencer, as an occasion to question if not attack the Royal Family and the resounding applause of members of the public not only augmented the force of his words but also represented an entirely innovative mourning practice. As her bereft brother, Earl Spencer was uniquely placed to reveal the 'truth' about Diana and her experience as a member of the Royal household. His act exemplifies what Seremetakis calls 'the relationship between the force of pain and the establishment of truth claims' (1991: 4).

We are therefore highlighting what Turner identifies as 'the power of the weak' (1974: 234); that is, the power which accrues to those who find themselves in liminal or marginal positions in relation to mainstream society. Bereaved people are commonly avoided by some of their neighbours and colleagues; however they may also discover unexpected privileges such as the waiving of customary demands or the granting of unexpected favours in light of the *force majeure* of a death. In parallel with the special status accorded to the 'last wishes' of the deceased, the requirements of their survivors may also be privileged, at least initially. Furthermore, individuals can profit from a bereavement: through witnessing the end of someone's suffering; through inheritance; through relief from the burden of care; through a belief that the deceased has made a transition to a better life of some kind; through the day-to-day absence of a demanding relationship; through the acquisition of the deceased's familial or professional status.

Some of these assets associated with deaths tend to be equated with criminal acts (gains through murder of a family member) or their attractions are marshalled as a reason why someone might want another dead and, as such, they also offer grounds for a powerful defence against making euthanasia available. But this stigmatizing representation of the more empowering and beneficial aspects of a death can obscure their everyday occurrence within the lives of those bereaved of loving or valued relationships. Pain and the expression of pain can provide them with a site of power, albeit disruptive power. Loss and its associated social and emotional 'weakness' can confer on them a special status. Practising a problem-focused, task-oriented approach to bereavement, like sleeping in Procrustes bed, potentially involves sheering off some of these after-effects of a death. Whilst heeding Nagel's warning (Chapter 1) that for human beings the subjective experience of being a bat is something of a closed book, we need to recognize that the models available to us, and the practices associated with them, may obscure far more of that experience than we realise. Accessing a bigger picture of grief and loss as something potentially more diverse and more powerful than is currently acknowledged is the task to which this book addresses itself.

References

Abrams, R. (1995) *When Parents Die*. London: Thorsons.
Ariès, P. (1975) *Western Attitudes Towards Death*. Baltimore, MD: John Hopkins University Press.

Armstrong, D. (1987a) Silence and truth in death and dying. *Social Science and Medicine*, 24: 651–7.

Armstrong, D. (1987b) Bodies of knowledge: Foucault and the problem of human anatomy, in G. Scambler (ed.) *Sociological Theory and Medical Sociology*. London: Tavistock.

Armstrong, D. (1997) Foucault and the sociology of health and illness: a prismatic reading, in R. Bunton and A. Petersen, A. (eds) *Foucault: Health and Medicine*. London: Routledge, pp. 15–30.

Benoliel, J.Q. (1988a) Institutional dying: a convergence of cultural values, techno-logy and social organization, in H. Wass, F.M. Berardo and R.A. Neimeyer (eds) *Dying: Facing the Facts*, 2nd edn. New York: Hemisphere Publishing.

Benoliel, J.Q. (1988b) Health care delivery: not conducive to teaching palliative care. *Journal of Palliative Care*, 4: 41–2.

Bluebond-Langner, M. (1978) *The Private Worlds of Dying Children*. Princeton, NJ: Princeton University Press.

Bowlby, J. (1979) *The Making and Breaking of Affectional Bonds*. London: Tavistock.

Bunton, R. (1997) Popular health, advanced liberalism and *Good Housekeeping magazine*, in A. Petersen and R. Bunton (eds) *Foucault, Health and Medicine*. London: Routledge.

Clegg, S. (1998) Foucault, power and organizations, in A. McKinlay and K. Starkey (eds) *Foucault, Management and Organisation Theory*. London: Sage.

Dineen, T. (1999) *Manufacturing Victims: What the Psychology Industry is doing to People*. London: Constable.

Eaton, L. (1998) Good grief? *Community Care*, 27 August: 24–6.

Exley, C. (1999) Testaments and memories: negotiating after-death identities. *Mortality*, 4(3): 249–67.

Field, D. and James, V. (1997) Dying, death and bereavement, in S. Taylor and D. Field (eds) *Sociology of Health and Health Care*, 2nd edn. Oxford: Blackwell.

Foucault, M. (1973) *The Birth of the Clinic*. London: Tavistock.

Foucault, M. (1977) *The Archaeology of Knowledge*. London: Tavistock.

Foucault, M. (1979) *Discipline and Punish*. Harmondsworth: Penguin.

Foucault, M. (1981) *The History of Sexuality*. Harmondsworth: Penguin.

Fox, N. (1997) Is there life after Foucault? Texts, frames and *differends*, in A. Petersen and R. Bunton (eds) *Foucault, Health and Medicine*. London: Routledge.

Fulton, G., Madden, C. and Minichiello, V. (1996) The social construction of anti-cipatory grief. *Social Science and Medicine*, 43(9): 1349–58.

Gordon, C. (ed.) (1980) *Michel Foucault: Power/Knowledge: Selected interviews and other writings 1972–1977 by Michel Foucault*. Hemel Hempstead: Har-vester Wheatsheaf.

Grayling, A.C. (1999) The last word on sorrow. *The Guardian*, 12 October, p. 12.

Harrison, P.R. (1992) Michel Foucault, in P. Beilhaz (ed.) *Social Theory*. Sydney: Allen & Unwin.

Hawkins, A.H. (1990) Constructing death: three pathologies about dying. *Omega*, 22: 301–17.

Hockey, J. (1986) The human encounter with death. Unpublished PhD thesis, Uni-versity of Durham.

Hockey, J. (1990) *Experiences of Death: An Anthropological Account*. Edinburgh: Edinburgh University Press.

Hopson, B. and Scally, M. (1989) *Lifeskills Teaching Programmes, No 1 How to Cope with and Gain from Life Transitions*. Leeds: Lifeskills Associates.

Humphrey, G.M. and Zimpfer, D.G. (1996) *Counselling for Grief and Bereavement*. London: Sage.

Illich, I. (1975) *Medical Nemesis: The Expropriation of Health*. London: Caldar and Boyars.

Kearl, M.C. (1995) Death and politics: a psychosocial perspective, in H. Wass and R.A. Neimeyer (eds) *Dying, Facing the Facts*. Washington, DC: Taylor & Francis.

Kellehear, A. (1990) *Dying of Cancer. The Final Year of Life*. London: Harwood Academic.

Kissane, D.W., Bloch, S., Dowe, D.L. *et al.* (1996a) The Melbourne family grief study, 1: perceptions of family functioning in bereavement. *American Journal of Psychiatry*, 153: 650–8.

Kissane, D.W., Bloch, S., Dowe, D.L. *et al.* (1996b) The Melbourne family grief study, 2: psychosocial morbidity and grief in bereaved families. *American Journal of Psychiatry*, 153: 659–66.

Kübler-Ross, E. (1969) *On Death and Dying*. New York: Macmillan.

Lendrum, S. and Syme, G. (1992) *Gift of Tears: A Practical Approach to Loss and Bereavement Counselling*. London: Routledge.

Lofland, L.H. (1985) The social shaping of emotion: the case of grief. *Symbolic Interaction*, 8(2): 171–90.

Lupton, D. (1997) Foucault and the medicalisation critique, in A. Petersen and R. Bunton (eds) *Foucault, Health and Medicine*. London: Routledge.

Lupton, D. (1998) *The Emotional Self*. London: Sage.

Maslow, A.H. (1968) *Motivation and Personality*. New York: Harper and Row.

Mills, C.W. (1940) Situated actions and vocabularies of motive. *American Sociological Review*, 5: 904–13.

Minuchin, S. (1974) *Families and Family Therapy*. London: Tavistock.

Oliviere, D., Hargreaves, R. and Monroe, B. (1998) *Good Practices in Palliative Care*. Aldershot: Ashgate.

Osborne, T. (1997) Of health and state craft, in A. Petersen and R. Bunton (eds) *Foucault, Health and Medicine*. London: Routledge.

Parkes, C.M. (1972) *Bereavement: Studies of Grief in Adult Life*. London: Tavistock.

Parkes, C.M. (1980) Bereavement counselling: does it work? *British Medical Journal*, 281: 3–6.

Parkes, C.M. (1981) Evaluation of a bereavement service. *Journal of Preventative Psychiatry*, 1: 179–88.

Parkes, C.M., Relf, M. and Couldrick, A. (1996) *Counselling in Terminal Care and Bereavement*. Leicester: British Psychological Society.

Payne, S., Horn, S. and Relf, M. (1999) *Loss and Bereavement*. Buckingham: Open University Press.

Penson, J. (1990) *Bereavement. A Guide for Nurses*. London: Chapman and Hall.

Raphael, B. (1977) Preventative intervention with the recently bereaved. *Archives of General Psychiatry*, 34: 1450–54.

Raphael, B. (1998) Bereavement and grief: an Australian perspective. Plenary address to International Work Group on Death, Dying and Bereavement, Sydney, Australia, 20 July.

Raphael, B. and Middleton, W. (1987) Current state of research in the field of bereavement. *Israel Journal of Psychiatry and Related Sciences*, 24: 5–32.

Reilly, D.M. (1978) Death propensity, dying and bereavement: a family systems perspective. *Family Therapy*, 5: 35–55.

Riches, P. and Dawson, P. (1996) Communities of feeling: the culture of bereaved parents. *Mortality*, 1(2): 143–61.

Riches, P. and Dawson, P. (2000) *An Intimate Loneliness*. Buckingham: Open University Press.

Roberts, H. and Oakley, A. (1990) *Miscarriage*. London: Penguin.

Rogers, C. (1951) *Client-Centred Therapy*. New York: Houghton-Mifflin.

Rose, N. (1993) Government, authority and expertise in advanced liberalism. *Economy and Society*, 22(3): 283–99.

Rutter, M. (1966) *Children of Sick Parents*. London: Oxford University Press.

Seremetakis, C.N. (1991) *The Last Word: Women, Death and Divination in Inner Mani*. Chicago, IL: The University of Chicago Press.

Silverman, P.R. and Worden, J.W. (1992) Children and parental death. *American Journal of Orthopsychiatry*, 62: 93–104.

Silverman, P.R., Nickman, S. and Worden, J.W. (1992) Detachment revisited: the child's reconstruction of a dead parent. *American Journal of Orthopsychiatry*, 62: 494–503.

Small, N. and Rhodes, P. (2000) *Too Ill to Talk? User Involvement in Palliative Care*. London: Routledge.

Spall, B. and Callis, S. (1997) *Loss, Bereavement and Grief: A Guide to Effective Caring*. Cheltenham: Stanley Thornes.

Sutcliffe, P., Tuffnell, G. and Cornish, U. (1998) *Working with the Dying and Bereaved*. London: Macmillan.

de Swaan, A. (1990) *The Management of Normality*. London: Routledge.

Truax, C.B. and Carkhuff, R. (1967) *Towards Effective Counselling and Psychotherapy: Training and Practice*. Chicago, IL: Aldine.

Tuffnell, G., Cornish, U. and Sutcliffe, P. (1998) Death of a parent in a family with young children: working with the aftermath, in P. Sutcliffe, G. Tuffnell and U. Cornish (eds) *Working with the Dying and Bereaved*. London: Macmillan.

Turner, V. (1974) *Dramas, Fields and Metaphors. Symbolic Action in Human Society*. Ithaca, MN: Cornell University Press.

Vachon, M.L.S. (1979) Staff stress in care of the terminally ill. *Quality Review Bulletin*, 6: 13–17.

Vachon, M.L.S., Lyall, W., Rogers, J., Freedman-Letofsky, K. and Freeman, S. (1980) A controlled study of self-help intervention for widows. *American Journal of Psychiatry*, 137: 1380–4.

Walsh, F. and McGoldrick, M. (1998) A family systems perspective on loss, recovery and resilience, in P. Sutcliffe, G. Tufnell and U. Cornish (eds) *Working with the Dying and Bereaved*. London: Macmillan.

Walter, T. (1999) *On Bereavement: The Culture of Grief*. Buckingham: Open University Press.

Wass, H. and Balk, D.E. (1995) Resources, in H. Wass and R.A. Neimeyer (eds) *Dying. Facing the Facts*. Washington, DC: Taylor & Francis.

Worden, J.W. (1982) *Grief Counselling and Grief Therapy: A Handbook for the Mental Health Practitioner*. New York: Springer. (2nd edn published in 1991).

Worden, J.W. and Silverman, P.R. (1996) Parental death and the adjustment of school age children. *Omega*, 33(2): 91–102.

7

The skills we need: bereavement counselling and governmentality in England[1]

ARNAR ÁRNASON

Over the past decade bereavement counselling has emerged as both an institution and activity of great importance in England. It is arguably now central to the way in which the English manage death and grief (see Árnason 1999). This chapter provides a critical account of the work of Cruse – Bereavement Care, the largest voluntary bereavement counselling organization in the UK. I briefly describe the history and organization of Cruse and the way in which it provides its services. In particular, I focus on the skills that counsellors are encouraged to master and discuss what they reveal about the organization's working models of grief. The aim of counselling is to help clients to explore, express and understand their emotions. I show, first, how these are influenced by a particular Western 'ethnopyschological' (Kirkpatrick and White 1985) understanding of the emotions. Second, I contend that bereavement counselling is an example of what Foucault (1988: 18; see Rose 1989) calls 'technologies of the self' that 'permit individuals to effect by their own means or with the help of others a certain number of operations on their own bodies and psyches, thoughts, conduct, and way of being. This is in order to transform themselves and so attain a certain state of happiness, purity, wisdom, perfection, or immortality'. I contend, finally, that bereavement counselling is also an example of what Foucault (1991) terms 'governmentality', the 'practices and relations of power that operate well beyond the state' (Cruikshank 1994: 32). These do not act directly and immediately on people but seek to govern through people's wishes and desires. 'This mode of government links the subjectivity of individuals to their subjection' (Cruikshank 1994: 32).

My description is based on fieldwork (1995–8) with two North Eastern local branches of Cruse where I trained and later worked briefly as voluntary bereavement counsellor. That fieldwork was part of a larger (Árnason

1999) anthropological study of the workings of bereavement counselling and the experience of the bereaved.[2]

A history of Cruse

Cruse was founded in 1958 by Margaret Torrie as a support group for widows (Torrie 1987: 1–2). Torrie, a Quaker, describes her inspiration as a 'call' (Torrie 1987: 10) after which she advertised in her local paper and invited widows to come to a meeting. The widows brought with them stories of inconsolable and uncontrollable children, pensions, exploitation, poverty and loneliness. Torrie arranged for friends of hers to provide the widows with help in the matters they had raised (Torrie 1987: 4).

In 1959 Cruse was registered as a charity. Amongst the aims and objectives were (Torrie 1987: 11–12):

1 The relief of poverty, suffering and distress among widows and their dependants.
2 To undertake research into the special problems of widowhood.
3 To collect and publish information about the social services and other matters that are of benefit to widows.
4 To establish a panel of counsellors to visit widows and advise them.
5 To alleviate the isolation and loneliness of widows by assisting in forming Cruse clubs of widows around the country.

Following lobbying in parliament the Government in 1974 allocated Cruse a three-year grant of £23,000 a year, intended to cover the administrative costs of the organization over that period and to cover the salaries and expenses of a national organizer. The job of the national organizer involved advising local branches on practice and organization and helping set up branches in areas where none had been established. In the late 1980s Cruse underwent a fundamental change when its remit was redefined and anyone bereaved by death could be a potential client. The following years saw a rapid expansion and now Cruse is established as a truly national institution. At the time of writing, it receives roughly £1,000,000 yearly in grants from various government offices and national businesses, the Queen is Cruse's Royal Patron, while other prominent patrons include the Archbishop of Canterbury, the Chief Rabbi, and Cicely Saunders, the founder of the Hospice movement. Cruse's current president is Colin Murray Parkes, who for 25 years has been Britain's leading authority on bereavement.[3]

The organization of Cruse

As set down in its mission statement a typical branch will aim:

- to give a service of the highest standard of counselling, information and social support to anyone who has been bereaved by death;
- to offer training, support, information, and publications to those working to care for bereaved people;
- to increase public awareness of the needs of bereaved people through education and information services;
- to constitute an organization that uses trained volunteers supported by specialists in the fields of social work, welfare, and mental health.

Cruse is therefore a national, voluntary, bereavement care organization that offers, as Cruse puts it in a publicity brochure, 'a comprehensive service of counselling by trained and selected people, advice on practical matters and opportunities for social support'. The headquarters, Cruse House, is an umbrella under which about 190 local Cruse branches work all over Britain. Local branches have autonomy in their affairs but the policies and standards of work are issued by Cruse House. In the past few years Cruse has been 'standardizing' its counselling practices and bringing them up to the levels of the British Association for Counselling. The consequences of this and of the expansion of Cruse's remit appears to be that counselling is now the most important part of Cruse's work. Those who counsel for Cruse do so as volunteers. Prospective counsellors have to complete a training course on grief, a course on counselling skills and meet the requirements of a selection process and an interview before they are taken on as probation counsellors. They are required to attend monthly training meetings and monthly supervision sessions. During supervision counsellors bring in any concerns or problems they may be having, share them with their supervisor and receive advice.

Counselling appointments may be held in the client's home if that is convenient for both client and counsellor. Local branches normally have access to counselling rooms in cases when the client's home is unsuitable as a place to meet. Counsellors generally wish to meet their clients alone. Appointments usually last one hour and counsellors are encouraged to keep the session quite strictly to the hour as this maintains the focus on counselling. One appointment a week is deemed appropriate in most cases and counsellors are encouraged to 'contract' a number of sessions with the client at the start of the counselling relationship. Cruse counselling is free.

Every Cruse branch has a telephone number through which potential clients can contact the branch. Clients are channelled to counsellors through the referral system. Cruse prefers clients to refer themselves but if referral is from a third party this must be with the full consent of the prospective client. It is common that doctors, priests, social services and even probation officers refer their clients to Cruse. All referrals must go through the referral secretary who keeps a list of all the counsellors affiliated with each local branch and decides which counsellors are able to take on which clients.

The training of new counsellors

Every two years or so local branches of Cruse will hold courses on 'aspects of grief and bereavement counselling'. The explicit aim of these courses is to enlighten the public about death and grief but an implicit aim, one that is jovially acknowledged, is to find volunteers for Cruse.

Some of the people who enrol on a Cruse course are looking for charitable work to occupy their time and put something back into the community. Others come out of interest in bereavement as such; still others because it is directly relevant for their work. Then, there are the people who are trying to forge for themselves a career in counselling. What is of particular importance here is that Cruse counsellors do their counselling under supervision since those with professional goals require a certain number of supervised sessions to qualify for registration as a counsellor with the British Association for Counselling.

About 30 people attended each of the two courses on bereavement counselling in which I participated. Most of them were middle-aged, professional people and were predominantly women. The courses were 'facilitated' by trained, experienced counsellors who are members of Cruse and are involved in the workings of a local branch. Though teachers may thus be responsible for most of the teaching on their courses they will call on 'experts' in particular fields to lecture on their particular subjects, for example loss through miscarriage.[4]

Both of the courses I attended were held once a week, for about two hours and the courses ran for nine weeks. Each session was usually organized around a particular theme on the subject of death and grief, such as: grief through suicide, abnormal grief, terminal illness, loss of a child, loss of a partner.

On the first night of the training courses the participants were made to get to know each other. This is thought important because a course like this may 'bring up issues relating to the losses' participants themselves have suffered and 'open up old wounds'. We were told that participants have to feel able to discuss these difficult issues 'openly' and that is only possible in the 'safe environment' provided by the company of people you know and trust. The importance of this was captured in the 'ground rules' that were established at the very beginning of the courses, written down on a big piece of paper and put where everybody could see them for the rest of the courses. We were told that for the environment to be safe anything 'personal' said during the course must remain confidential and whatever any one participant said had to be treated sensitively and with respect. These rules became the basis of our interactions during training and they reflect the values of Cruse's counselling. Here we can see the capillary nature of power, trainee counsellors taking on the imperatives of disclosure and trust, which they in turn will make known to their clients, a process which then feeds out into a prevailing popular culture of grief.

The skills we need

Cruse practises person-centred counselling with Rogers's (1951; see Mearns and Thorne 1988) three core conditions of 'congruence', 'unconditional positive regard' and 'empathic understanding'. During training 'congruence' was explained to us as the counsellor's ability, and duty, to be honest, 'to be herself'. Clients have to be able to trust their counsellor and they can only do so if the counsellor is honest. Also, if counsellors are congruent this conveys the message to the client that it is 'ok to be yourself'. 'Unconditional positive regard' means to accept the client for who he is, whoever he is. The client should be made to understand that his experiences are valid and his emotions bearable, no matter how devastating they seem.

'Empathic understanding', involves trying to 'enter the client's frame of reference'. It is like 'stepping into another person's shoes and seeing the world through their eyes without losing touch with one's own world'. It is a continuous effort whereby the counsellor attempts to lay aside her way of experiencing and tries to 'sense' the experiences of the client. Empathy helps the client to feel that he is understood. This, it was stressed, is particularly important in the case of bereaved clients who so often have to suffer in isolation. They may be overtaken by 'weird' feelings – anger and resentment, for example – that do not figure in their expectations of bereavement and which may lead them to fear that they are 'going mad'. If the counsellor can communicate that she understands the client's feelings she sends him the broader message that his feelings are understandable and normal. Empathic understanding is the counsellor's way to seek to normalize the client's experience.

Apart from the core conditions, counsellors need to master particular counselling skills. It was emphasized in training that grief is 'messy' and that each grief is unique. Nonetheless, we were also told that bereavement counselling involves roughly three phases.[5] On the first meeting the counsellor has to establish a contract with the client specifying the frequency and number of sessions. The counsellor must explain to the client the nature of the counselling relationship. In particular the counsellor should make it clear that the client should be in charge of the sessions and that the sessions should be focused on working on the client's 'issues' and ensure the client about Cruse's rules regarding confidentiality.

Then, the counsellor must make the client feel that she is dedicated to trying to understand him. She must strive to show empathy and unconditional positive regard, she must attempt to create a 'safe environment' in which the client can 'explore' his emotions.[6] The basic building block of a safe environment is congruence. Finally, the counsellor must gather the history of the client, his relationship to the deceased, the circumstances surrounding the death and its aftermath.

At this initial stage the counsellor needs skills such as 'active listening and attending', 'staying with the feeling', 'open-ended questioning', 'paraphrasing', 'reflecting feeling', 'clarification', and 'summarizing'. During training counsellors are told that 'active listening' is the most important part of counselling and that with that alone they would do their clients no harm and probably considerable good. It is a continuous attempt to 'really listen to what the client is saying' without ever jumping to 'our' conclusions. This establishes the client's experience as the most important part of the counselling session; allows the client to express his emotions; and allows the counsellor to learn the history of her client. Here the counsellor also relies on clarification and summarizing. Clarification refers specifically to the task of making clear certain aspects of the client's story. A client will frequently populate his account of events with a large number of characters whose relationship with the client may not be obvious. At an appropriate moment the counsellor may want to clarify precisely who is who. This is often done in conjunction with summarizing. When there is a lull in a long story the counsellor may take the opportunity to summarize what the client has already said. Summarizing may also encourage the client to reflect on and assess his story.

Here the ability to ask open-ended questions, to paraphrase and reflect is important. An open-ended question would be, for example: 'I wonder what that felt like?' In contrast with closed questions, which limit the range of possible answers and thus force on the client a certain way of experiencing, open questions encourage the client to express 'their experience'. By then paraphrasing the counsellor 'returns' to the client something that they have said. The client may indicate strongly that he at some point felt very distressed without actually using the word distress to describe his emotion. The counsellor can return this with the words 'you say that this happened and it was maybe distressing'. Paraphrasing demonstrates to the client that the counsellor is 'actively listening' and allows the client to look again at what he has said, 'hold it up to view' and evaluate it.

Reflecting feeling involves 'picking up' the feelings that the client communicates and 'turning them back to the client'. The client may relate a story to the counsellor adding 'it was very sad'. The counsellor will pick this up and reflect it back to the client saying something of the sort: 'You say it was "very sad", can you tell me more about that?' At this stage the counsellor should try to 'stay with the feeling' and attempt to keep the feeling 'in the frame', using various techniques, like paraphrasing and reflecting, to encourage the client to 'explore' the meaning to them of feeling 'sad'. This encourages the client to actively reflect on his feelings: their origin, nature and consequences. It also gives the counsellor and the client a chance to identify those areas in which they may want to exhort most of their efforts. This, in turn, takes the counselling process onto a somewhat different stage.

Here the client and the counsellor seek to go 'deeper' into grief and 'work through the pain of grief' (see Worden 1991). The counsellor should encourage the client to 'actually feel the pain of grief in their body'. This is deemed important for the bereaved person to 'learn to live with the loss'. Counsellors understand that 'difficult emotions' might stand in the way of this and that part of their job is to address in particular anger and guilt. Many bereaved people feel intense anger over what has happened, anger that may be directed towards everyone and anyone, most problematically perhaps the deceased himself. The problem is that anger towards the deceased is not an acceptable part of bereavement in England. People therefore often suppress their anger and start to feel guilty over feeling angry.

These feelings may be part of what many bereaved people experience as having 'unfinished businesses' with the deceased. It is important to finish these businesses and this might be achieved by encouraging the client to recognize his feelings, to experience and express them. It might be necessary to work through these emotions if the bereaved person is to 'learn to live with the loss'. Some bereaved people may possibly depend too much on the deceased, which could cause the bereaved person to carry on behaving as if the deceased was still alive. Bereavement counsellors seem to think that it is not quite right, not quite dignified, for people to carry on for long like that. It would be as though people were not willing to live their own lives.

Now counsellors should be able to 'probe', 'challenge' and 'confront' their clients. To 'probe', 'challenge', or 'confront' requires the counsellor to take a more active role than the use of the skills mentioned previously demands. During training counsellors are informed that in sessions they may pick up all sorts of things about the client without the client having expressed them. For example, a counsellor may 'pick up' a lot of anger from a client even though the client does not express this anger or cannot 'place it' anywhere. The counsellor may see signs that the anger is in fact directed towards say the client's dead husband and may 'probe' by asking the client if she is angry and against whom the anger is directed. The counsellor may 'challenge' the client more directly by asking, for example: 'Are you angry with your husband?' Alternatively, the counsellor may even 'confront' the client by saying straight out: 'I think you are angry with your husband?'

Probes, challenges and confrontations, we were told, are very powerful and potentially dangerous tools. If a challenge is 'spot on' it can be very fruitful and open up for the client new and previously not 'explored' 'issues'. Here precisely might lie the emotions, the 'anger' and the 'guilt' that can prevent a client from 'moving on'. If it fails it can set the counselling relationship back a long way. Accordingly probes, challenges and confrontation tend to be presented as the preserve of more experienced counsellors and trainees are advised to be careful in using these skills. Only when a 'safe environment' has been built can counsellors start challenging and confronting their clients.

Bereavement counselling, technologies and governmentality

The material above describes the content and practices of the training courses I participated in as part of my study. What do these data tell us about Cruse's idea of grief? While bereavement counsellors are not very willing to distinguish between right and wrong ways of grieving, we were often advised to focus on 'emotion-self-now', on how the client is feeling in the present. The skills described above clearly aim at that. So within the model of grief, which underpins the world of Cruse, emotions are understood to be the most important aspect of bereavement, and those emotions are imagined as a force located within the individual mourner. Particularly 'difficult emotions' may even be 'buried deep' within the individual, a notion shared by Anderson's (see Chapter 8, this volume) interviewees. In this way Cruse's ideas reflect what can be called the Western 'ethnopsychology' (Kirkpatrick and White 1985) of the emotions (Lutz 1988), and differs from the ethnopsychology of some non-Western people where emotions are understood as being located in the social relationships between people (see Rosaldo 1980; Abu-Lughod and Lutz 1990). This is why bereavement counsellors prefer to meet their clients alone so that he can be isolated from his social environment and thus focus his attention more intently on his own mind rather than his relationship with those around him.

However bereavement counselling, I would argue, is more than an example of a particular ethnopsychology. The counselling skills of 'clarification', 'paraphrasing', 'reflecting', 'probing', 'challenging' and so on, are examples of 'technologies of the self' (Foucault 1988) through which the client, with the help of the counsellor, trains his attention on his own subjectivity and attempts to affect a change in his being. As a technology of the self, bereavement counselling is also an example of governmentality, that is, of government at a distance. It is relevant here that the financial support that Cruse receives from the Government is provided under 'Section 64', which aims to tap into the experience and expertise of the voluntary sector to meet the Government's goal of promoting the health and well-being of individuals and the community (this information is based on telephone interviews with Department of Health personnel). What Rose (1992: 159) calls 'postmodern governmentalities' are characterized by the fact that all shades of political opinion agree that 'democratic government must engage the self-activating capacities of individuals'. The technologies for doing so, Rose continues, make it possible 'to govern in an advanced liberal way, providing a plethora of indirect mechanisms that can translate the goals of political, social and economic authorities into the choices and commitments of individuals'. Barbara Cruikshank (1993: 331) rephrases Foucault (1983) to the effect that: 'Democratic government, even self-government, depends upon the ability of the citizens to recognize, isolate and act upon

their own subjectivity, to be governors of their selves'. Bereavement counselling can be seen as an example of the mechanisms to which Rose and
Cruikshank refer. The skills it employs help people to explore, isolate,
express and understand their emotions, to bring those under some control
so that its clients can 'learn to live with their loss'. But it is through these
acts of exploration, isolation and expression that the client is made to
become a subject for himself; through these acts the very states that counselling seeks to uncover are brought into being.

Bereavement counselling is a difficult and demanding task. Bereavement counsellors are generally highly trained, dedicated, professional
people whose support many bereaved people find extremely helpful. For
counselling to work it must seek to adjust its clients to the social reality
under which we live. That is both normal and natural and this criticism –
if that is what it is – is in fact something with which counselling is quite
comfortable (see MacLeod 1993). I have suggested here, though, that we
need to look a little bit further and see counselling as being implicated in
the construction of the very social realities to which it seeks to adjust its
clients.

Notes

1 Thanks are due to: Michael Carrithers, Lonisa Elvira Belaunde, Bob Simpson,
  Jenny Hockey, Sigurjon Hafsteinsson and Hulda Sveinsdottir who as supervisors,
  examiners, editors and friends have helped greatly. Especially I thank the people
  at Cruse. Fieldwork was funded by Durham Research Scholarship and the chapter written while I received Monbusho scholarship from the Japanese government. I gratefully acknowledge both.
2 I will sometimes talk about Cruse and sometimes about bereavement counselling
  generally. That should be taken with the regular anthropological grain of salt,
  that my discussion is based on more localized fieldwork, supported by other
  research. I have also for the sake of saving space, collapsed the discussion of the
  two branches of Cruse about which I know. I still believe my account to be
  accurate. In places I use ' ' around words to denote terms that were frequently
  used by counsellors during my fieldwork.
3 This information was gathered in 1996 and some of it updated in 1998. Some
  details may have changed. The point is that Cruse enjoys the support of the
  people in the top echelons of British society.
4 I use the terms 'teachers' to refer to the people who were in charge of the two
  courses I attended. This is my imposition, during the courses they would simply
  be referred to by their first names by everyone involved.
5 Our teachers were quick to add that not all counselling relationships would
  go through the same phases or in the same order, these were only rough
  guides.
6 For the sake of clarity, I use 'she' when referring to the counsellor and 'he' when
  referring the client.

References

Abu-Lughod, L. and Lutz, C.A. (1990) Introduction: emotion, discourse, and the politics of everyday life, in L. Abu-Lughod and C.A. Lutz (eds) *Language and the Politics of Emotion*. Cambridge: Cambridge University Press.

Árnason, A. (1999) 'Feel the pain'. Death, grief and bereavement counselling in North East England. Unpublished PhD thesis, University of Durham.

Cruikshank, B. (1993) Revolutions within: self-government and self-esteem. *Economy and Society*, 22: 327–44.

Cruikshank, B. (1994) The will to empower: technologies of citizenship and the war on poverty. *Socialist Review*, 23: 29–55.

Foucault, M. (1983) The subject and power, in H.L. Dreyfus and P. Rabinow (eds) *Michel Foucault: Beyond Structuralism and Hermeneutics*, 2nd edn. Chicago: University of Chicago Press.

Foucault, M. (1988) Technologies of the self, in L.H. Martin, H. Gutman and P.H. Hutton (eds) *Technologies of the Self: A seminar with Michel Foucault*. Amherst, MA: The University of Massachusetts Press.

Foucault, M. (1991) Governmentality, in G. Burchell, C. Gordon and P. Miller (eds) *The Foucault Effect: Studies in Governmentality*. London: Harvester Wheatsheat.

Kirkpatrick, J. and White, G.M. (1985) Exploring ethnopsychologies, in J. Kirkpatrick and G.M. White (eds) *Person, Self, and Experience: Exploring Pacific Ethnopsychologies*. London: University of California Press.

Lutz, C.A. (1988) *Unnatural Emotions: Everyday Sentiments on a Micronesian Atoll and their Challenge to Western Theory*. Chicago, IL: University of Chicago Press.

MacLead, J. (1993) *An Introduction to Counselling*. Buckingham: Open University Press.

Mearns, D. and Thorne, B. (1988) *Person-centred Counselling in Action*. London: Sage.

Rogers, C. (1951) *Client-Centred Therapy*. London: Constable.

Rosaldo, M.Z. (1980) *Knowledge and Passion*. Cambridge: Cambridge University Press.

Rose, N. (1989) *Governing the Soul: The Shaping of the Private Self*. London: Routledge.

Rose, N. (1992) Governing the enterprising self, in P. Heelas and P. Morris (eds) *The Values of the Enterprise Culture: The Moral Debate*. London: Routledge.

Torrie, M. (1987) *My Years with Cruse*. Richmond: Cruse.

Worden, J.W. (1991) *Grief Counselling and Grief Therapy: A Handbook for the Mental Health Practitioner*, 2nd edn. London: Routledge.

8

'You have to get inside the person' or making grief private: image and metaphor in the therapeutic reconstruction of bereavement

MICHAEL ANDERSON

Introduction

In recent years, there has been a careful sociological and anthropological exploration into various aspects of emotionality, which has taken various forms (e.g. Jagger 1989; Jackson 1993; Heald and Deluz 1994). It is curious, however, that the emotion of grief has yet to be keenly considered as a social, rather than just a private, mental process. While death as a ritualized event and the bereaved as a social category have long been established on the sociological and anthropological agenda, the nature of grief has rarely been examined as a socially constructed process. One exception however has been Rosaldo's (1989) moving account of Ilongot grief in the Philippines and its relation to his own experience of bereavement. Whether this is because it is thought too sensitive an area for the social sciences to analyse and speculate on, or whether it has simply not stimulated commentators in the way that other emotions have is not entirely clear. One clue reveals it may be the former: 'We all believe we know what death is because it is a familiar event and one that arouses intense emotion. It seems both ridiculous and sacrilegious to question the value of the intimate knowledge and to wish to apply reason to a subject where only the heart is competent' (Hertz [1909] 1960: 27).

Although the contents of what Westerners see as the most intimate province of the self may commonly be considered as definitively non-public (and even non-social), this chapter is an attempt to examine how personal emotions are constructed publically and socially through language and conversation. Hence 'making grief private' is an attempt to show how what we refer to as personal and private grief, and the way counsellors construct it, is in fact premised on a very public and social discourse. This is to say, feelings are grounded in the social and cultural discourses within which they occur.

The observations and reflections on which this discussion is based have been collected over a number of years and began with research (Anderson 1993) which involved interviews with bereavement counsellors and those in the care of bereaved people. The metaphoric use of language was a striking theme in counsellors' own imaging of their work with bereaved people and in their reported conversations with them. This was evident both in informal interviews as well as in formal, authorized texts. An analysis of these provides a study of how words and language not only express but construct the experience of grief.

The death event and the reconstruction of grief in counselling

The form of grief counselling, its contents and the process of 'overcoming' or 'resolving' grief is commonly thought to proceed through a series of strategic conversational stages. Although these are not necessarily sequential stages they follow a familiar pattern, and each stage can be returned to at any point during the entire course or process. Beverley Raphael (1984: 362–7) summarizes these (conversational) stages as a series of counselling questions addressed to the counsellee, abbreviated but encapsulated as follows:

1 Can you say a little about the death? What happened that day?
2 Can you tell me about your relationship with the deceased?
3 What has been happening since the death? How have things been . . . ?
4 Have you been through any other bad times like this recently . . . ?

By relating the sequence of events leading up to the death of the loved one the client relives the story of the loss of their loved one. All conversational roads lead up to and from the moment when the death was realized, like spokes to and from the hub of a wheel. Temporally related activities are remembered in minute detail – dialogues, conversations, and otherwise insignificant routine domestic activities. Other events may serve as 'points of return' for the counsellor–counsellee conversation – 'moments' that the counsellor can use as purchase and leverage to new directions for the grief 'story'. Thus, within the conversational process private thoughts and feelings are socially re-invented and reconstructed, seen anew and afresh by counsellor and client. Private trauma and public self come to cohere in the counselling process so as to effect 'cure'.

Language and conversation

Stevi Jackson maintains that 'We create for ourselves a sense of what our emotions are . . . We do this by participating in sets of meanings constructed, interpreted, propagated and deployed throughout our culture, through learning scripts, positioning ourselves within discourses, constructing narratives of self' (1993: 212).

As a verbal distillation of social life, words, language and conversation do not merely give expression to a socially constructed experience but, and the point being made here, accomplish and create it. This is tangentially reminiscent of Durkheim's sentiments: 'Men do not weep for the dead because they fear them; they fear them because they weep for them' (1965: 447).

That is to say, actions have the potential to produce emotions. Actions are not merely the results of emotions. Words, language and conversation act as metaphoric catalysts of experience (and not just expressions of it) and therefore as evocative components not only for managing grief but for constructing it also. As Rapport maintains 'Through language individuals become origins of action upon the universe and centres of experience within it' (1993: 152).

Blumer is more specific on conversation in relation to personal meanings with which emotions are laden. He says 'if human beings act toward things on the basis of the meanings things have for them, and these meanings are the *sine qua non* of the social existence of things *per se*, then it is in conversation with their fellows, in the processes of interaction that this construction of meaning takes place' (1969: 3).

Language and conversation construct and control experience and meanings, not least that of grief. Through an analysis of specific concepts, words, and images in counselling activities it will be demonstrated *how* such construction takes place in ways acceptable to the cultural and conventional norms of 'professional' practice.

Metaphors, emotions and counselling

Counselling was born of the psychoanalytic tradition and inherits many of its theoretical and methodological characteristics. Models of the person (in neurosis, in crisis, in trauma, in grief) have been developed through engagement with these. Their schools of thought have now long been established as theoretical paradigms of the self.

These models, inherited and developed by grief counsellors, have established more specific metaphoric themes within which their therapeutic vocabularies and conceptual aims are couched. Among these are the metaphors of 'depth', 'letting go', (grief) 'work', 'disengagement', 'resolution' and so on. Here, I want to comment on some of these since they provide the key conceptual pivots on which the unwelcome and unwanted state of the person in traumatic grief is brought 'back' to cohere with the conventions of social acceptability, and because they establish the building blocks to an interpersonal narrative or story, which functions to construct private grief in a way that is more controllable for the bereaved person.

The metaphor of 'depth'

Metaphor causes us to image one thing as another, to make the inchoate choate (Fernandez 1982: 28), the intangible more tangible. The movement from the insecurity and danger of the unknown, or rather unfamiliar (in this case grief) to the comforting familiarity and certainty of the known (through conversation with others) is necessary for people to act competently (Fernandez [1972] 1986: 8).

Hastrup (1995: *passim*) has also argued that metaphor is a prime element in our structuring of experience. In coming to terms with grief, metaphors provide us with a range of images that enable us to picture a shattering event and a fragmented self in a way that repositions or cements the shattered pieces and fragments (themselves oft-used metaphoric images) into a once again bearable, narrative whole. Essential to this process, and a premise of the counsellor's model of the self, is that of the person as container and its attribute of 'depth'.

The metaphor of depth was first used professionally by Freud who saw himself as constructing an 'archaeology' of the mind. The idea that counsellors and therapists are in some way getting at information that is deep within individuals' psyches is the key justification for the role of the counsellor and therapist in their extraction of grief to the 'surface' of the self where it is made available to language and where it can be observed and 'treated'.

As an illustration of this metaphor, one counsellor interviewed used the following expression 'You have to get inside the person . . . draw out their real feelings and thoughts . . . I try to get them to reflect on these . . . make them aware of their true selves and then to open them out so we can work on them together . . . to resolve them . . . before they begin to do damage . . .'

The metaphor of depth is combined with, and premised on, the metaphor of the self as *container* (Lakoff and Johnson 1980) and provides a concept that is apt for the tacit allusion to a self which, in the state of grief, is an unhappy 'Pandora's box' of unpredictable and undesirable thoughts, feelings and potentially uncontrollable acts, but whose eventual contentment lies somewhere near the bottom or 'deep within'. Yet from which other impostor, or 'false' selves/aspects (denials?) must be evacuated before the 'real' one can emerge.

The suggestion is one of a receptacle of proper and improper selves, a platonic cave of 'illusionary' shadows, which the bereaved person is socialized to confront during their therapy precisely through its conversational method, and its allusion to 'real' and 'true' identities. The process conspires to separate out false selves from the true ones before the former take over and 'begin to do damage' as the counsellor suggests. Another counsellor comments 'Each person is unique and I tend to encourage my clients to speak about the death, sometimes over and over again . . . their feelings, thoughts . . . it's cathartic . . . If these things aren't dealt with (spoken about) . . . they'll come back and haunt the person in later life . . .'

Thus, there may not only be false selves but recurring phantoms too, each of which must be 'talked through' and dispelled through the metaphorical re-imaging of memories and feelings within the conversation. To 'speak about' is to expose the dark depths of feeling to the surface light of language.

The metaphors of 'work'

Bereavement counselling is justified by the cultural classification of grief as an unwelcome intrusion (or violent interception) into the normal efficient running of everyday life. Stroebe *et al.* hold 'Grieving, a debilitating emotional response, is seen as a troublesome interference with daily routines, and should be "worked through". Such *grief work* typically consists of a number of tasks that have to be confronted and systematically attended to before normality is reinstated' (1996: 32).

These 'tasks' amount to a conversational negotiation of the processes of grief. The invention of 'inappropriate' grief processes and *grief work* has provided the justification for the professional realm of practitioners who theorize and prescribe on the appropriateness of feelings and actions following the death of a loved one. Taking one example of this, another counsellor comments: 'It's not only that some people can't stop grieving it's often that they can't start. The point of bereavement counselling is to try to get the person to talk about their feelings . . . to focus on their relationship with the deceased and try to get them to let go . . .'

Not being able to 'start' grieving is a curious notion and hints at the apparent lack of emotional feeling and vocabulary perceived by the counsellor on the part of the bereaved, confirming that certain types of behaviour following death are appropriate (better) and others not (worse). By implication it also suggests a new or different vocabulary, which must be learnt; an appropriate response into which clients must be socialized through the counselling conversation.

The notion that unrequited grief, or even uncommenced grief, is often perceived to take the form of an undesirable attachment is not uncommon. Indeed, this has dominated therapeutic theory for many years (e.g. Raphael 1984; Sanders 1989). Indications as to its 'resolution' are not uncommonly sought in the bereaved person's resort to tears. A lack of tears can be interpreted as 'denial' whereas profuse weeping or crying within a set period of time after the death, and perhaps sporadically afterwards may be

seen as 'desirable', 'letting it out', 'not bottling it up'. This suggests a verit-
able plumbing metaphor of emotional expression wherein pain is flushed
out – a measurable volume of tears providing evidence of successful grief
work.

The 'unblocking' of the container self is deemed to require an emotional
plumber (counsellor) for the job of returning it to normal. Ensuring the
free flow of emotion in the right direction, without it overflowing or leaking
at the wrong times and in the wrong places, lends for a peculiar model
of the self and emotional life. Moreover, the necessity for 'work' appears
to have about it the requirement of the completion of certain tasks. This
resonates with the ordinary concept of work in the West, which while often
mundane, hard and even painful will reap beneficial rewards in the long
term.

Unsuccessful grief work on the other hand (inappropriate grieving or
'denial') are deemed to lead to pathological states from severe depression to
heart attacks in which the bereaved person may die as a consequence of the
stress brought on by the loss – the so called 'broken heart' syndrome (Parkes
et al. 1969). There is an implicit threat, which hangs over those who do not
get it right – a sense that the contents of the container of the inner self will,
in time, react in deeply pathological ways if not given the right means of
expression at the right time. But also for the right period of time, not too
short (as to be abrupt) and not too long (as to be morbid). An extended
period of grief in the West may be interpreted as morbidity whereas in
other cultures grieving may continue for many months or years and with
little thought of the consequences (Muslims in Bali and Egypt are examples
of this, see Wikan 1988).

Metaphors of 'disengagement' and 'letting go'

'Disengagement' from the deceased has long been thought to be the goal of
grief counselling and talking the means of achieving this. This is linked to
the idea that once a loved one is no longer alive, emotional attachment to
that person, which continues for a longer than particular length of time,
can be deemed pathological (see, for example, Parkes and Weiss 1983;
Sanders 1989).

Klass *et al.* (1996) trace this tendency to the value of independence and
individualism in Western culture. They also draw attention to the positivist
thread in Western scientific thought and that only what is observable is
of value to scientific and therefore medical thought. Subjective feelings and
meanings are not observable and therefore are dismissed as potential con-
taminants of genuine knowledge. Thus, clinging to the memory of the deceased, to the unobservable (that is not 'letting-go'), culminates in the view
of a failure of sufficient independency. Stroebe *et al.* again comment:

Principles of grief counselling and therapy follow the view that, in the course of time, bereaved persons need to break their ties with the deceased, give up their attachments, form a new identity of which the departed person has no part, and reinvest in other relationships. People who persist in retaining a bond with their deceased loved one are in need of counselling and therapy to achieve emotional withdrawal from the deceased

(Stroebe et al. 1996: 34)

Klass et al. (1996), however, argue that aims which implicitly invoke this dismiss strong, prolonged feelings toward the deceased as mere barriers standing in the way of a more fruitful life. While short-lived clinging is acceptable, long-term 'inability to let go' is thought unhealthy. This is challenged head on by Klass, Silverman, and Nickman (ibid.: 22), 'We suggest that the dominant model of grief is based on inadequate assumptions about the nature of the self and is based in inappropriate social scientific methodology used to study bereavement . . . because the model is based in the unexamined assumptions of our age'.

Klass et al. are not directly critical of the counselling process but clearly question the assumptions underlying current counselling conventions and aims. Moreover, work by Walter (1996) compares different kinds of talking and language usage during bereavement: that which aims (therapeutically) at letting go, and that which actually strengthens the bond between the bereaved person and the deceased. Traditionally, grief counselling has predominantly exercised the former in which the counsellor is trained in the art of a particular kind of conversation which is designed to strike the right balance in the management of personal feelings and to create some kind of emotional distance between bereaved and deceased.

Through the words of therapeutic conversation the bereaved person is 'brought back' from the messiness of 'unresolved grief' or 'denial' or the deepest and darkest recesses of the self to the daylight outside and the clarity of conversation and community. This is the world of social others towards which the bereaved are directed both within and through talking. The counselling conversation provides a necessary story, a narrative of the restoration of personal dignity and identity; an elevation of feelings through words and the construction of social (conversational) communion over individual isolation.

Summary

The purpose of this chapter has been to say that grief is not merely an inner or private emotion but is socially constructed through metaphor and that the grief counselling process is particularly illustrative of this. To talk of grief is to make it both social and private, shared and personal. It is made personally resonant and socially salient through language in conversation. Yet its personal resonance and social saliency are accountable for its public construction as a private emotion. Emotionality receives its personal and private meanings through social interaction in language, gesture and sign; otherwise public recognition of it as such would be impossible. That is to say, words, language, narrative and conversation construct and control private grief in terms of the public system of symbols, which makes those experiences both resonant for, and communicable to, others.

References

Anderson, M. (1993) Managing death: aspects of control in death and bereavement. Undergraduate dissertation, University of Edinburgh.

Blumer, H. (1969) *Symbolic Interactionism*. Englewood Cliffs, NJ: Prentice Hall.

Durkheim, E. (1965) *The Elementary Forms of the Religious Life*. New York: Free Press.

Fernandez, J. (1982) The dark at the bottom of the stairs: the inchoate in symbolic inquiry and some strategies for coping with it, in J. Maquet (ed.) *On Symbols in Anthropology: Essays in Honour of Harry Hoijer*. Malibu: Udena Publications.

Fernandez, J. ([1972] 1986) Persuasions and performances: of the beast in every body and the metaphors of everyman, in *Persuasions and Performances: The Play of Tropes in Culture*. Bloomington, ID: Indiana University Press.

Hastrup, K. (1995) *A Passage to Anthropology: Between Experience and Theory*. London and New York: Routledge.

Heald, S. and Deluz, F. (1994) *Anthropology and Psychoanalysis*. London and New York: Routledge.

Hertz, R. ([1909] 1960) *Death and the Right Hand*. New York: Free Press.

Jackson, S. (1993) Even sociologists fall in love: an exploration in the sociology of emotions. *The Journal of the British Sociological Association*, 27(2): 204–20.

Jagger, A. (1989) Love and knowledge: emotion in feminist epistemology, in A. Jagger and S. Bordo (eds) *Gender/Body/Knowledge: Feminist Reconstructions of Being and Knowledge*. New Brunswick, NJ: Rutgers University Press.

Klass, D., Silverman, P.R. and Nickman, S.L. (eds) (1996) *Continuing Bonds: New Understandings of Grief*. Washington, DC: Taylor & Francis.

Lakoff, G. and Johnson, M. (1980) *Metaphors We Live By*. Chicago, IL: University of Chicago Press.

Parkes, C.M., Benjamin, B. and Fitzgerald, R.G. (1969) Broken heart: a statistical study of increased mortality among widowers. *British Medical Journal*, 1: 740–43.

Parkes, C.M. and Weiss, R. (1983) *Recovery from Bereavement*. New York: Basic Books.

Raphael, B. (1984) *The Anatomy of Bereavement*. New York: Basic Books.

Rapport, N.J. (1993) *Diverse Worldviews in an English Village*. Edinburgh: Edinburgh University Press.

Rosaldo, R. (1989) *Culture and Truth: The Remaking of Social Analysis.* Boston, MA. Beacon Press.

Sanders, C. (1989) *Grief: The Mourning After.* New York: Wiley.

Stroebe, M., Gergen, M., Gergen, K. and Stroebe, W. (1996) Broken hearts or broken bonds?, in D. Klass, P.R. Silverman and S. L. Nickman (eds) *Continuing Bonds: New Understandings of Grief.* Washington, DC: Taylor & Francis.

Walter, T. (1996) A new model of grief: bereavement and biography. *Mortality*, 1: 7–25.

Wikan, U. (1988) Bereavement and loss in two Muslim communities: Egypt and Bali compared. *Social Science and Medicine*, 27(5): 451–60.

9 Supporting bereaved children at school

JEANNE KATZ

In the UK very little attention has been given to the need to incorporate into teacher training some understanding of children's responses to death and also the basics of bereavement counselling skills (McWhirter *et al.* 1998). Indeed, both in the UK and the US, the focus has been on developing crisis intervention models to deal with the possibility of multiple deaths in a school (Aspinall 1996) or in another type of environment, rather than providing education both for teachers and for students about death, dying and bereavement amongst different age, racial and ethnic groups. Even training about how to deal with adolescents who are likely to experience the death of one or more of their peers through accidental death or suicide has not been adequately addressed in teacher education. Furthermore, little attention has been paid to acknowledging the needs of children bereaved in their home environments, despite findings that up to 70 per cent of schools have at least one bereaved child at any given time (Holland 1993).

This chapter looks at the issues relating to caring for bereaved children at school. It surveys current views about children's understandings of death and bereavement patterns and suggests a number of possible strategies that could be developed by schools in the United Kingdom and the United States on how best to deal with (1) school children bereaved at home and (2) survivors of tragedies befalling a group of children from the same school.

Methods

Over a five-year period as part of a programme of regularly updating students studying the Death and Dying course presented by The Open University, the course team (Jeanne Katz and BBC producer Alison Tucker) carried out semi-structured interviews with those working with bereaved children in schools. Those interviewed included: school teachers attending a bereavement course for teachers held at St Christopher's Hospice as well as those delivering this course; the head teacher and school counsellor attached to a small village primary school; the head teacher and several teachers at a secondary school which had experienced the deaths of 12 children and a teacher in a mini-bus accident (interviewed three times over five years); Dorothy Judd, a psychotherapist specializing in bereavement in children; volunteers and professionals running Winston's Wish aimed at supporting bereaved children and their families; Shirley Payne who coordinated the 'Gone Forever' project – a programme to train adults, primarily teachers, working with bereaved children; an official in a local education authority developing a policy for dealing with bereavement in schools; and Jacqueline Walsh who coordinated the Snowdrop Campaign to ban handguns following the massacre of school children and their teacher in Dunblane, Scotland in 1997.

One of the unifying features of the data emerging from these interviews was the lack of training for teachers in many areas relating to bereavement and loss. In particular a paucity of knowledge of what children of different ages understand about death.

Children's understandings of death

How do children interpret the meaning of death and to what extent is this relevant to a classroom situation? Maria Nagy (1959) undertook the first major study of the ways in which children of different ages respond to death in Hungary during the 1950s. She interviewed children between the ages of two and nine years and asked them to describe their views of death. Her work was based on Piaget, who focused primarily on the conceptual capabilities of the child's developing brain.

She identified three stages (quoted in Kastenbaum 1977: 28–9):

1 Stage 1 (till about age five). Children are curious about death and focus on the fate of the body. Dead people don't differ much from living people – they are often seen as asleep, which can create anxiety for the child; children at this stage usually do not grasp the finality of death.
2 Stage 2 (from five to about age nine). Death is now seen as final and life has ceased. Nagy noted that children at this stage saw death as an individual, who often visits at night. Death was seen as avoidable and lucky people might fool death and escape.
3 Stage 3 (from ages nine to ten onward). Death is now viewed not only as final but also as inescapable for all living things.

Nagy's work still forms the basis for most studies of this area but has been criticized on a number of grounds; for example, Myra Bluebond-Langner

(1978) critiques these developmental, age-graded models: 'They share the tacit assumption that at some point in the maturation process (some researchers argue that it occurs as early as age three, others as late as nine), the child casts aside "immature", "childish" concepts in favour of "adult", "scientific" conceptions of death.' She also disputes the idea that adults do not share children's macabre fantasies of death, including visions of hell and death.

Kastenbaum developed Nagy's work further, providing guidelines for what one can expect a child of different ages to grasp in relation to death. It is clear from his work and that of others that children do dwell on death (Kastenbaum 1977). However, children's interpretations of death depend on a variety of factors. Kastenbaum identified four different kinds of information which he thought important (1977: 25–6).

1 Developmental level: This relates to the child's age, but clearly varies according to the maturity of the individual. Chronological age roughly indicates the extent of developmental functioning. However, this is an important indicator of the child's ability to comprehend regardless of the content of the information.
2 Individual personality: Like adults, children differ in personality and their individual characteristics contribute to their understandings of death.
3 Life experiences: The death of a parent is often associated with problems experienced by the child later in life. But other life experiences also influence a child's interpretation of death; for example, extended separations from family members, or encounters with serious life-limiting illness can influence a child's understanding of death.
4 Communication and support: A child's interpretation of death also relates to the general patterns of communication within the family or social network. A child who feels comfortable sharing concerns within the family and feels listened to, is more likely to discuss anxieties about death. The reverse is also likely to be true.

Myra Bluebond-Langner (1978) suggests that Kastenbaum's criteria for understanding a child's concept of death are too narrow. She and others (quoted in Worden 1996) suggest that children between the ages of six and ten express mature understandings of death. In addition, it could be said that the developmental view does not adequately take into account life experiences and self-concept, which in turn are related to gender and possibly class. Other criticisms of Kastenbaum's criteria include the observation that they are ethno-centric and do not incorporate cultural and religious influences. Children whose culture or religious structure has clear parameters regarding death are likely to incorporate these into their own understandings of death.

With regard to adolescents, Kastenbaum's categories are also difficult to apply but so is the normal 'adult' concept of death and its principal subconcepts found in adults as described by Speece and Brent (1996):

Subconcepts embraced by the concept of death include:

- Universality
  All-inclusive
  Inevitability
  Unpredictability
- Irreversibility
- Non-functionality
- Causality
- Non-corporeal continuation

Researchers have questioned the applicability of these concepts to adolescents, suggesting that although adolescents appreciate the consequences of death, their responses to it differ from those of adults (Noppe and Noppe 1997). First they 'experience tension with their concept of death' and this is evidenced by their attempt to defy, flirt with or cheat death (Noppe and Noppe 1997).

Second, although adolescents can accept death in the abstract, they do not easily imagine their own death. Third, adolescents tend to participate in group activities, which in itself could include risk taking and create internal and external conflict. Fourth, adolescents experience developmental feelings of loss at the same time as a heightened sense of being alive. These ambivalent responses to death reflect their wide-ranging attitudes and behaviour – this is exemplified by music shared by adolescents regardless of gender, class, culture or nationality. This music (like some classical music) often describes death and loss. Despite being aware of the risks they take at some level, many adolescents are not necessarily inured to the possible dangers (Corr et al. 1997). They tempt death through risk-taking behaviours, from experimentation with drugs to driving at high speed. Over three-quarters of deaths among American adolescents are a result of accidents, homicide or suicide, and therefore include components of trauma or violence (Corr et al. 1997). In the UK the high number of accidents (which sometimes result in death) in adolescence and young adulthood are indicated in the Table 9.1.

Thus children's and adolescents' understandings of death vary according to age and stage and may vary considerably within these. Their responses to loss are also hard to categorize.

Children's responses to bereavement

The work of Kübler-Ross can be seen as having the greatest influence on the lay perceptions of what are the 'normal' responses to dying, regardless of age group (Kübler-Ross 1983). Her framework has also been taken by many to apply to bereavement as well. Furman (1974) and others have

Table 9.1   Major accident rates[1]: by age and gender, 1995

England	Rate per 100 population[2]	
	Males	Females
16–24	42	23
25–34	34	13
35–44	18	12
45–54	17	12
55–64	11	13
65–74	8	14
75 and over	11	19
All aged 16 and over	21	15

1 An accident for which a hospital was visited or a doctor consulted. Some adults may have suffered more than one accident.
2 Average annual rate based on how many accident respondents had had in the six months prior to interview.
Source: Health Survey for England, Department of Health (Social Trends 28, 1998, Table 7.12)

emphasized that a child's ability to mourn depends to some extent on receiving permission from a 'consistent' adult, who satisfies the child's reality needs and enables the child to give expression to sad feelings.

William Worden (1991) developed a model of tasks of mourning in adults and has adapted them to children (1996). He is clear that children do need to mourn but that this can:

> only be understood in terms of the cognitive, emotional, and social development of the child. Loss through death is experienced and expressed in different ways at different developmental phases. For example, a child who has not developed the cognitive abstractions of irreversibility and finality will have difficulty with Task I, accepting the reality of loss. When dealing with the emotional impact of the loss (Task II), a child aged 4 or 5 with magical thinking may believe that he or she caused the death to happen and must deal with guilt from this belief. This is less likely to happen once the child moves beyond the magical thinking stage. A young child with less well-developed coping skills may take longer than an older child to adjust to an environment where the deceased is missing (Task III). Children negotiate the relationship with their dead parent over time, as they pass through the various developmental mileposts . . . And this affects the way they deal with Task IV, emotionally relocating the deceased.
>
> (Worden 1996: 12)

Dealing with bereaved children in school

Studies exploring teachers' attitudes towards bereavement have suggested that teachers take this area seriously, noting physical and psychological problems manifested in bereaved children. Teachers seek help particularly from church or social services (Holland 1993), yet still note a gap in available resources as well as in their own training.

Although teacher training includes considerable study of child development, the impact of this in relation to bereavement is not covered and, by extension, is not specified in the national curriculum. Why it is not in the national curriculum *per se* is in itself interesting – there are many places in which it could appear, for example when considering literature. Some bereaved children relate their own experiences to loss in fiction (Leaman 1995) and this can open up opportunities to discuss their feelings, but often this is not taken up by teachers. Shirley Payne of the 'Gone Forever' project questions 'who' is seen as the expert in bereavement in schools:

> Often it is hived off to the RE person – well it must be about religion so we'll give it to the RE person. It's an aspect of science, because the development of the life style includes death, and so you can make a case for it, but teachers are so busy delivering the competencies against which they are going to be measured themselves and producing paperwork for those inspections . . .

Thus the consensus of opinion from those interviewed in my study was that most teachers in the United Kingdom had insufficient preparation to deal with bereaved children and no specific remit to raise these issues.

> I think bereavement was something that was just not tackled at at all. I certainly never encountered it in my training. My immediate concerns were that I could envisage the scenario of me having to sit and tell the children something that I was too distressed – I didn't know how I was going to do it myself, and I felt that it would be necessary for other people to be there to share the burden.
>
> (Primary school head teacher)

In addition to not knowing about children's responses to bereavement, teachers suggested that they knew little about bereavement in general.

> I really don't know anything about bereavement. Neither does anybody else in the school, no one has really tackled it. For instance, I have got in one of my teaching groups a girl from Bosnia, so we've got a few refugee children in the school, and you find that for a lot of reasons they might be tearful or not attending school regularly. I feel this is one of the issues that needs to be attended to properly.
>
> (Primary school teacher)

A couple of years ago a girl came to me, she said that her father had died, he'd had a heart attack in the street totally unexpectedly, and could she come and talk to me about it. I got the shock of my life because this was the first time I'd had to deal with something like that, and I said, 'Yes, well of course you can', as you would. I'm not going to turn the poor girl away, and she came and talked. I just felt totally inadequate because I had nothing to say in reply over and about your sort-of-common sense. You are left there as the teacher who the child will come to and say, this has happened, what do I do about it, and you don't actually know, and there is no answer, and you don't know what to say.

(Primary school teacher)

As the quotes above indicate teachers do not feel confident about dealing with children's grief (interview with Shirley Payne). This area causes even more concern if one accepts the hypothesis proposed by Leaman (1995) who has written extensively on this subject and suggests that 'most teachers are even more reluctant to get involved in this area of discussion than other members of the public, and that they share the disinclination of the middle class to explore their own feelings about death in any detail or to any depth' (p. 31).

Another area of concern is that of touching distressed children. Shirley Payne notes that 'When someone is grieving you want to put your arm round them, and hug them and men as well as women are conscious of the worries about touching'. However, the question of touching children in the classroom has become increasingly problematic and teachers need to seek guidance on what is acceptable.

Distressed children are also disruptive in class (Holland 1993) and do not progress academically if their needs are not met in the school environment. They are likely to pose questions that need answers:

Often quite young children, when they ask these sorts of questions, they want honest open answers. They're not taken in by the airy-fairy stories of somebody drifting off onto a cloud, and being away for a long time on holiday. It's so important for the child who's asking to enable them to understand exactly what their feelings are, it's so important for the adults to be honest, and be able to say to them, well, no, I'm sorry he or she won't be coming back again, but we can do this and that (gives e.g. of activities) and for the adult to be there and give the honest answer plus the obvious support and guidance that the child needs.

(School counsellor)

Although there are no longitudinal studies of bereaved children, retrospective studies suggest increased vulnerability to adult psychiatric disorders, especially depression (Black 1998). Suggestions about ameliorating this situation include preparing (where possible) the child for the bereavement, supporting parents and caretakers after bereavement and talking openly with children about their experiences (ibid).

Teacher or counsellor?

Teachers recognize inherent conflicts between their role as teacher, and being listeners and confidantes. They suggest that as educators their students expect them to retain control and to impart knowledge – that the flow of information should go from teacher to child and not in reverse. Counselling on the other hand employs listening as the primary skill and therefore suggests that the student would be providing the information for the teacher to distil and possibly interpret. Teachers tend to see the role of educational psychologist or school counsellor as quite separate, requiring specific skills and being divorced from the classroom dynamics. Dorothy Judd a child psychotherapist specialising in bereavement explains:

> There is a dichotomy between the usual teacher role, which is obviously directive and somewhat controlling at times, as opposed to a counselling role. I think there are ways that teachers can improve in their ability to step out of the teacherish role and become more of a so-called counsellor. I would think that one of the main difficulties is in giving the task adequate time and setting, and it's giving it the importance that it deserves – a quiet room, and if possible the same place every week at the same time – those sorts of things about regularity and boundaries, of knowing how long you have, so it's giving that safety, those parameters that gives the child a space within which he or she can express the reality, perhaps at times frightening or fragmented feelings and confused feelings that they may be having.

The teachers interviewed for this study expressed concern that without training in counselling they could cause more damage through their interactions. In addition they suggested that students would find it difficult if they also expressed their emotions. Shirley Payne notes that 'We've pressurised teachers into thinking that teachers know all the answers, teachers can put everything right, and that's not true – it's a different approach, an openness and sharing and giving information, because if children don't get information they'll make it up, and what they make up will be wrong, and probably frightening for them'.

A number of teachers were uncertain whether providing bereavement counselling was indeed part of their remit, and suggested that it might be preferable to refer bereaved children to specialists. 'I wonder to what extent, maybe, our role is to refer children to a counselling service rather than actually to deal with it ourselves, if we're not properly equipped and trained to do so' (secondary school teacher).

However, not every school has access to a permanent school counsellor who is familiar on a day-to-day basis with the school culture. Some teachers complete courses in counselling or even bereavement counselling yet they still question their skills as well as whether it is appropriate for them to engage with bereaved children.

> One of the things the course taught me was how poor my counselling skills are, and I think that's partly due to the fact that as teachers we are used to providing answers, we're used to directing, we're not used to this mode of listening, empathizing, prodding, but letting the pupils have the autonomy. I've been very grateful that we've had a team of counsellors in from outside because I have felt utterly at sea, and incapable of helping in a significant way. I'm not sure to what extent a teacher can be, in terms of the training we have, in terms of the lack of time we have. To me it's an open question, to what extent can teachers in fact act as effective counsellors?
>
> (Secondary school teacher)

Schools' responses to types of bereavement

Individual loss

Two distinct types of bereavement are encountered in school environments – children bereaved in their personal lives or bereaved within the school community. Teachers differentiated between the types of responses required for these different situations. In the former case teachers felt responsible for, yet unqualified and untrained to address the child's needs. St Christopher's Hospice has designed courses specifically for teachers to help them work with bereaved children. The purpose of the course is as follows:

> We help parents to understand that it's not possible *not* to communicate with children, and I think a lot of teachers have that issue too. Are we going to talk to the children about what's happening or not? As if there's a choice – there in fact isn't a choice because children pick up messages in all sorts of ways. It's much better that information is given in a controlled and caring way.
>
> (Principal social worker)

A lot of teachers simply need reassurance that the things they thought they were going to do are appropriate. For example, recognizing openly with a child that a death has occurred, or talking to the child about the difficulties that they're experiencing because someone is very ill. They also want advice on the sorts of things it's proper to tell other children in the child's class. Are there any helpful books for the teacher to read, or to give to the parents to read to the child, or to give to the child directly?

(Social worker, St Christopher's Hospice)

A school counsellor assigned to a village school in which a child was diagnosed as terminally ill acknowledged the teachers' feelings of inadequacy and placed her skills at their disposal: 'Initially what I did was provide a book list and some ideas and the offer of the phone number of being there, if you like, so that in any emergency the school knew that there was at least somebody there who could come out fairly quickly'.

Multiple deaths

The second bereavement challenge facing teachers relates to tragedies that befall the school environment. These include both accidental and violent occurrences, some of which are seen as national tragedies. The Aberfan disaster 40 years ago where children died when a mountain of mining residue engulfed their school prompted much concern as to the impact on the survivors as did the shooting of Israeli schoolgirls by a Jordanian soldier in 1996 or the mass murder of schoolchildren in Dunblane by Thomas Hamilton. Training in crisis management is generally not incorporated into teacher training except insofar as it may relate to physical evacuation of school premises. The school community's (as well as the local community's) responses to violent or accidental multiple deaths are often haphazard and unplanned and resemble national or local responses to tragedies in other situations, e.g. the 1989 fire in King's Cross underground station in London, which killed commuters. In many instances the impact of these events has long-term implications for both the staff and student populations.

Several articles in the professional literature suggest that preplanning crisis intervention responses can minimize the long-term impact for all concerned. Implications might include symptoms of post-traumatic stress disorder in children and their parents (Parker *et al.* 1995). In the UK, few school communities have such contingency plans and tend to rely on outside services to provide support. Paul Hill the headmaster of Hagley Roman Catholic secondary school described how local services spontaneously co-ordinated to provide support for the school community when in November 1993, eight school girls and their teacher were killed in a minibus accident.

By the time I arrived here at 8 o'clock (I was) met by the Director of Hereford and Worcester County, the Chief Education Officer and also a whole variety of counsellors and priests who were already in the school. They were able to do group counselling in the early hours of that day, and for the first couple of days, more or less saying, look we're going to set up shop in this classroom and eventually we refined the system of getting appointments. For the first few weeks you're talking about hundreds of appointments taking place in a week and eventually that just tailed off, as perhaps their own resources, their own strength, their own faith perhaps and the input that the school was giving from a spiritual point of view in terms of prayer and our own beliefs; perhaps this caused the numbers to attenuate. There were three different sets of counsellors: one from Kidderminster General Hospital, the clincial psychologist was in charge there; there was social services; and the third group were the educational psychologists, and one or two support helpers. It became clear that there was a need to get all the bereaved parents together to help them. The police also provided a liaison officer for each of the families. What we tried to do within school was to make sure that each family had a support teacher and it was the teacher's job to coordinate the arrangements for the funerals.

(Paul Hill Headmaster Hagley School)

Teachers share the distress expressed by the children. However they may not always welcome the invasion of counsellors/support agencies. Indeed, support from outside agencies might not initially be perceived as necessary as explained by a child psychotherapist specializing in bereavement: 'When there's a disaster on a large scale there is often a sense that the survivors cling together and often get quite a lot of support from each other, with the feeling that nobody else could understand, they haven't been through it, which is true. And I think that the people working with them can only facilitate a very natural process'.

For up to 18 months support was forthcoming both for students and staff at Hagley School. Thereafter, most of the counselling support was provided for teachers. This being a Catholic school, religious counselling was also available from the church priests – Mr Hill estimated that about 50 per cent of the counselling was provided by members of the clergy or local Catholic counsellors. The long-term impact on the school has been considerable, several teachers took early retirement and some children left the school because of the memories. However, for most of the school community, the emphasis on religious belief and practice has sustained and in some ways contained the distress. Several memorials to the children have been built, included a stained glass window and benches that enumerate their names, and also a new music centre. An annual memorial mass is held on the anniversary of the tragedy, which also serves to unite the school community in commemoration.

Tragedies like that which befell Hagley School and also reactions to violent atrocities perpetrated in Dunblane and in Denver in 1999, where schoolchildren were murdered by peers, have generated a considerable literature debating whether and how communities ought to be prepared. The

American work suggests that schools need to have clearly defined crisis plans which include critical incident stress debriefing (Ohara *et al.* 1994).

Strategies for dealing with future tragedies and bereavements

Development of guidelines

Some guidelines have been developed for schools both in the UK and the US to deal with mass tragedies (Capewell 1999; Holland 1999). Sorensen (1989) suggests that crises caused by sudden deaths could be diminished if a team approach for dealing with such events is preplanned. Guidelines have been developed to help schools respond to deaths (e.g. Winston's Wish nd). These guidelines usually focus on the teaching staff in order to reach the children and also on how to cope with external pressures, such as press interest. One useful principle is to see the school as a system rather than work through individuals *per se*. The following list summarizes the plans used in many crisis documents:

1 Work through head teacher – without his or her support little will be achieved.
2 Initiate contact (this might not come from the school, but they are likely to welcome this).
3 Focus on senior staff and head teacher.
4 Help them acknowledge the tragedy.
5 Focus on integrating tragedy into everyday life of school and normalize life within this new reality.
6 Help school community see grief as natural response and do not pathologize it.
7 Do not be prescriptive!
8 Should bereavement training be part of teacher training?

If the figures are correct that most schools have at least one bereaved child at any given time it would seem appropriate that teachers acquire some knowledge about bereavement patterns in children. It would seem sensible therefore to include bereavement issues in induction courses for trainee teachers and also for senior staff and head teachers. As part of this it would also seem appropriate to incorporate counselling skills into teacher training.

Headteachers and senior staff should also be provided with guidelines on issues relating to

1 Dealing with their own grief
2 Handling death in the classroom
3 General mental health issues (these are being developed)
4 Resources available that can provide counselling and other support when tragedies occur

If teachers have some training on how to deal with these difficult issues, it might reduce the level of distress experienced by them and by the whole school community.

A final suggestion is to incorporate death education in the school curriculum as a clearly defined subject (Stevenson and Stevenson 1996). Within the UK, personal and social education curriculum may be an appropriate vehicle. Aspinall (1996) argues that a crisis intervention model is not enough, a more educative approach is required. School staff, including school psychologists and counsellors encounter death and bereavement issues too often to ignore them. If issues relating to death were to be raised as part of the curriculum with students at school, teachers would feel more competent to recognize needs that they could incorporate into their role and which needs required outside intervention and know-how to coordinate this. And most important of all, students would be enabled to deal with loss and grief within the social context of the school (McWhirter et al. 1998).

References

Aspinall, S.Y. (1996) Educating children to cope with death: a preventive model. *Psychology in the Schools*, 33(4): 341–8.

Black, D. (1998) Bereavement in childhood, in C.M. Paker and A. Markus (eds) *Coping with Loss*. London: BMJ Books.

Bluebond-Langner, M. (1978) *The Private Lives of Dying Children*. Princeton, NJ: Princeton University Press.

Capewell, E. (1999) Disseminating the concept of crisis intervention into education: mapping the process. Paper presented at 4th International Children and Death Conference, Bristol, September.

Corr, C.A., Nabe, C.M. and Corr, D.M. (1997) *Death and Dying, Life and Living*. Pacific Grove, CA: Brooks/Cole.

Furman, E. (1974) *A Child's Parent Dies*. New Haven, CT: Yale University Press.

Holland, J. (1993) Child bereavement in Humberside primary schools. *Educational Research*, 35(3): 289–96.

Holland, J. (1999) Bereavement and Schools in Kingston upon Hull and area. Paper presented at 4th International Children and Death Conference, Bristol, September.

Kastenbaum, R. (1977) Death and development through the lifespan, in H. Feifel (ed.) *New Meanings of Death*. New York: McGraw-Hill.

Kübler-Ross, E. (1983) *On Children and Death*. New York: Macmillan.

Leaman, O. (1995) *Death and Loss: Compassionate Approaches in the Classroom*. London: Cassell.

McWhirter, J., Wetton, N. and Hantler, A.-M. (1998) Preparing children for loss and bereavement, in R. Weston, T. Martin and Y. Anderson (eds) *Loss and Bereavement: Managing Change*. Oxford: Blackwell Science.

Nagy, M.H. (1959) The childs view of death, in H. Feifel (ed.) *The Meaning of Death*. New York: McGraw-Hill.

Noppe, I and Noppe, L. (1997) Evolving meanings of death during early, middle, and later adolescence. *Death Studies,* 21: 253–75.

Ohara, D.M., Taylor, R. and Simpson, K. (1994) Critical incident stress debriefing. *Educational Psychology in Practice,* 10(1): 27–33.

Parker, J., Watts, H. and Allsopp, M.R. (1995) Post-traumatic stress symptoms in children and parents following a school-based fatality. *Child: Care, Health and Development,* 21(3): 183–9.

Sorensen, J.R. (1989) Responding to student or teacher death: preplanning crisis intervention. *Journal of Counseling and Development,* 67: 426–7.

Speece, M.W. and Brent, S.B. (1996) The development of children's understandings of death, in C.A. Corr and D.M. Corr (eds) *Handbook of Childhood Death and Bereavement.* New York: Springer.

Stevenson, R.G. and Stevenson, E.P. (1996) Adolescents and education about death, dying and bereavement, in C.A. Corr and D.E. Balk (eds) *Handbook of Adolescent Death and Bereavement.* New York: Springer.

Winston's Wish (no date) *Positive Responses to death: A Strategy for Schools.* Gloucester.

Worden, J.W. (1991) *Grief Counselling and Grief Therapy.* New York: Springer.

Worden, J.W. (1996) *Children and Grief.* New York: Guilford Press.

10 The Child Death Helpline

◼ JEAN SIMONS

The Child Death Helpline is a confidential freephone service for anyone affected by the death of a child, staffed by volunteer bereaved parents working in partnership with professional staff who offer training and supervision. Callers to the Child Death Helpline may be parents, relatives, friends, teachers, nurses; anyone who has been affected by a child's death in whatever circumstances, from miscarriage to the death of an adult child, however long ago.

The Helpline opened at Great Ormond Street Hospital in 1992 amalgamating with the Alder Centre Helpline in 1995 to form the present nationally available service. A Steering Group consisting of professionals and bereaved parents working in partnership originally developed the Helpline, and this group continues to guide all operational and policy decisions concerning the activities and service offered. The ethos by which the Child Death Helpline operates is that people who have themselves been bereaved by the death of a child can empathize with and normalize the experiences of the caller, uniquely, and the volunteers offer befriending and support in confidence. Their skills may be referred to as counselling or listening skills, but the contact is distinct from a counselling relationship. The Helpline can also offer a gateway service, and an adjunct to other support, which the caller may also be receiving.

The inception and development of the Child Death Helpline has taken place in the last decade. This has happened in the context of prevailing theories about grief and bereavement, and also within a particular political and demographic climate.

It is helpful to examine in more detail the context in which the Child Death Helpline has developed and expanded.

Professional responses to parental grief

Several authors have reviewed critically the way in which thinking about bereavement and loss has developed historically. These key works have helped shape contemporary practice in bereavement support and counselling. John Bowlby (1980) offers a psychological perspective through his work on attachment theory. Colin Murray Parkes (1988) in his extensive work and research writes of psycho-social transitions, the fact that bereaved people have to make great changes in their assumptions about how the world operates. These changes take courage and energy and can affect every aspect of life. Elisabeth Kübler-Ross (1969) identified denial, anger, bargaining, depression and acceptance, as stages in work with patients who were known to be terminally ill. These 'stages of grief' came to represent a linear model of grieving, which was ascribed, erroneously, to her.

More recently William Worden (1991) described four tasks of mourning, confirming that grief work is tiring and not passive, and giving a useful guide to the kinds of achievements that have to be made before a person can be considered to be resolving their grief. The four tasks of mourning maybe summarized as:

1 Accepting the reality of death.
2 Feeling the pain of grief.
3 Learning to live without the deceased.
4 Reinvesting emotional energy.

Worden acknowledged that these tasks of mourning are not achieved in a linear progression, but people may experience any or all stages sequentially, simultaneously or repeatedly.

Klass et al. (1996) wrote about 'continuing bonds', a concept extremely accessible to bereaved parents who know only too well that 'letting go' is at odds with the idea of forgetting, an inappropriate end point of grieving. More appropriate, as Tony Walter (1996) writes, is incorporating the loved person into one's own autobiography.

Stroebe and Schut have delineated a dual process model of grief (1999), and write of the oscillation between the expression of emotion and the need to take practical action as a way of surviving grief. They align this dual process to the usual ways of grieving of men and women; men being the practical doers often at the expense of acknowledging their emotions, and women being the more likely to wish to find emotional expression in talking about their feelings and about the child.

Within the past decade there has been an increasing focus on parental grief being shared as narrative. Many parents have written, overtly as a tribute to their own child, of their own experience, and the universality of their experience has been enormously helpful for other bereaved parents to recognize (see, for example, Monckton 1994). Other writers and professionals in the field, not necessarily bereaved parents themselves, have also written in a more narrative style about the experience of bereaved families with whom they have had contact (see, for example, Helen Wilkinson 1991; Celia Hindmarch 1993; Sister Frances Dominica 1997). Their work has been written for professionals to gain an understanding of the expressed needs of bereaved parents, but bereaved families have also gained great comfort and support reading of the experiences and feelings described, which so clearly match their own. The latter three authors do not on the whole prescribe or follow any kind of recognizable bereavement theory, but promote the need for empathic support, 'standing alongside' the grieving person.

Statistical and demographic issues

In the case of child death, the Office of National Statistics (ONS) states that '12000 children between the ages of one and 19 die from all causes each year in the U.K.'. This of course takes no account of the fact that many children who die are over the age of 19, or indeed under the age of one, and grief for the death of a child of any age is no less acute. Approximately 20 per cent of calls to the Helpline concern a 'child' of more than 19 years of age, perhaps not surprisingly considering that the age group (15–27) represents the section of the population most likely to die a sudden and traumatic death, for example from road traffic accident, homicide, and, increasingly, suicide, especially among young males. Statistics, of course, do not give any real idea of how many people are affected by the death of a child of any age. Grieving families join a cumulative total, as naturally they do not only grieve for the child in the year of his or her death, but for the rest of their own lives.

In the developed world the death of a child is still seen as a thankfully rare occurrence, but in the parts of the world where poverty, famine and war are common, millions of children still die from preventable causes. In Ethiopia for example, half of the total child population do not live beyond their fifth birthday (Baum 1994).

Historical perspective

Up until the twentieth century before effective control of now preventable diseases, and particularly in wartime when so many families suffered a bereavement, there seems to have been little professional attention paid to the feelings and needs of bereaved parents, except perhaps an emphasis on the desirability of a stoical attitude.

Present calls to the Helpline indicate how important it is to parents to remember and talk about a child however long ago he or she died. In 1995,

50 years after the end of the Second World War, at the time of the VE Day celebrations and Services of Remembrance, many elderly parents contacted the Helpline, and doubtless other bereavement support services, to discuss the death of a child 30, 40 or more years ago, obviously wishing to re-emphasize the importance of their own bereavement, which happened at a time when they would not have been encouraged to talk about their child's death. The death of a partner or spouse, or the terminal illness of an elderly person facing their own death, commonly provokes the need to talk about the long ago death of a baby or child so that someone, apart from themselves, will hear about and remember that person. This has been written about by, among others, Williams who contributed to in-house bulletins and newsletters in the mid-1990s and whose observations about 'releasing the past to help the present' were frequently referred to. This is a recognized phenomenon among those involved in hospice or reminiscence work.

Attitudes to bereaved families following the deaths of children in disasters have also changed in the last half of the century. A tragic event involving civilians during the Second World War in Europe was the sinking of the evacuee ship, *City of Benares*, in 1942 (Jackson 1985). This ship was carrying children from the UK to North America and Canada. Many families had sent their children reluctantly in response to government 'propaganda' current at the time, and several families lost more than one, and in some cases all of their children. A total of 260 passengers died of whom 84 were children. The authorities informing the bereaved families first concealed the extent of the tragedy, this action being considered in the public interest. Later they imparted the information impersonally by telegram, the normal way of notifying bereavement in wartime. No particular follow-up was suggested or offered to most of the families concerned.

Twenty-four years later, in 1966, at Aberfan, 116 children and 28 adults died when a village school was engulfed by a slurry tip. The event was acknowledged as a national tragedy and the media were quickly involved and much more proactive. Information about the event spread rapidly throughout the UK and abroad, and the site of the tragedy was visited by politicians, media figures and the royal family. Thirty years later a book was published, written contemporaneously by one of the survivors who was then a child herself (Madgwick 1996). Although psychiatric assessment and help was offered and provided for the child survivors and siblings, the majority of the grieving parents were not offered, or did not accept such support, and many were unable to express their feelings or speak about the tragedy. Madgwick reveals the shame felt by many families to admit their grief, and the very great need of those involved in the community to provide their own mutual support and not express their grief and need for help. This attitude was especially apparent among the men. The damaging consequences of this lack of openness are documented, for example, marital and family breakdown and rifts among those remaining in the area and personal psychological problems. 'Thirty long years have passed and there are still scars, the wounds remain unhealed . . . My dad was very bitter, and never spoke to anyone about his feelings . . . years later (they) have suffered post-stress that still has many people in Aberfan on medication' (Madgwick 1996). The special cemetery at Aberfan containing the graves of all the children who died also includes a surprisingly high number of graves of their parents who died well before the end of their own expected life span, though in most cases the cause of death is not stated (DoHalmos, personal communication 1966).

After a series of tragedies at the end of the 1980s and into the 1990s, for example the sinking of the ferry *Herald of Free Enterprise*, the Hillsborough stadium disaster, the Kings Cross fire, the Kegworth plane crash, and the Lockerbie PanAm plane explosion, the public have become accustomed to media reporting of private and public emotion and have become more or less familiar with such topics as post-traumatic stress disorder and the presumed need for support and possibly counselling following involvement in or witnessing of such terrifying and disturbing events.

By the time of the Dunblane tragedy in 1996, when a gunman entered a Scottish primary school and shot and killed 17 children and one of their teachers, it had become standard practice for the press to report that 'counsellors' were on the scene in order to attempt to offer help to grieving and shocked families. In Dunblane, the families themselves pleaded for privacy and sensitivity on the part of the media and the general public so that their recognized needs could be addressed with care and dignity within their own community. Recognizing the need for immediate information and support, a helpline was set up in the locality, as is generally now the case in any disaster or major incident.

During the 1980s and 1990s, it has become the case that the death of a child, whether from a rare illness or a sudden traumatic cause, is usually the subject of media interest and publicity, whether welcomed by the family or not, and several children's deaths have led to campaigning by press and interested professional or volunteer groups for changes in the law or public attitude or promotion of awareness of social issues. For example, Ben Hardwick, a little boy who required a liver transplant in 1987, had his case taken up by a well-known media personality and great public interest followed his illness, treatment, and finally his sad death and the ensuing events in his family.

Leah Betts, a teenager, died in 1996 following an experiment with the drug ecstasy and her parents spearheaded a campaign to promote awareness, particularly among teenagers, of the dangers of drug taking. Jamie Bulger, a toddler, was abducted and murdered on Merseyside in 1993 by assailants who were themselves children leading to public outrage at the law as it applies to children who commit crimes and their need for care and treatment. In these instances, and many others less nationally publicized, the grief of the family concerned and the feelings of individuals are often trivialized by some sections of the media or truncated into such phases as 'grieving mum', or 'tragic tot', tending thereby to sensationalize the event but not explain or individualize the feelings of the families involved.

The grief that parents actually experience after the death of their child probably remains as frightening and inaccessible to most of the public, and indeed to a great many professionals, as it ever was. It is perhaps not surprising that many grieving parents themselves turn to others who have suffered in the same way, or use their campaigning energies to help and inform, and hopefully to prevent similar tragedies occurring in future. For example, the self-help groups of the Compassionate Friends, or the informative campaigning of the Suzy Lamplugh Trust.

Service development

Key advances in the medical treatment of children's cancers, the second most common cause of death after accidents in children aged between one and 19 (Office of Population Census and Surveys), all drew attention to the psycho-social issues and bereavement needs of families thus affected. The work, for example, of the Malcolm Sargent Cancer Fund (now Sargent Cancer Care) emphasized the psycho-social, emotional and practical needs of families alongside the emphasis on clinical and nursing care, and employed specialist social workers in children's cancer treatment centres from the end of the 1970s. The organization CLIC (Cancer and Leukaemia in Childhood) began to employ specialist nurses during the 1980s and also started to acknowledge the needs of families to have comfortable family-style accommodation when in hospital with children who were suffering from a life-threatening illness. The CLIC house in Bristol was the first of its kind rapidly followed by other charitable provision around the country, such as that of the Sick Children's Trust. This kind of provision and the founding of the first children's hospice, Helen House, in Oxford in 1982 represented the beginnings of the children's palliative care movement. The focus was, and remains, on the holistic care of the dying child and his or her family and social network. Health care workers, sometimes including trained volunteers, accord expert status to the parent or carer, and facilitate their care of the child as opposed to dictating it. The emphasis is on the totality of the family's needs throughout the child's illness and the eventual bereavement. A definition of children's palliative care emphasizes 'an active and total approach to care embracing physical, emotional, social and spiritual elements'. It focuses on enhancement of quality of life for the child and support for the family and includes the '... provision of care through death and bereavement ...' (Joint Working Party Report of ACT and the RCPCH 1997).

In keeping with these developments in children's palliative care, the Symptom Care Team opened at Great Ormond Street Hospital in 1986. The team was based, as were so many developments at this time, within the field of paediatric oncology, and embodied ideas of partnership with and between professionals and parents, in order to facilitate the parents' care of their child within their own home and within the community.

The Alder Centre, a pioneering setting for multi-focused and multi-professional support to those affected by the death of a child, opened in 1989 in Liverpool. Although counselling from professionals was offered at the Alder Centre, there were also drop-in services and self-help and mutual help between those similarly affected. Chapter 11 in this volume describes the Candle Service, initiated from this Centre.

The ideal of parents, volunteers and professionals working in partnership was embodied in 1993 by the formal constitution of ACT (Association for Children with Life-Threatening or Terminal Conditions and Their Families), which, as an umbrella group working in conjunction with the Department of Health, steered the distribution of grants under the Department's Pilot Project Programme for children with life-threatening illness (DoH 1998); the present author becoming one of the Pilot Project fund holders for the development of the Child Death Helpline. The multi-professional Terminal Care Group at Great Ormond Street Hospital had recognized the need to fill a gap in a very *ad hoc* service to bereaved families. Most paediatric oncology units provided a good service, as did other specialist units, for example Cardiac and the intensive therapy unit (ITU), but on the whole provision was patchy, with many families returning home from hospital, especially those who had experienced their child's sudden death, without any knowledge of where to turn for help, support and follow-up.

Ethos

The proposed development of the Child Death Helpline incorporated the desire of bereaved parents to receive support from others who had had a similar experience, with the proviso that parents and professionals worked in partnership as supporters not counsellors, emphasizing current thinking that grief is a normal response and resisting the pathologization of expressed feelings. The apparently irrational feelings and behaviours so commonly recognized can worry those who do not often encounter people affected by the death of a child. If a friend, family member or health care professional feels, as many do, overwhelmed by the needs of the bereaved parent, they may encourage referral to a 'counsellor', without any clear idea of what this means or entails.

Almost all those who speak to others, similarly bereaved, on the Child Death Helpline are relieved to know that their frightening and apparently inexplicable feelings find ready acceptance from other bereaved parents. There is also easy recognition of the life-long nature of grief (not the same as pathology); an idea expressed by Cooper (1991). The widespread effects of a child's death, not only on the grieving parents but on many other family and friendship group members, confirms the appropriateness of providing the Helpline service for anyone affected by the death of a child. Many callers who are not themselves the parents of the child, may not feel 'entitled' to receive their own support in their grief (for example, aunts, childminders, grandparents) but may welcome the opportunity for discussion and acknowledgement of their own feelings if this is offered.

The group of callers who are grieving for the child who died many years ago would also not normally consider themselves to be needing a bereavement counselling service. Their support needs are often only recognized or realized in other circumstances; for example, as mentioned earlier, the recent death of a partner.

The opportunity for these callers to share remembrance of an anniversary, or memories of the child whom no one else remains alive to remember, is highly valued, something often expressed to Helpline volunteers.

Those who are grieving an adult child commonly feel that their needs are secondary to the surviving partner if there is one. Some concentrate instead on helping the grandchildren, if they exist. The ability to recognize, express and have acknowledged their needs as bereaved parents in the informal conversation on the Child Death Helpline is extremely valuable. Common features of grief for the death of a child of any age, in any circumstances, are readily acknowledged and to a great extent normalized.

Many callers will acknowledge the essential selfishness, particularly of early grieving and the wish to be exclusively listened to, as opposed to having to listen to others (for example in the setting of a support group). Other callers highlight the value of an instantly accessible listening ear, as opposed to the responsibilities involved in making and keeping appointments if engaged with a more formal bereavement support service. Others value the anonymity of the Helpline if feeling, as many do, that they do not want the responsibility of the developing relationship that they would inevitably make with a counsellor.

Those who are grieving the death of a child in circumstances often considered 'stigmatizing', such as suicide or homicide, may particularly value the anonymity and accessibility of the Child Death Helpline alongside any other support they may be receiving. The particular stresses of the criminal justice system and its impact on the grieving families, for example the necessity for repeated post-mortems, evidence giving, delays to the funeral, inquests and police investigation, as well as media attention, may be intolerably stressful. Any support offered, no matter how sensitively, by those who are 'stake holders' in the investigation may be difficult to accept as truly disinterested. For example, Family Liaison Officers may be simultaneously supporting family members of a murdered child, while their colleagues may have to investigate the same family members.

Even if there is no conflict of interest, bereaved parents and families may be reluctant to voice their doubts and concerns about, for example, the speed of an investigation, or its thoroughness to those whose colleagues are conducting the investigation. Similarly, a family receiving follow-up from hospital staff, no matter how supportive previously, may be reluctant to express concern, founded or not, about the nature of the care received, to those who were part of the treatment team. The Helpline may therefore provide a necessary adjunct to services being received appropriately in the family's own community. It may also provide a valuable gateway service to other forms of support, whether within the caller's local community or from other appropriate sources, for example the Cot Death Helpline (operated by FSID) for those who have suffered bereavement by the sudden and unexplained death of their infant.

The emphasis on the mutuality of the support offered between bereaved parents should not cloud the recognition that disinterested guidance and support to those offering the service, is vital. The potential pitfalls of unguided or unsupervised self-help groups are recognized by professionals and bereaved parents who have offered or received such support (Child Death Helpline volunteers, personal communication) and any service, while not becoming 'over professionalized' must be organised in a professional manner. There must be recognition that support and befriending are not the same things as ordinary friendship. The Scottish Befriending Development Forum Code of Practice (1997) defines befriending as a 'service' while defining a friendship as a 'private, mutual relationship'. This code of practice goes on to say 'Befriending is a relationship between a volunteer and a recipient which is initiated, supported and monitored by a voluntary or statutory agency'. The volunteer service provider must understand and acknowledge the tenets of confidentiality and must gain skill and confidence in recognizing when a caller's need for specific support is not appropriate to the Child Death Helpline. It is important that a supportive professional can carry out a competent bereavement assessment and depression screen for the quite small proportion of callers who do actually need medical or psychiatric help. It is extremely important not to confuse the concept of 'volunteer' with 'amateur'.

Recruitment and training

Since the Helpline's inception, a system of training, supervision and on-going support has been developed, changing and refining itself over time according to the perceived needs of the developing service. Its Person Specification simply requires potential volunteers to be bereaved parents of three to four years standing, who undertake to attend preparation classes and to abide by the operational guidelines of the Child Death Helpline. They must also be able to come to Great Ormond Street or the Alder Centre in order to operate the Helpline, as the service does not allow calls to be taken by the volunteers in their own homes. The 'necessary' period of bereavement before applying to become a volunteer has been lengthened in the past three years to the present three to four year mark. The service began in 1992 with the more usual two-year cut-off point, but unfortunately it was apparent that the volunteers who were accepted onto the Child Death Helpline at that point needed to take a break from duties quite early on or, in three cases, gave up Helpline work as it was perceived to be too stressful. It was agreed that responsible management of the Helpline, and support for those operating it, meant discouraging volunteers, no matter how keen and how appropriate they appeared to be, only two years after their child's death.

An application form is required from each potential volunteer, followed by a personal interview and the taking up of two references. If the training course is then completed, a second interview still allows the potential volunteer to withdraw or rethink. If the person continues on to become a Helpline volunteer, a probationary period of six months operates followed by an annual review with the Coordinator.

All volunteers are allocated a supervisor who is there to help them develop and extend their skills and to promote their interest in ongoing training. Supervision is normally offered in a group, which also provides peer support. There is an opportunity to attend a quarterly Meeting, which offers social activity, mutual support and further education. Workshops and training days or sessions are provided either 'in-house' or by other organizations relevant to the work of the Child Death Helpline. Volunteers are encouraged (and expenses are paid) to attend courses that interest them.

As mentioned above, the preparatory training course for becoming a volunteer on the Child Death Helpline, has been developed, changed and refined over the years. Classes are loosely topic-based, concentrating variously on the silent, inarticulate or extremely distressed caller, or the specific issues for the caller whose child has died a violent or traumatic death. It is generally acknowledged that the potential volunteer does not need to know a lot of facts about particular illnesses or situations that the callers might present. More important is the ability to listen, and the emphasis therefore is on experiential exercises to practise listening skills, particularly through the use of simulated phone calls.

There is opportunity in the class to discuss the volunteer's own bereavement and reactions, although it is made clear that the class does not provide therapy for the potential volunteer. The volunteer needs to see what it feels like to be listening to stories and situations and expression of feelings that they themselves have perhaps not experienced, but with which they can empathize. Accordingly, volunteers undergo a skills-based training around issues of cue recognition, the asking of open questions and the eliciting of psychological and emotional concerns.

These are the kind of interactive skills promoted by Faulkner and Maguire (1994) and are seen as having the greatest relevance for the volunteer's work. They are often referred to as basic counselling skills, but are not to be confused with a training in counselling.

There are some rules and policy guidelines with which the potential volunteer must be familiar and these concern the caller who may be in imminent danger of suicide or of harming a child. Confidentiality prevents any supervisors or professionals listening in to calls once the volunteer begins work on the Child Death Helpline, and therefore, unlike in some organizations the new volunteer cannot start with 'easy' cases. Right from the beginning they must be able to listen to any caller who phones.

The nature of the service

What can the callers expect?

First, the caller can expect to be heard by someone who can empathize with the situation without needing to be given a lengthy explanation. If, for example, a person contacts the Child Death Helpline and opens with the words 'today would have been his birthday', this is not a surprise to the volunteer receiving the call, and the conversation can begin instantly on an accepting and empathic level.

Volunteers are a representative sample of parents bereaved in all manner of ways, and should not express horror, revulsion or (maybe worst of all) incomprehension, at any of the feelings described. In short the volunteer can empathize and normalize. The 'unacceptable' emotions, anger, bitterness, blame, hatred, despair, can be expressed anonymously if necessary. The caller's story, however horrific, can be told again and again to a Child Death Helpline volunteer, whereas the patience of family and friends may run out, or their own pain may be too great for them to listen repeatedly. The confidentiality and anonymity may be easier for those grieving a 'stigmatized' death. If the details are very painful, friends, neighbours or even professionals may fear or avoid offering support.

Other bereaved parents may feel isolated by the lack of acknowledgement of their grief and loss among friends and colleagues. For example, a person who has suffered a miscarriage may find that the expected date of delivery is a particularly difficult time, perhaps as difficult as the birthday of an older child who has died, yet the parents' grief may well not be understood as such by friends or even family.

Of great value is the chance to express all the very difficult and frightening thoughts, feelings and fears that many bereaved parents keep to themselves for fear of the listener confirming their own worries that they are mad, unusual or wicked. The volunteer may have experienced at least some of the thoughts and feelings that the caller describes. The very presence of the bereaved parent volunteer at the Child Death Helpline can confirm to the caller, who may not believe it at the time of their call, that survival following the death of their child is possible.

Caller profile

The caller profile has changed little over time, though since the advent of the nationally available Freephone number in 1995, there has been an increase in calls from other relatives and friends, as well as parents. The majority of callers are still bereaved mothers, 75 per cent, bereaved fathers account for 10 per cent of calls and the other relatives, friends and professionals form 15 per cent.

The types of bereavement discussed are along the lines of the nationally available statistics (OPCS, ONS) indicating that approximately half of child deaths are a result of a sudden event or accident, and approximately half are a result of a longer illness. The proportion of calls concerning the death of the adult child is about 15 per cent, and there is a similar proportion of calls about long ago death. Sadly, there is also a recognizable numerical increase in calls about the suicide of young adults and deaths related to drugs. Callers who mention this type of death often need to call repeatedly, and therefore become recognized by several of the volunteers.

Most of the calls concerning suicide or drug-related deaths concern those in the 15–27 age group; the group given by the Office of National Statistics as linked with an increase in these types of deaths.

The Child Death Helpline has produced figures showing that the age of the 'child' at death has ranged from 22 weeks gestation to 58 years, the time since death has ranged from the same day to 50 years. The mean length of call is calculated at 45 minutes.

Although since the Freephone service began there have been nearly 8000 calls, it is not really useful to think in terms of absolute numbers as some callers will want to talk for hours, and some callers will be making a brief query. It is appropriate, however, to say that during the times the Helpline is open, the phones are busy and there is very little airtime 'space'.

Challenging callers

In common with all other support services, especially those provided by a telephone helpline, the Child Death Helpline has noticed an increase in callers with apparent mental health problems, not necessarily due to their bereavement, although the bereavement may be one feature in the caller's constellation of problems. There is an observed increase in bereavements reported due to drink- and drug-related causes, and also in the number of callers who, by their own admission, suffer problems in connection with substance or alcohol abuse.

There are also a number of callers, both regular/recognized and intermittent, who themselves are in need of care in the community by the mental health services, but whose needs seem to be beyond the scope of, or are not able to be addressed by, psychological and psychiatric services.

In a few instances, with the caller's permission, discussion has ensued between the Child Death Helpline and the caller's Social Services Department, and has resulted in an agreement in two instances that the confidential support provided by the volunteers of the Child Death Helpline appears to be the most appropriate support available to the caller in their present circumstances. Many of these callers have serious personality disorders (diagnosed and stated) but, although challenging, they are deemed appropriate for the Child Death Helpline if they are bereaved parents, in some instances because of their own actions towards their child. These callers obviously make severe demands on the sympathy and empathy of the volunteers, who need careful support and supervision.

In 1996, immediately after the Dunblane tragedy, the Child Death Helpline suffered several weeks of extremely difficult calls from a few particular callers who were showing evidence of, and later proved to be perpetrators of Factitious Disorder by Proxy. The Helpline was thus alerted to the challenges of offering sympathetic volunteer support to callers whose mental or psychological symptoms should more appropriately be addressed by psychiatric or social services, or even dealt with by the police.

A paper detailing the situation of three particular callers, and the challenges they posed to the Helpline, was presented at the Royal College of Paediatric and Child Health Annual Meeting at York in March 1999 by the present author (Goldman and Simons 1999). At first these callers were confused with other suspected 'hoax' callers, for example youngsters giggling in phone boxes, or callers telling such tall tales that volunteers would quickly be alerted to the fact that the story did not 'ring true'.

However, such was the florid and horrific nature of some of the descriptions given, and the apparently knowledgeable details of symptoms, that the volunteers quickly distinguished between the usual hoax callers, whom they do not find particularly disturbing, and these very challenging callers who pose a severe threat to the volunteers' own emotional and psychological equilibrium. Almost all volunteers had been taken in at some stage by one or other of these challenging callers and their sympathies and empathic support engaged and exploited. The realization, after investigation, that the stories of all of these callers were false and in two cases the caller had actually killed their child, caused many of the volunteers to feel themselves to be naïve and to doubt their own judgement about all of the callers. Many greatly disliked the feeling in themselves that the trust and authenticity, which they wished to extend to all callers, was mixed with their desire not to be duped in the future, and this made many of them feel careful, suspicious and distanced from the caller. After a special support group, much peer discussion and some individual supervision, all volunteers remained within the Child Death Helpline despite some initially having felt threatened enough to wonder whether continuing was appropriate.

It was also very helpful, following these events, that a PhD student, undertaking a qualitative evaluation of the work of the Helpline, ran a series of workshops examining the limits and boundaries of the volunteers' role within the Child Death Helpline and the guidelines and policies by which the Helpline operated. It became apparent that most volunteers felt that anyone who was a bereaved parent had the right to use the Helpline as they wished and to be heard non-judgementally.

Others concluded that callers who were known to be hoaxers, personality disordered, or were otherwise misusing the time and resources of the Helpline, should not be listened to uncritically. They wanted the professionals from the Helpline to negotiate with the caller, or the caller's professional supporters, in order to agree in partnership the appropriate time that could be devoted to the caller's need for contact. The latter course was chosen by the Joint Management Group and there are, at the time of writing, two callers who are subject to time-restricted contact with the Helpline, after negotiated agreement with the callers themselves and the relevant involved professionals.

The Child Death Helpline Coordinators contribute to an informal group of helpline operators who come together regularly to discuss calls to their respective services, particularly calls that trouble the volunteers. A small group of psychologically disturbed callers has quickly been identified as using several helplines, and the ability to track these callers and to make decisions in their best interests, is of great benefit to the volunteers, who feel thereby that they are not isolated or deskilled, but that they are playing a responsible part in the appropriate support, inadequate though it may be, that can be given to these callers.

Health service providers are increasingly recognizing that paternalism and professional secrecy may lead to dissatisfaction and even litigation, and that the kinds of interactive skills more usually evinced by psycho-social professionals and volunteers are increasingly appropriate.

Parents expect to have the opportunity to express their feelings and concerns, to have appropriate information to enable them to make proper choices and decisions, and those offering support must do so in partnership with those receiving it.

Conclusion

These current challenges in health care of clinical governance and risk management are applicable to bereavement support services, making it increasingly inappropriate for support to bereaved parents to be offered in an *ad hoc*, unstructured and unsupervised manner. This is neither to the benefit of the volunteers offering the service nor to the bereaved person receiving it.

At the time of writing the Bristol Royal Infirmary Inquiry (1998–1999) was underway, with the remit '. . . to inquire into the management of the care of children receiving complex cardiac surgical service at the Bristol Royal Infirmary between 1984 and 1995, and relevant related issues . . .' (including support available to bereaved parents).

The volunteers and Coordinators of the Child Death Helpline have provided support to the bereaved parents, and advice and expert witness to the Panel of the Inquiry, and in so doing have confirmed the recognized value of accessible, empathic professionally organized volunteer support to anyone affected by the death of a child.

References

Baum, J.D. (1994) Introduction: the magnitude of the problem, in A. Goldman (ed.) *Care of the Dying Child*. Oxford: Oxford Medical Publications.

Bowlby, J. (1980) *Attachment and Loss: Vol. 3. Loss: Sadness and Depression*. New York: Basic Books.

Cooper, D. (1991) Long term grief. *British Medical Journal*, 303: 589–90.

Department of Health (1998) *Evaluation of the Pilot Project Programme for Children with Life-Threatening Illness*. London: NHS Executive, Health Services Directorate.

Dominica, F. (1997) *Just My Reflection*. Darton: Longman & Todd.

Faulkner, A. and Maguire, P. (1994) *Talking to Cancer Patients and Their Relatives*. New York: Oxford University Press.

Goldman, A. and Simons, J. (1999) Hoax calls to the Child Death Helpline; another manifestation of Factitious Disorder by Proxy? Paper presented to the Annual Meeting of the Royal College of Paediatrics and Child Health, York, March.

Hindmarch, C. (1993) *On the Death of a Child*. Oxford: Radcliffe Medical Press.

Jackson, C. (1985) *Who Will Take Our Children?* London: Methuen.

Joint Working Party Report: Association for Children with Life-Threatening or Terminal Conditions and Their Families and Royal College of Paediatrics and Child Health (1997) *A Guide to the Development of Children's Palliative Care Services*. London: ACT and Royal College of Paediatrics and Child Health.

Klass, D., Silverman, P.R. and Nickman S.L. (1996) *Continuing Bonds: New Understandings of Grief*. Washington, DC: Taylor & Francis.

Kübler-Ross, E. (1969) *On Death and Dying*. New York: Macmillan.

Madgwick, G. (1996) *Aberfan: Struggling out of the Darkness*. Blaengaarw: Valley and Vale.

Monckton, G. with Burden, H. (1994) *Dear Isobel: Coming to Terms with the Death of a Child*. London: Vermilion.

Parkes, C.M. (1988) Bereavement as a psychosocial transition: process of adaptation to change. *Journal of Social Issues*, 44(3): 53–65.

Scottish Befriending Development Forum (1997) *Code of Practice: Working Together to Promote Good Practice in Befriending.*

Stroebe, M.S. and Schut, H. (1999) The dual process model of coping with bereavement: rationale and description. *Death Studies*, 23: 197–224.

Walter, T. (1996) A new model of grief: bereavement and biography. *Mortality*, 1(1): 7–25.

Wilkinson, T. (1991) *The Death of a Child: A Book for Families*. London: Julia MacRae.

Worden, J.W. (1991) *Grief Counselling and Grief Therapy: A Handbook for the Mental Health Practitioner*. London: Routledge.

11 A place for my child: the evolution of a candle service

JO HESLOP

My Anchor

For some months now I have been upset by advice given to me. 'All things change', I was told, and shouldn't I go forward and grow as a person. These statements made me unhappy because to go forward is to leave something behind.

I have been struggling with these thoughts for some time, and I have finally managed to sort the situation out, regarding myself.

I am aware that things will change that I have very little control over most aspects of life. The idea that I have come up with is perfect for me, it allows for change, but gives stability as well.

I imagine that my grief, my loss of my beloved Clare, is an anchor, to which I am attached by a long chain. I can move around my anchor, to allow for change, but wherever I am I will always be close to my anchor. This idea has helped me get my emotions into some sort of order.

(John Gosney 1992)

A memorial service for an adult is normally held once. When somebody famous dies the funeral service is often followed a few months later by a memorial service, attended by friends and colleagues to remember and honour the person who has died. This memorial service is not usually repeated at regular intervals. Similarly, relatives of those who die as patients of a hospice may be invited to a memorial service organized by staff of the hospice. Typically invitations will be extended to relatives of all those who have died over a particular period, but such an invitation will be sent once and not on an annual basis. The Candle Service, organized by staff and parents of the Alder Centre in Liverpool, is different. The service, which takes place each December, is to remember children who have died and is attended by many families year after year.

Why should this be? What does this service provide to parents that draws them back each year? In order to try to address these questions interviews with five parents, of four children, all of whom had different deaths, were undertaken. Despite the small number of interviewees a number of themes emerged, the strongest of which was the continuing relationship with the child who had died.

The death of a child is one that is overwhelming in the grief and pain it brings (Sanders 1993). It has come to be regarded as a death that is untimely, which upsets the natural order of life (Littlewood 1992). Parents bereaved of a child often speak of the loss as one from which there is no recovery (Klass 1996), describing instead a process of learning to survive without their child. It would be unnecessary and perhaps foolish to seek to quantify the grief of those bereaved of someone they love by claiming that the loss through death of a child is the most difficult death to face. Each bereaved person's grief, whatever their relationship to the person who has died, is the most difficult for them. It does seem, however, that there are some elements in the death of a child which make it different from the loss of a partner, parent or friend. In contemporary Western society it is a normal expectation that children will live longer than their parents. Death in childhood is rare and few parents will have to face the death of their child. This means that it is unlikely that those who do will know any other bereaved parents who understand how they feel. Guilt, often felt in bereavement (Parkes 1972), can be especially difficult for parents, who may feel that they had not done enough to protect or save their child (Sanders 1995). Friends and family may feel afraid to talk about the dead child, and so bereaved parents often feel isolated and alone, 'When your child dies the world shuts you out' (Broadcasting Support Services 1990: 2). Children represent their parent's future, and when they die, parents lose something of that future, something of themselves (Sanders 1995).

The Alder Centre

How then do bereaved parents survive? How do they find a place for their dead child within their lives? The Alder Centre, at The Royal Liverpool Children's NHS Trust, was set up in 1989 to help those affected by the death of a child. Each year, some 120 children on average die at the hospital and work with bereaved parents showed a clear need for sustained support. An important feature in the setting up of the Alder Centre was the involvement of bereaved parents, who worked in partnership with a multidisciplinary team of professionals to plan the services that are on offer today. The Centre undertakes many activities: it provides individual counselling, formal groupwork and informal drop-in facilities. A telephone helpline, staffed by bereaved parents trained in telephone counselling, has been developed. A library has been put together and a newsletter is produced. The Centre provides support not just to parents, but to anyone affected by the death of a child.

The Centre has also paid attention to the spiritual needs of bereaved families with the development of an annual memorial service, the Candle Service. It is the introduction and evolution of this service of remembrance, and its meaning for some of the parents who are involved with it, that is my focus here.

The Candle Service

The first Candle Service was held in December 1989, some six months after the Alder Centre opened. It was with some trepidation that professional staff at the Centre first began to talk about such a service. Christmas is a time of celebration and a time for families. How would parents bereaved of a child feel about attending a service to remember their dead children at such a time? Would it be helpful or would it simply magnify their pain? The obvious way to address these questions was to include parents in the planning of the service. This 'parents and professionals in partnership' approach was already well established. Bereaved parents had been members of the Core Group, which had worked to plan and establish the Centre. In a radical move bereaved parents were included on the interview panel for the Centre's professional staff, and parents also have full representation on the Centre Users Group, which meets regularly to offer support to the Centre Manager.

Parents who were consulted about the inauguration of a memorial service felt that this would be a positive thing to do and it was not hard to find a group of parents who wished to be involved in the planning of the service. The first Candle Service was held in an outpatient clinic waiting room area at Alder Hey Children's Hospital. The service was attended by some 40 people, bereaved families and hospital staff who had known children who had died. During the service those who attended were given the opportunity to write the name of the child they had come to mourn on a small card. The children's names were read out and candles were lit and placed behind a frosted glass screen, to symbolize the fact that although the children were no longer in view they were not forgotten and love for them continued. This service had a Christian basis, with prayers, readings, hymns and a final blessing. The religious element continued for the next two years, after which it was abandoned in favour of a general spiritual approach, in order that those who had a faith other than Christianity, or who were of no religion, would feel welcome and included. Although the service has evolved to a form that has no clear religious affiliations, a strong spiritual element remains; indeed the continued use of the word 'service' indicates the importance of this spirituality.

From its small beginnings the Candle Service has grown to a gathering of some 1200 people and is now held in one or other of Liverpool's two Cathedrals. The service has evolved to a point where it has a recognizable framework, which remains the same from year to year. Elements of the service that make up the framework include a large candle being taken to the front of the cathedral by one family, the reading out of children's names and the lighting of a single candle for each name. Every year a theme is identified by the planning group and readings and songs flow from there. The service usually begins with a sad reading or song and then lightens as it moves on. There is always a speaker, often someone who has personal knowledge of the death of a child.

Interviews with bereaved parents

Clearly the Candle Service is an event that touches the emotions of those who attend. Not only do they remember a particular child they love, but they also hear the names of over 400 other children who have died read out, surely a painful experience. Equally clearly the fact that the service has grown into such a large event shows that it provides bereaved parents with something valuable. Interviews with five parents enabled a number of important themes to be identified. The children of the parents interviewed had all died in different circumstances. Jim and Sarah's son Daniel died of the malignant childhood cancer, neuroblastoma, shortly before his second birthday; Helen lost her baby after the termination of a pregnancy following medical advice from her doctor; Christopher's 10-year-old son, Ewan, was killed by a car as he played with his friends; and Margaret's daughter, Amy, who had had a chronic blood disorder for six years, died suddenly of a brain haemorrhage. Semi-structured interviews were used to find out how these bereaved parents view the Candle Service.

Three themes were common to all the parents: spirituality; a bond with other parents bereaved of a child and a sharing of grief; and a continuing relationship with the child who has died. There was also recognition that the service would mean different things to different people. Christopher said that 'there are millions of reasons why people go', and Margaret pointed out that 'people go for different reasons, and get different things'. She went on to talk about the different circumstances of those who had had a still-born baby and those who had lost an adult child, feeling that they might have diverse needs that the Candle Service could fulfil in different ways. Jim felt that 'what affects me most is the music, not necessarily the words', whereas for Helen the words of the songs and reading are very important; she is 'very grateful that the words of the songs are in the service sheet'. Christopher said that the Candle Service served 'a need to keep the child vivid – you have to make an effort and the Candle Service helps', whereas Margaret felt she needed no aid to remember details 'that is part of me anyway'. Helen and Margaret, who had both been involved in the organization of the service felt differently about the way participation had affected them. For Helen 'involvement has had a really powerful effect', and, because of her experiences, she wished that more parents would take part in presenting the service. Margaret, on the other hand, had been involved in the service for the first nine years it was held and, although she had gained a great deal from this, had felt 'slightly detached, because of the responsibility of making sure everything ran smoothly'. She wasn't involved in the organization of the most recent service and so had been able to concentrate more during the service itself.

Spirituality

All the parents involved spoke, either directly or indirectly, of the importance of the spiritual nature of the service. Sarah felt that a spiritual element was an important part of the service and noted that 'In the planning meetings there have been people who are spiritual and people who are not, so there is a good cross-section'. The spiritual nature of the service 'takes people away from just facts'. The notion of a search for meaning was important. Margaret did not feel that 'God and religion were much part of it', but also noted that 'At times when people can't help, in extreme times, people call on God, not the doctor, not the fireman, not the policemen – why do we do that'? Christopher spoke of the fact that 'bitter experience leads you to ask questions [of the church]. The idea of a random element is challenging to the church, who tell you that 'there is a reason but we don't know what it is yet'. Margaret talked of people's search 'for meaning, for truth when the church has let them down', and felt that spiritual meaning was found in 'each other, the solemnity of the occasion, the readings and the children's choir'. Christopher also felt that spiritual meaning was derived from the company of other bereaved parents and described a move away from thinking of God as a distinct personality towards thinking of God as the good in people. 'People will do things with no apparent expectation of anything in return – that could be God in people – rather than simply to help you so that you will help them'. Margaret suggested that 'perhaps the Candle Service is so successful because it doesn't work to rules and regulations. It allows people to express themselves, to experience spirituality'. The importance of solemnity, together with the symbolism of such features as the lighting of candles, was noted by Jim. A sense of the emotions of the occasion was given by Helen, who spoke in a very moving way of the feeling of being surrounded by dark clouds. The service helped her to feel that the clouds were parting and she felt 'love and sadness mixed' and said that the Candle Service had given meaning to her baby's death. In a similar way Margaret spoke of 'a real moment, a genuine moment'.

Given the enormity of their loss it is not surprising that parents will seek to make sense of what has happened to them or that this will not be an easy process. The death of a child can result in questioning of a previously held faith, or cause a search for the possibility of an existence after death. 'To survive, we must reconcile our loss with our worldview and our belief in God or a power greater than ourselves. We must be able to place our child somewhere beyond the grave' (Talbot 1997–98: 51). The Candle Service provides the opportunity for parents to think about these things and also serves to value the lives of the children who have died.

A bond with other parents bereaved of a child and a sharing of grief

It was important for parents to share the occasion with others in the same situation. Given our knowledge of the isolation and sense of being set apart from the rest of society, which bereaved parents feel (Sanders 1995), this is not an unexpected finding. Parents liked to see others benefit from the service as well as gaining support for themselves. Jim spoke of the community of families, describing the part of the service where one family makes their way to the front of the cathedral carrying one large candle, symbolic of the loss of all the bereaved families. 'This makes you feel you are not alone.' Margaret also talked in this vein, telling me of the 'invisible strength' which is found in the service. 'We give to each other by being there and sharing.'

A continuing relationship

A continuing relationship with their child who had died was of great importance to all the parents. Christopher was very clear that the Candle Service is more than simply a service of remembrance. 'It's not merely remembering. There is a continuous relationship, making a history with your child.' Margaret too knows that her relationship with her daughter continues. 'It is about remembering the living part and taking the living part forward. The Candle Service is keeping the link and taking it forward, keeping her part of the family.' Helen, who had never known her baby, spoke of the love which nevertheless continues. Her baby has been given a name, one which would be suitable for either a boy or a girl as the baby's gender was never known, and she continues to love and remember her child, having the name read out in the same way as all the other parents do. The notion of the service being a time for the child who had died was very strong. The children were felt to be part of the family all the time, but this service acts as their special time. 'He is always part of the family, but this is a time to focus on Daniel as part of the family', said Jim, 'People need it. This is a time for the family with the child they've lost, which normally doesn't happen. Jenny and Susie [Daniel's sisters] have always come'. Margaret echoed this 'Amy is part of the family, the Candle Service is her time'.

The fact that the Candle Service is held shortly before Christmas each year was also seen as important, giving the opportunity to devote time, love and thought to the children, making a place for them within the family activity at Christmas time. Margaret spoke of the Candle Service as 'keeping her part of the family, just before Christmas. I give to her and she gives to me. I can then cope with Christmas and the rest of the family'. Jim too felt that the time of year was important. It is a time of the year when families get together and children who have died should not be excluded from that.

Much bereavement literature talks of the bereavement process, which works towards 'resolution' of grief, and a 'letting go' of the person who has died (Parkes 1972; Bowlby 1979; Raphael 1984). It is clear that the parents in this study have no need or intention to 'let go' of their children, but instead have worked to find a place for their child within their continuing family lives. 'To reinvest in life we must overcome the fear that we will forget our child . . . find ways to maintain a connection with our child and incorporate our learning's from motherhood and bereavement into a new identity which encompasses both caring for others and caring for ourselves' (Talbot 1997–98: 52). This is not an easy task. There is much personal pain to endure and there is the difficulty of living in a society that is afraid to speak to a parent about a dead child, or which believes that 'time will heal' and 'you will get over it'. It seems that the Candle Service provides one place where parents can, in a way which is both public and private, maintain their bond with their children. The end of grief is not severing the bond with the dead child, but integrating the child into the parent's life and into the parent's social networks in a different way than when the child was alive' (Klass 1996: 199).

That many parents return year after year to the Candle Service is not in doubt. That the service will mean different things to different people is likely to be the case. However, the five parents, all of whom have attended the service for a number of years, identified three areas that were of particular help to them: the spiritual nature of the service, sharing the experience with other parents, and a place in which to keep the continuing bond with their children alive. It is perhaps in this last respect that this memorial service for children differs from a memorial service for adults, a difference that may reflect the difference between grieving for a child who has died and mourning an adult.

References

Bowlby, J. (1979) *The Making and Breaking of Affectional Bonds.* London: Tavistock.

Broadcasting Support Services (1990) Notes to accompany *40 Minutes: A Place for Tom*, BBC2 television programme, January.

Gosney, J. (1992) My anchor, in M. Shawe (ed.) *Enduring, Sharing, Loving.* London: Darton, Longman and Todd.

Littlewood, J. (1992) *Aspects of Grief.* London: Routledge.

Klass, D. (1996) The deceased child in the psychic and social worlds of bereaved parents during resolution of grief, in D. Klass, P.R. Silverman and S.L. Nickman (eds) *Continuing Bonds: New Understandings of Grief.* Washington, DC: Taylor & Francis.

Parkes, C.M. (1972) *Bereavement: Studies of Grief in Adult Life.* London: Tavistock.

Raphael, B. (1984) *The Anatomy of Bereavement: A Handbook for the Caring Professions.* London: Hutchinson.

Sanders, C.M. (1993) Risk factors in bereavement outcome, in M.S. Stroebe, W. Stroebe and R.O. Hansson (eds) *Handbook of Bereavement.* Cambridge: Cambridge University Press.

Sanders, C.M. (1995) Grief of children and parents, in K.J. Doka (ed.) *Children Mourning, Mourning Children.* Washington, DC: Hospice Foundation of America.

Talbot, K. (1997–98) Mothers now childless: structures of the life-world. *Omega*, 36(1): 45–62.

PART III

12 Changing death rituals

JENNY HOCKEY

Introduction

The chapters in this final part of the volume present examples of contemporary death ritual. As such, their starting point is what people do when someone dies, rather than what they feel. Death ritual, or mourning, describes observable and often public behaviour: grief is private emotion (Lofland 1985). Chapter 1 provided a comprehensive critical appraisal of theories of grief. Chapter 6 and the examples in Part II of the book showed how these are expressed in particular forms of care for bereaved people. This opposition between grief and mourning, although useful, is however problematized in the present chapter. Difficulties in understanding how – or whether – mourning practices shape the experience of grief; or conversely, whether grief is the spur that shapes mourning practices, can be seen to arise from a convention which separates inner experience and outer behaviour.

The chapter begins by mapping the landscape of changing Western death ritual in the twentieth century, before concluding with a critical examination of the relationship between mourning and grief, which reviews the ways in which anthropologists and sociologists have understood it. Chapters 13–18 go on to provide accounts of disposal and memorialization, as exemplified in the work of Doris Frances, Leonie Kellaher, and Georgina Neophytou and Mary Bradbury; forms of death ritual developed by particular groups or for particular circumstances, as Shirley Firth demonstrates, and the changes associated with the practices of professionals after a death as exemplified in the work of Glennys Howarth and Philip Gore. Brought together in this collection, these local and specific examples point to the diversity of contemporary Western death ritual. They raise the question of whether social scientists should even attempt to provide a coherent account of this aspect of contemporary life. Walter has argued that within the recent 'revival' of death, two strands predominate: the late-modern experts who provide ever more refined advice and theories about dying, death and bereavement and a postmodern position that privileges the needs and wishes of the individual, whatever they may be (1994, 1996). In his view, we may now be managing loss outside any collective wisdom or set of practices, yet we remain social beings and, as the chapters to follow demonstrate, contemporary society is characterized by a diversity of *shared* rituals at the time of death (Walter 1996: 204).

Current variation in practice can be seen as the outcome of changes in Western death ritual, which have taken place during the twentieth century and a critical, historically located account of this period requires an examination of the social, economic and environmental shifts that have gathered momentum during this period. These include factors such as the secularization and diversification of religious belief and practice; social and geographical mobility; the growth of both consumerism and environmentalism; changing conceptions of home and hygiene; the manner and scale of death in two world wars and the professionalization of care of the dying and disposal of the dead. However, it is difficult to describe death ritual without acknowledging a now familiar set of questions. These ask, in composite form, has death ritual all but disappeared and, if it is still in place, has it has become meaningless and, if it still has some point, should this privilege religious faith, philosophical understanding, mental health, personal identity, community membership or national feeling? Any account of death ritual will be filtered through the kinds of answers the author might offer in response to these questions. For example, the author's definitions of death ritual will determine the material to be included. In addition, available accounts of death ritual are not neutral, but instead reflect the disciplinary and practice backgrounds of their authors, many of whom evaluate and indeed prescribe rather than just describe the behaviours that are their focus. The following account of changing ritual practices therefore needs to be read with these caveats in mind. It forms the basis for a later, more focused engagement with the composite question above, concerning the nature and purpose of death ritual put forward.

Two world wars and one world cup

Familiar on the terraces at England versus Germany football matches, this England supporters' taunt sums up their country's twentieth century victories over Germany in war and sport. Condensed in a single phrase, these events encompass a 50-year period during which both the expression of emotion and gender relations have undergone significant shifts. In late twentieth-century wars and sporting events men have allowed their tears and their anger to become publicly visible. From the time of the Falklands War, the emotional distress of servicemen has been exposed and indeed become a focus for litigation. Even General Schwarzkopf, commander of the American forces in the Gulf War, cried in public (Boscagli 1992/1993, cited in Lupton 1998: 134). On the 'playing field', once the site at which school boys learned 'muscular Christianity', with its stress on aggressive spirituality and physical prowess' (Bourke 1996: 13), key figures such as Paul Gascoigne, Eric Cantona and John McEnroe lost control of their tears and their anger before media audiences in their thousands. If mourning customs are, at least in part, an expression of emotion, then recent changes in the perception of emotionality during the twentieth century need to be taken account of. Here gender is an important aspect.

From the late nineteenth until the mid-twentieth century, emotional control was expected of men. Circumstances where it might be undesirable, or prove impossible, were relegated to the feminized sphere of domestic life (Lupton 1998: 110). When it came to expressing grief, women in the late nineteenth century complained that they bore the burden of mourning: '. . . the custom of mourning presses far more heavily on women than on men. In fact, so trifling are the alterations made in a man's dress . . . that practically the whole burden of mourning wrappings would seem to have fallen on women . . . they [men] positively manage to mourn by proxy . . .' (Women's World 1889, cited in Morley 1971: 63). If gender was important in shaping mourning practices, social class had an equally important role to play. Working-class women and men paid dearly for funerals that resembled those afforded by the emergent middle class – funerals that in themselves replicated the practices of a former aristocracy: 'persons in inferior conditions and of limited means, who are governed by examples of those above them, and who are put to ruinous expenses', complained the Committee of 1843 (cited in Morley 1971: 12). If we examine death ritual in the twentieth century we find that these forms of social differentiation continue to be in evidence.

Nineteenth-century gender relations were characterized by separate spheres that opposed men, reason, paid work and public space to women, emotion, family and private space (Davidoff et al. 1976). Grief, as noted, was located at the site of women, as evidenced in the wearing of mourning dress. By the end of the twentieth century – and after two world wars – shifts in this division of emotional labour had taken place. However, in the four-year period between 1914 and 1918, 9.5 million men died in young adulthood, leaving behind an estimated three million widows (Winter 1995: 46). The death ritual of this period is described in Gorer's autobiographical introduction to *Death, Grief and Mourning in Contemporary Britain* (1965). His mother wore elaborate mourning dress from 1915 until 1917 after the deaths of his non-combatant father and grandfather. The widows of the war dead dressed similarly, yet by 1918 what Gorer describes as 'the full panoply of public mourning' had become the exception (1965: 6). In his view, the volume of war dead had made it unfeasible since the idea that so many women's emotional and sexual lives were over was not 'socially realistic' and, moreover, evidence of the scale of death had to be kept from soldiers returning on leave. His argument is not entirely persuasive. Although the nation could not adequately reproduce itself if so many young women withdrew into mourning for an extended period, this does not explain individual women's decisions not to mourn publicly. His point about morale has more weight, yet Cannadine's work on public memorialization and spiritualism after the First World War shows that, although dress may have altered, war death was anything but hidden (1981).

Bourke's study of the effects of this war on masculinity provides an additional, in-depth account of its implications for death ritual (1996). She argues that nineteenth-century death ritual was intimately bound up with dying at home, regarded as the appropriate haven for affective family relationships. The 1832 Anatomy Act made the bodies of those who died without a home the material for the anatomists rather than the focus of a funeral. First World War soldiers who died far from their homes with bodies so damaged that they lost all marks of personal identity similarly became institutional property; Bourke notes that '[i]n death, white soldiers turned blackish and black Sengalese soldiers turned whitish' (1996: 214). Families lost control of their dead to the War Office who were unable to support the return of bodies to the UK. Winter describes similar struggles in France where the Ministry of the Interior refused families access to the bodies of dead servicemen even when they offered to pay for exhumation and transportation (1995: 23). Death ritual could not therefore be staged in their homes and local communities with the bodies of the deceased present. Worse, many bodies were buried in mass graves, 200,000 being lost without trace or even used to patch up the trenches. If individual rituals were enacted at the battlefields, the words might be drowned out by the sound of the shelling and a named grave might be opened up so that clothing and blankets could be stolen. Yet despite this scale of 'disorderly' dying, Bourke does not share Gorer's view that the war was decisively the source of change in ritual practice. Like Morley (1971) and Cannadine (1981), she identifies strong evidence of much earlier resistance to the ostentatious death ritual of the nineteenth century. For example, the Church of England began a campaign of funeral reform in the 1830s on the grounds that the funeral had begun to incorporate pagan imagery and symbolism (Howarth 1997: 124) and by 1875, the National Funeral and Mourning Reform Association (Morley 1971), the Church Burial, Funeral and Mourning Reform Association and the Church of England Funeral Reform Association (Bourke 1996) had all been founded. Nonetheless, Bourke notes that 'as the war progressed and black clothes began casting a shadow over public places, the bereaved were implored to adopt cheaper and more varied mourning apparel' (1996: 221). Issues of morale, simplicity and economy would therefore seem to be intertwined at this point. Even the spirits of dead servicemen were enlisted to this cause and Bourke quotes the message of a spirit called Bob: 'beg the mourners to stop crying and to cease wearing black clothes' (1996: 222). Howarth (1997: 125) cites the *Undertakers' Journal* of 1910, which reported that the 'parade of private grief' had become unfashionable, many people 'refuse[ing] to make themselves conspicuously sorry'.

Changes in death ritual subsequent to the First World War also cluster around the notion of solicitude for the corpse as both threatened and threatening. Morley (1971) documents mid-nineteenth century concerns about the fate of the corpse, showing how belief in the resurrection of the body contributed to protest about the overcrowding of churchyards and demands for more consecrated ground in which the body might be protected. However, the perceived threat to the living from the bodies of impoverished cholera and typhus victims had already led to the establishment of secular cemeteries at a distance from densely populated areas. The Church itself refused to found new cemeteries, at least in part because of the lost burial fees. However, as Morley also suggests, this refusal signalled its decline as a core social institution (1971: 41). Cremation was one solution to the problem of disposing of a growing number of bodies in urban society and from 1874 onwards the Cremation Society had advocated this method as a way of curbing the supposed spread of disease from accumulated corpses. Bourke notes that public and personal awareness of bodies deteriorating in the battlefields of Northern France fuelled the growing popularity of cremation in the name of purity: purification by fire rather than pollution by burial became a compelling cremationist slogan in the wake of the First World War (1996: 224).

In the details of Bourke's account of the setting up of crematoria – 'the new Romanesque architecture, dignified chapels in subdued colours, comfortable seating' (1996: 225) – and the uniform, Modernist architecture of the war cemeteries in North France, we can make out the profile of a simpler, Modernist aesthetic of death ritual. Of the war cemeteries, she says: 'many of the bereaved in fact approved of its Modernist designs. By emphasizing the contrast between the worlds of war and peace, the uniformly constructed cemeteries were an attempt to console the bereaved and for many people they were successful' (1996: 227). The unsavoury links between celebratory representations of death in battle and the fate of paupers provided a spur in the development of simplified mourning practices, which emphasized the civilian status of the deceased.

Bourke's account helps make sense of a growing sanitization of death ritual, yet this trend later came to be seen as a problematic dimension of late twentieth-century funerary practice. C. Davies (1996), for example, argues that the growing popularity of cremation in Britain represents an avoidance of decay. The American display of the embalmed corpse is a more extreme response, which, in Davies's view, constitutes a denial of deterioration by a nation that regards cleanliness as a key aspect of religious and cultural identity – and which consumes far more deodorant than countries with similar climates. Davies's problematization of contemporary death ritual is a not uncommon view among late twentieth-century theorists. It is often expressed in parallel with concerns about the professionalization of care of the dying by doctors and the management of the corpse by funeral directors. In his review of the sociology of death, Kellehear (1990), for example, describes the medicalization of death and its sequestration in nursing homes as contributing to the stigmatizing of death. He refers to 'radical decreases in exposure to death and dying and subsequent to this, of information about it. This has resulted in embarrassment and secrecy around death for nearly three quarters of this century' (1990: 12).

This distancing of human mortality does, however, need to be set within an historical context of public conflict about the ostentation of nineteenth-century death ritual and religious concerns about the fate of the resurrected body. As indicated above, issues of gender and class were prominent here, concerns about 'the Woman Question' (Evans 1982), as well as the volatile nature and boundaries of the class structure being implicated in resistance to heavy mourning dress and traditional sites of disposal. Most powerfully, we need to take account of 9.5 million lives lost in a manner that could not be incorporated within the beliefs and practices of nineteenth-century life – or indeed those of many preceding centuries. While young men have always died in battle, previous strategies that celebrated the deaths of heroes were thoroughly undermined in survivors' inescapable confrontation with evidence of the pointless and degrading squandering of lives in the mud of Flanders. Bourke points out that censorship failed to stop the circulation of photos of dead soldiers and their content revealed the unseemly fate of their bodies (1996: 211).

Despite persuasive arguments that this combination of circumstances paved the way for a Modernist aesthetic in death ritual in the early years of this century, they do not explain the current diversity of practice. To see it merely as a rejection of simplicity and control is inadequate. A linear view of history as a chronologically discrete series of events, each one triggering the next, comes close to a functionalist balancing act: too much austerity automatically breeds a desire for elaborate symbolism, and so on. As noted in Chapter 6, Foucault (1977: 16) has shown how factors such as tradition, spirit and evolution support a misleading perception of historical continuity within the events of the past. In light of this, we here focus on competing approaches to death ritual throughout this century. Thus, while Bourke (1996) details spurs towards a Modernist aesthetic in funerary and commemorative practices, Winter (1995) takes a very different view. Of mourners' responses to mass death in the First World War, he says, 'A complex traditional vocabulary of mourning, derived from classical, romantic or religious forms, flourished, largely because it helped mediate bereavement. The "sites of memory" . . . faced the past, not the future' (1995: 223). This use of forms derived from Romanticism echoes the nineteenth-century practice of erecting monuments in secular cemeteries, which allowed the middle class to separate themselves off from the poor whose bodies crowded urban churchyards. The most revealing representation of what went on after the First World War is Bourke's statement about the Imperial War Graves Commission's difficulties in designing war cemeteries: 'the tension was the funereal equivalent to the Modernist versus anti-Modernist tension within the language of mourning. The commission was opting for the stark realities of modernity while many of the bereaved sought the romantic myths of tradition British funeral practices' (1996: 226). As her sources indicate, however, the emergence of an aesthetic of Modernity was no mere top-down imposition, but was welcomed among some bereaved families. In seeking to understand the patterning of mourning customs at this time we therefore need to recognize the parallel influences of modernism and Romanticism. And, indeed, when it comes to making sense of contemporary practice we will find that both continue to flourish.

As regards the years after the First World War, Richardson's interviews with older adults who had lived through much of the twentieth century are revealing (1984). Her findings support Cannadine's argument that both memorialization and spiritualism, as attempts to rescue servicemen from 'disorderly' deaths, led to a widespread preoccupation with death between the wars (1981). The older adults who had grown up during these years were reluctant to participate in elaborate death ritual, something that she attributes to their satiation in mourning practices at an early stage in life. Following Bourke (1996), we might add that a distancing or sanitizing of some aspects of death might be predictable among people whose early years involved a massive exposure to the body's vulnerability to destruction and decay.

Recent challenges to this generation's Modernist response to death and dying can be made sense of in the context of late twentieth-century expectations of the gendered expression of emotions. Lupton (1998) identifies a contemporary privileging of the emotions as core to self-identity and personhood within Western societies. This has undermined the previous gendered compartmentalization of emotionality that applauded men's ability to master their emotions, both in demanding intellectual endeavours and in challenging physical activities, such as going into battle or venturing into unknown parts of the world. However, she also contrasts this compartmentalization with the prevailing Romanticism of the early nineteenth century, which accommodated overt affective relationships between men as well as between women. Citing the work of Yacovone (1990), she notes that by the end of that century 'the rejection of sentimentality, rapid industrialisation, massive immigration, economic transformation and disloca- tion "produced a culture that worshipped muscle and might"' (Yacovone, cited in Lupton 1998: 116). Her point echoes Bourke's argument that the health and fitness of men for work and for battle became an increasing focus of concern towards the end of the nineteenth century, a trend that persisted in forms of discipline and surveillance such as public health and industrial psychology (1996: 251–2). The body's capacity to represent 'hardness', 'dryness' or integrity was therefore linked with the management of emotionality from the second half of the nineteenth century onwards when the medicalized foregrounding of the 'flows' of women's reproductive lives shored up an image of fluid, emotionally volatile and *unreliable* fem- ininity. This association between women, emotionality and flow persists in the twentieth-century gendering of emotionality. Lupton cites Patthey-Chavez *et al.*'s 1996 study of the representation of gender differences in women's erotic fiction where men experience hot fiery passion, in response to which women melt and dissolve (1996: 119). At the end of the twentieth century, as Lupton notes, men continue to gain kudos through their ability to control their feelings and think rationally; yet in a world where self-authenticity or the 'true self' have increasingly become associated with the emotions and their expression, men also acquire respect when showing themselves moved by strong feelings. Thus, emotional expressiveness and sensitivity, while still being strongly associated with femininity in both thought and practice, have become a new source of status or superiority, laid claim to not just within feminist literature but also by men themselves. Lupton's (1998) history of 'the emotional self' during the twentieth century supports Walter's representation of the current 'revival of death' in which Modernist expertise sits sometimes uneasily alongside a postmodern valuing of indi- vidual choice (1994). Modernism and Romanticism continue to influence emotionality in general and death ritual in particular. While Lupton fails to take account of the diversity of masculinities, she does pinpoint a trend among some men that reveals the combined influences of these two major philosophical and aesthetic trends.

To sum up, at the end of the eighteenth century as well in the present day we can trace a resurgence of Romantic ideology, which posits emotion as the only solid basis for moral and ethical judgements and which regards those who are emotionally sensitive as getting more out of life (Lupton 1998). Whether men's recent emotional expressiveness reflects a distressed crisis of masculinity, engendered by economic depression and a reconfigured, empowered femininity; or whether they willingly enter into their feelings having been persuaded that emotional expressiveness will enhance their sense of self is unclear. It is within this context that the contemporary diversity of mourning practices needs to be viewed.

Death ritual and the professional

In his work on the social distribution of sentiments at the time of a death, Prior (1989) examines the death notices in Belfast newspapers. On the basis of these data he argues that, 'grief is overwhelmingly regarded as the preserve of the immediate family (the "sorrowing family circle", as it is frequently referred to)' (Prior 1989: 146). This, he argues, supports Ariès's argument that there has been a historical shift away from community-based grief towards the privatization of 'hidden death' within the immediate kin group (Ariès 1983, cited in Prior 1989). Nonetheless, Walter (1994), describing the contemporary 'revival of death' highlights the Modernist rationalization of death, which, in its various forms, has served to distance death from the personal and intimate sphere of family life. While grief may remain 'an intensely personal sense of loss', many aspects of death are managed through a series of expert discourses and practices (Walter 1994: 9). The result is a schism between private emotion and public discourse, which, in Walter's view, the current 'revival' of death seeks to bridge.

It is the public rationalization of death through the offices of experts that we now focus on. Medicalization, secularization and individualism all refer to processes that have removed death from the environs within which the lives of the dead took place. In Walter's view, the moral opposition between 'good' and 'bad' death was superseded by the normal/abnormal dualism of early nineteenth-century medical science, with the requirement that all deaths be categorized and registered (1994: 10). Through the work of doctors and coroners, the cause and nature of death is now decided and defined, and an associated proliferation of bureaucracy frequently overwhelms bereaved families. During the period immediately after a death, they are not engaged in care of the body and/or religious observance; they are 'running about', the phrase through which many describe the bureaucratic demands set in train by a death (Hockey 1996b). Unfamiliar bureaucratic practices may also foster the need for an extra layer of professional help, and doctors and funeral directors not only deal with the dying and dead body but also help families with the associated paperwork (Walter 1994: 11). Whether we are talking about medicalized re-definitions of human mortality as a 'terminal illness' and grief as 'normal' or 'pathological', or the cremation of corpses as a way of alleviating local authorities' financial and administrative burdens, the rationalization of death serves to abstract it from knowledge and expertise held within the immediate family and their wider community. State control over the nineteenth-century paupers' corpses and early twentieth-century servicemen's corpses are examples of 'special' cases of rationalization; but if we examine recent practice we find a more generalized sequestration of the dead body. Bereavement theorists have argued that the professional removal of the corpse from family care has produced problems for survivors in that the grieving process may not take place if they are distanced from the reality of corporeal death (Worden 1991). Walter (1994) highlights the question of who possesses the body and shows this to be central to the professionalizaton of death ritual. Once death has occurred hospitals, funeral directors and coroners' exert considerable control over access to the body. Coroners, for example, are empowered to take possession of the body for the purposes of their inquiry, a practice that can produce difficulties for families who wish to draw their own conclusions about its fate through extended contact, regardless of how damaged it might be (Hallam *et al.* 1999: 87–103).

When we speak of the rationalization and sequestration of death we imply that it is somehow removed from the social arena. However, a growing number of studies document the *social* aspects of expert service delivery; as well as the persistence of death ritual that occurs outwith professionalized discourse. Many of them take dying as their focus and provide insights into the work of hospitals (e.g. Sudnow 1967) and hospices (e.g. Lawton 1998). Although this volume focuses on the period *after* death, we nonetheless need to consider what happens at the site of dying. While hospitals draw on routinized practices to manage the immediate post-mortem events, the question of whether this inevitably excludes or disempowers the bereaved remains debatable. Komaromy (2000), for example, identifies the ways in which the sight of the corpse is hidden but the sound of it being lifted from the bed onto the trolley are not only audible but unmistakable. Her work, like that of Sudnow (1967) and Howarth (1996), reveals the performative aspects of professional ritual, families and other observers often participating in the representation of death, which the 'expert' organization or individual is seeking to stage. Sudnow's data show how visitors to the hospital, expecting news of a relative's death, accede to the institution's hierarchy of who may or may not announce the news to them, apparently taking no account of other hospital personnel who are quite evidently in full possession of the information they are waiting for. Similarly they were never observed to question the truth status of an announcement of a death (Sudnow 1967). Hallam *et al.* (1999) similarly describe a collusion between the mortician and the family in which visitors were observed not to challenge or reality-test the professional representation of the dead relative at the site of the corpse: 'Workers utilise theatrical techniques to stage the desired image, and families, not searching for the secrets, refuse to look for the props. To raise the coverlet, for example, or to glimpse beneath the body's clothing would destroy the image' (1999: 136). Material of this kind suggests that many bereaved people accept the role of professionals in staging death ritual on their behalf. Indeed we cannot ignore evidence that they appreciate expert help. Walter cites one testimony to the welcome intervention of the funeral director: 'He was marvellous – he took all the pressure off . . . All we had to do was pay the bill' (Office of Fair Trading 1989, cited in Walter 1994: 17).

If we wish to look critically at the proposition that the rationalization of death has involved a problematic professional take-over of key aspects of domestic/community life, there are a number of studies now available. However, these provide varying accounts. Adams's work on the role of the neighbourhood layer-out in Foleshill, Coventry between two world wars shows how the development of hospital and funeral directing services brought women's informal community-based networks of care to an end (1993). Previously this community had been excluded from professionalized systems on financial grounds. Adams describes Foleshill women operating according to a rationality of care, rather than the medical rationality of institutional care, a distinction that destabilizes any simple opposition between Modernist rationality and Romantic emotionality. Her data also throw into question the notion that informal care is unorganized: 'the system of informal care developed in Foleshill seems to have been organised, the women knew where to go for help and the role or task each was likely to undertake' (Adams 1993: 156). As women went about their domestic work within the neighbourhood they gained extensive and organized informal knowledge about the needs of families in the area, whenever a birth or a death was imminent. No regulated system of payment was in operation; rather, reciprocal arrangements pertained, money, goods and favours being exchanged in ways that were sensitive to the resources and the needs of those concerned.

In remoter areas, community-based expertise persisted well into the post-war period. While Clark's (1982) study of the management of death in a remote fishing community provides evidence of the gradual professionalizing of community practice, some traditional approaches remained in place. For example, villagers often owned the clothing they planned to wear in their coffin; the local laying-out board remained in use; and the family of the deceased continued to provide a funeral tea for everyone in the community. However, the death itself was likely to have occurred not in the home but in a hospital or nursing home; the coffin was supplied by the Co-operative Funeral Director rather than the local carpenter; and the corpse was cremated in an industrial centre some 40 miles away (Clark 1982).

Distaste, if not fear, of the corpse is said by professionals to underlie the need for their services. In Chapter 13, for example, Gore cites the growing unwillingness of families to accommodate the dead within the home. One of Adams's informants describes the practice of placing the coffin in the front room as 'not very pleasant in them days, 'cos if you'd got no hall entrance you had to come in that way'. In the summer the smell of a corpse was unsupportable in the home and it would be removed to the carriage master's stables (Adams 1993: 161). She cites Leaney's suggestion that the language of cremationists in the late nineteenth century served to generate this kind of distaste for the body, bringing about a 'feeling of intense loathing for the physical remains of the dead' (Leaney 1989, cited in Adams

1993: 162). By the 1930s the families of Foleshill were able to send their dead to Chapels of Rest attached to funeral directors' premises. Not only did this relieve them of the 'smell of death' reported to have permeated crowded working-class homes during periods of up to a fortnight before a funeral; it also allowed them to show respect for the deceased by drawing on the services of a professionally trained mortician (Adams 1993: 165).

With any consumerist development, evidence is often limited or uneven as to whether it has been driven by the professionalizing, profit-oriented motives of providers or by changes in the lifestyle and tastes of consumers themselves. Ariès's work clearly documents the shift towards the exclusion from the home of dirt, particular that related to the human body (1981: 568–72). Similarly, Lupton (1998) shows that up until the sixteenth century the body in life and in death had been seen as open and permeable, a 'public' rather than private entity. Bodily functions were carried out in the public sphere and the body's orifices were seen to be linked with the external environment, an aspect of the embeddedness of the individual within wider social networks. During the sixteenth and seventeenth centuries, bodily regulation took hold and Lupton describes the body becoming privatized and invisible, a source of potential shame and embarrassment (Elias, cited in Lupton 1998: 77). She links this with the Reformation when rational thought gained precedence over magic and the supernatural, the 'Word of God' epitomizing the experience of worship, rather than the more embodied sensations that made up a multi-dimensional ritual. In the Enlightenment period, which spanned the late seventeenth and early eighteenth centuries, the perspectives introduced by the Reformation became consolidated and in the following century the Industrial Revolution and associated processes of urbanization meant that individuals increasingly lived – and died – at close quarters with those from different social classes. As noted, the establishment of cemeteries on the peripheries of cities reflected middle-class concerns about the piling up of working-class corpses in overcrowded churchyards, a practice said to produce dangerous miasmata or noxious fumes, which put health at risk. In the language of hygiene, issues of class were negotiated (Morley 1971).

In this changing cultural and social environment where the body lost its unproblematically public position within networks of social relationships, the post-Reformation soul also became detached from the care of survivors who were forbidden to pray for its safe transition to God's care. No longer dependent upon their mediating practices, it made a speedy transition either to salvation or damnation. As Howarth (1997) notes, the clergy's role in orchestrating the individual's safe passage from life to death diminished and two other professionals took over. Rather than the priest, it was the doctor who became the intermediary between life and death, their respective roles in relation to death having shifted from one of management to one of prevention or even 'cure' (Illich 1975). Once death had taken place, the priest was no longer needed to orchestrate the requiem mass and the care of the corpse fell to the undertaker. Howarth charts the growth of the undertaking profession during the eighteenth and nineteenth centuries when the fear of body-snatching drove the families of the dead to the services of professionals who would safeguard a loved one's body. In addition, the middle-class taste for funerals that aped the trappings of aristocratic her-aldic funerals – mutes, plumed horses, velvet palls – required the resources of a well-organized professional. Morley cites the 1843 Supplementary Report into the Practice of Interment in Towns: 'Are you aware that the array of funerals, commonly made by undertakers, is strictly the heraldic array of a baronial funeral, the two men who stand at the doors being supposed to be the two porters of the castle . . .' (Morley 1971: 19). From the 1870 *Cassell's Household Guide* he also cites 'the full middle class complement' of '[h]earse and four horses, two mourning coaches with fours, twenty-three plumes of rich ostrich-feathers, complete velvet covering for carriages and horses, and an esquire's plume of best feathers . . . two mutes with gowns, silk hat-bands and gloves; fourteen men as pages, feathermen and coachmen . . .' (Morley 1971: 19).

The site of burial for nineteenth-century middle-class dead was likely to be a private or municipal cemetery at some distance from urban centres, a location which again required professional help if the funeral journey was to be conducted with sufficient grandeur (Howarth 1997: 123). As regards the urban poor, they were an untapped market until funeral directors began to invest in the burial club movement, an economic strategy so pop-ular among working-class communities that it survived until well into the twentieth century: '[I]n return for weekly payments the club guaranteed a funeral according to custom' (Howarth 1997: 123). Thirty years into the twentieth century, war deaths recurred but not those of servicemen in another country. The civilian deaths as a result of bombing lent a fragile quality to everyday life and funerals were scaled down for a society busy with managing warfare on its front step (Howarth 1997). Meanwhile under-takers had worked hard to gain respectable status, changing their name to funeral director in 1940 and seeking equal status with doctors and the clergy. Stricter codes of conduct were enforced by professional organiza-tions and a quasi-medical status was assumed through a growing emphasis on embalming as a form of 'hygienic treatment'. The increasing popularity of cremation, now featuring in more than 70 per cent of funerals (Jupp 1993), meant that funeral directors were less involved in the construction of expensive, bespoke coffins for burial, paving the way for larger compan-ies to take over smaller businesses and so tap into mass produced prod-ucts. Howarth concludes that while funeral directors struggled to achieve respectability by promoting their services as a way of sanitizing death ritual, current qualms about the distancing of death represent a new challenge to the profession, one which, in her view, can only be met by representing themselves as sources of care and emotional support (1997).

Mourning and grief

With a focus on twentieth-century death ritual, this chapter has presented historical material which gives key insights into the recent privatization of mourning customs. However, in tracing the twin influences of Romanticism and Modernism it becomes possible to make sense of what Walter (1994) has termed the contemporary 'revival of death'. It also become clearer as to why we might currently be experiencing a curious mixture of approaches whereby expert bodies of knowledge are instructing us to follow our individual hearts when it comes to death ritual. This raises the question of what the implications of mourning might be for the emotional experience of grief. In 1985 a paper by Lyn Lofland asked whether the experience of grief was universal. Her aim was to show that 'grief may be profoundly socially shaped and thus highly particularized across time and space' (1985: 173). She attributes the lack of answers to this question to the fact that most of the relevant data are limited to clinical encounters, first person accounts and interviews with bereaved Westerners. When it comes to the majority of the world's population the data are more likely to describe mourning – the observable behaviours that follow death. In her view these data do not tell us how people actually feel at that time. However, while we seem to know a lot about how Westerners feel, we remain confused about what they are likely to do when someone dies. For example, the argument that Westerners actually do very little after someone dies has been both contested and reinvented since Geoffrey Gorer published his critique in 1965. By contrast, although numerous theories of grief have been posited and then demolished since Freud's work in 1917 (see Chapter 1), the variety, intensity and duration of emotions stimulated by bereavement in the West have been well documented (Marris 1958; Lewis 1961; Parkes 1972; Collick 1982; Riches and Dawson 1996, 1997; Lovell 1997). Apart from these accounts of the experiences of the Western minority, there is only limited evidence of what people actually feel after a death. A similar gap concerns the bereavements of another majority – those individuals who predeceased us and so escaped the research interview and the clinical encounter. We have records of what they did at funerals and we have the objects they created and exchanged after deaths had occurred. We may have their personal diaries or letters – or books prescribing death-related behaviour – but we are not able to examine this material in context and so engage at first hand with the emotions to which it might refer.

Two points can be developed from this. First, Lofland's fascinating observation that while we repeatedly examine our own psyches via data that describe Western grief, we stand aside and watch when it comes to non-Western bereavement. This suggests an absence of any easy, universal language of feelings or shared tradition of emotional 'confession'; it also highlights the distancing or exoticizing of the 'foreigner' whose inner world we hold back from scrutinizing. Here we might note that much of the literature, which does describe – and often critique – Western death ritual, excludes the practices of Western 'foreigners', whether their differences be of ethnicity or social class. White middle-class death ritual is often the assumed reference for authors who pine for something more elaborate, meaningful and, now, lost. When it comes to the 'internal world' of the Western grief experience, a similar social hierarchy of appropriate inter-viewees is evident in the relative absence of men, those 'strangers' to emotional confession, and children, who must be protected from passion. Only in the 1990s has men's grief begun to form a focus (Thompson 1997). The new sociology of childhood has not so far explored children's experience of grief. Interestingly the best known study of children and death has been conducted by an anthropologist, Myra Bluebond-Langner (1978). Though the dying children who appear in her work are social actors with undeni-able agency, it is their actions rather than their emotions that are explored, an approach which aligns them with the foreign 'others' who provide the traditional focus for ethnography.

One explanation for the focus on grief among Westerners and mourning among non-Westerners is Lofland's suggestion that the Western relationships that become a focus for grief are private and based on emotional express-iveness and closeness. They pertain to the inner world of the individual and can be contrasted with the 'personal' relationships that characterize traditional societies. The latter are typically sited within the public sphere of the community, are multiple and less individually complex (Lofland 1985: 175–7). This view throws light on investigations of the former via the confessional interview, since public behaviours may not shed light on very private loss. Meanwhile, the latter have been accessed most directly via the public rituals, which quite appropriately represent the loss of community-based relationships.

The second point to be developed from Lofland's paper concerns her comfortable acceptance of a distinction between the observable behaviours we call public mourning and the internal feelings we know as private grief. Indeed she is concerned to highlight the potential for dissonance between these two domains, warning the observer against making inferences about informants' inner feelings on the basis of observable behaviour. Nonethe-less, whilst discounting any straightforward correspondence between what is visible and what is felt, she believes explanations for variation in the experience of grief are to be found in the *social* realm. Her thesis is there-fore that there is a relationship between mourning and grief which can be described as the 'social shaping of emotion' (Lofland 1985: 173). However, whilst wishing to explore this link, she maintains a clear distinction between inner and outer worlds, the inner world consisting of some kind of affective raw material that can be moulded by forces residing within the outer world. Working from this basis, her article argues for a social shaping of grief on the basis of three clusters of variables that differentiate experiences of loss: what kind of relationship has been severed as a result of the death; what does death mean within the individual's cultural framework; how accustomed is the individual to being bereaved; how separate or embedded does the individual feel in relation to other members of their society; does the individual have the time and space to give extended attention to the memory of a deceased person.

Writing in 1985, Lofland called for a more adequate account of cultural variation in the experience of grief and, in particular, for a persuasive explanation of the mechanisms through which cultural and social factors shape the individual's emotional life. Chapter 6 discussed Foucault's account of how a particular mode of subjectivity is constituted in social practice (see Fox 1997: 41). When theories of grief are reviewed from this perspective we gain insight into the operation of power via the drawing up of the boundaries of normality. Huntington and Metcalf's (1979) review of work on death ritual and the emotions, however, warns against reading off the feelings of bereaved people from their ritual behaviours: 'we can assume neither the universality of particular modes of feeling nor that similar signs of emotion correspond to the same underlying sentiments in different cultures' (1979: 24). This explicit acknowledgement of the difficulty of interpreting emotional experience from observable behaviour seems almost to absolve the anthropologist from venturing any further into that terrain.

While earlier anthropologists did attempt to provide accounts, Huntington and Metcalf problematize their theories: they ask what evidence the structural functionalist Radcliffe-Brown could muster for his belief that the display of emotion – as in context-specific weeping – fostered the feeling which it demonstrated (1979: 26). Ceremonial weeping, in his view, affirmed the bonds between society's members and therefore fulfilled the function of maintaining social solidarity. Huntington and Metcalf point out that there is no way of knowing what the weeping person is actually feeling but acknowledge that Radcliffe-Brown did usefully identify the symbolic role of weeping as a marker of social membership and an affirmation of its value. Further, he developed this insight by making sense of funeral weeping in the context of other circumstances where weeping was required, so constructing a culturally-specific account that initially refused any universal explanation. Nonetheless, he then went on to generalize from this observation to argue that all ceremonials have the function of promoting particular sentiments which ensure the survival of societies.

Huntington and Metcalf also highlight the influence of Durkheim's work on Radcliffe-Brown (1979: 28). In Durkheim's view, collective ritual had a

key role in integrating individuals into society. For example, the requirement that even those who were barely related to someone who had died
should join in the ferocity of Australian death ritual was read as evidence of
ritual operating to strengthen social ties (Durkheim, cited in Huntington
and Metcalf 1979). Prior (1989) notes that both Hertz (1907) and Durkheim
(1912) made claims about the *social* production and distribution of mourning and grief at the very beginning of the twentieth century. While this
insight was incorporated within anthropology it was 'absolutely and entirely ignored by those who studied the manifestations of grief in Western
cultures – a study which, incidentally, fell under the control of a normalis-
ing psychology' (1989: 133). Prior's commentary aptly illustrates Foucault's
account of how particular knowledges come to hold sway, the individual,
their society and the prevailing form of disciplinary power forming a temporary and unstable nexus.

Although Radcliffe-Brown ultimately veered towards generalizing theory,
his practice of seeking to understand emotionally expressive behaviour within
its specific structural context has been taken up in many ethnographic
accounts of death ritual. Du Boulay (1982), for example, explains the fear
felt by Greek villagers at the time of a death in terms of a wider structure
of kin relations and patterns of dance. Whether on marriage or at death,
the individual has to be steered towards an appropriate right-handed spiral
movement into the next kin group or the next life. Failure to accomplish
this passage correctly risks both the inauspicious 'returning of blood' to the
kin group and the fearful return of the dead in the form of a vampire,
which will suck out its relatives' blood. While Du Boulay's anthropological
account of mourning customs is appropriately context specific, its focus is
death ritual rather than bereavement, a trend that Rosaldo (1989) critiques
as part of ongoing debates about how mourning and grief might be related.
He recounts his personal experience of returning to his field study among
the Llongots of northern Luzon, Philippines, after the accidental death of
his wife in a fall. Previously he had had little understanding why, for the
men he was interviewing, 'grief, rage and headhunting go together in a self-
evident manner' (1989: 1). Whilst not wishing to posit universalizing models
of emotion, he argues that his own overwhelming rage when he discovered
his wife's body helped him grasp the experience of Llongot men. He questions anthropological accounts that fight shy of the emotions of the bereaved,
criticizing them for their over-tidy, intellectual models of 'ritual', which
take little account of 'the informal practices of everyday life' (1989: 16).
Death ritual, in his view, may contain both 'a culture's wisdom' as well as
'brim(ming) over with platitudes' (p. 15). Its relationship with the experience
of grief is not contained in the moment but instead unfolds across the months
that follow. What he finishes by pointing out is that the anthropologist is a
socially positioned outsider to the field within which they are working. As
such their personal experiences can allow certain aspects of what they observe

to be made sense of, and others to remain a mystery. Here we might note a parallel between the anthropologist's interpretation of their data and the psychiatrist's reading of Shakespeare. As noted in Chapter 1, references to Malcolm's injunction to 'Give sorrow words' within contemporary Western therapeutic literature draw out its implications for using talk to stimulate emotional catharsis, a reading that reflects an established Freudian standpoint. Yet as Small points out, Malcolm goes on to advise bereft Macduff to 'let grief convert to anger; blunt not the heart, enrage it', words that echo the 'grief reaction' of both Rosaldo and the Llongot men.

In contrast with anthropological – and indeed historical – accounts of death ritual, which often overlook the actual experience of grief, material that focuses directly on the emotions associated with bereavement is, as Lofland (1985) argues, primarily Western in focus. As suggested, this reflects both a lack of identification with the inner worlds of historically remote or foreign 'others', as well as a distinction between the multi-stranded private relationships of Western families and the multiple, community-based relationships of traditional societies. In addition, as Cohen and Rapport (1995) argue in their work on the nature of the self, such distinctions between the 'inner' and 'outer' person are reinforced by disciplinary boundaries. Thus anthropologists have taken the outer person as their terrain – hence the proliferation of ethnographic accounts of death ritual in non-Western societies (Wilson 1939; Bloch 1971; Bloch and Parry 1982). When it comes to the inner person, the imagination is seen as the focus for literature or philosophy while other 'internal' aspects such as brain, personality and memory are the proper realm of psychology. Cohen and Rapport (1995) call for work from an anthropological or sociological perspective, which neither limits itself to the 'outer life of overt behaviours' nor assumes that the meaning of these behaviours can be read at face value. Instead it reminds the reader that, rather than an exclusive focus on the integrative power of social structures, individuals can be seen as 'intentional, interpreting, imaginative, conscious agents' (1995: 4). Their behaviour should not be seen simply as an effect of culture or the result of social forces, which are located prior to and outside the individual. Indeed, if externally derived beliefs and values did play such a determining role within human consciousness, the resulting observable behaviours could be very easily interpreted in that they stand in direct relationship to wider cultural patterns. In practice, as our common sense reminds us, individuals make choices and devise strategies, albeit through habit rather than explicit thought in many cases. What they do and what they demonstrate may be culturally specific, but its meaning is not transparent, being mediated by the individual's own agendas and priorities. This view challenges Radcliffe-Brown's assumption that the Andamanese, who had developed the ability to cry profusely at will, are necessarily experiencing the sentiment of attachment to the focus for their weeping (cited in Huntington and Metcalf 1979: 26).

Approaches to death ritual

Alongside the difficulty of knowing what it is people appear to feel, or appear *not* to feel during death ritual, there is a parallel confusion about what constitutes death ritual in the first place. The elaboration of the Victorian funeral described above, or the drama of the Indian funeral pyre, are easily put into the category of death ritual. They are complex, distinctive, ostentatious events, which reflect a shared set of religious beliefs about the fate of the deceased and the role of the bereaved. They only take place when someone has died and they provide a focus for collective, participative behaviour. However, if these criteria are taken as a yardstick for the identification and evaluation of death ritual, we soon find our way back to the familiar critique of the contemporary Western funeral as brief, austere, impersonal, professionalized, meaningless and poorly attended. Further, a number of authors have argued that idealized accounts of funerals in other societies, or in a Western past, actually tell the reader more about a Western preoccupation with the 'natural' emotionality of less 'sophisticated' peoples than they do about what actually took place (Martins 1983; Walter 1995; Hockey 1996a). Depending on who is critiquing contemporary death ritual, there are at least five subsequent moves that can be made.

First, there are a set of positions that reflect a commitment to the emotional needs of bereaved people. Authors have: expressed regret that Christian funerals have become 'an empty ordeal' for some mourners (Ter Blanche and Parkes 1997: 135); highlighted the need for better information and training for Christian clergy (Hockey 1992); and encouraged the development of alternative funerals that reflect different philosophies or beliefs (Albery *et al.* 1995). As noted already, Walter (1990) has identified the way in which the Anglican funeral problematically seeks to provide a religiously coherent and emotionally satisfying death ritual on the basis of what was merely the tail-piece of pre-Reformation funerals. Yet when the adequacy of contemporary funerals is discussed, the debate often hinges on the model of the elaborate, emotionally volatile death ritual believed to take place among traditional peoples or in earlier centuries. For example, a Catholic priest interviewed about his practice said:

> I think we need to look at the symbolism again, because funerals tend to be obviously morbid, desolate affairs and over-stark. Whereas the Catholic Church is a church full of symbolism and that is just as important at a funeral as it is at a baptism. At baptism we have white garments, oil, candles, all of which have a significance which can be explained. I think funerals are impoverished'. He went on, 'Those opportunities are there, because most people do need sights, sounds and smells and touches . . . we do need atmosphere and we do need something to hold on to afterwards
>
> (Hockey 1992: 36–7)

As a Catholic priest, his view echoes the ethos of the Counter-Reformation, which emerged in early seventeenth-century Europe and, as Lupton notes, 'sought to introduce a new sensuality into religious practice, with an emphasis on the emotional and the mystical rather than the cognitive (Mellor and Shilling 1997, cited in Lupton 1998: 78). This approach can be described as the enhancement or amendment of existing ritual practice.

Second, there are a group of social scientists who demand that we look more openly at all the events and processes that surround a death and expand the definition of 'ritual'. Rather than resurrecting past practices, which, from an anthropological perspective, make sense only in context, they argue for a more open-minded examination of what is actually done after a death – which, in their view, reveals the contemporary meaning of death. For them, the work of hospital staff (Sudnow 1967), hospice staff (Wright 1981; Froggatt 1997), bereavement counsellors (Arnason 1998), self-help groups (Riches and Dawson 1996, 1997), funeral directors (Prior 1989; Howarth 1996) and coroners (Howarth, Chapter 17, this book and 1997; Hallam *et al.* 1999) is viewed through the lens of 'ritual'. In managing this distressing or stigmatizing form of work, routinized behaviours are developed and one particular set of meanings predominates (James and Field 1992). This approach is exemplified in Helman's (1990) account of medical encounters in general, which represents them as a form of ritual that has symbolic as well as instrumental goals. In a similar vein, his account of dissection (1991) is constructed via metaphors such as journeying and participating in a religious service. Similarly Littlewood (1993), in asking whether rites of passage persist as a way of managing death in contemporary society, identifies private behaviours such as undergoing another rite of passage – marriage or childbirth – after a bereavement, or the maintenance of active bonds with the deceased, as forms of ritual behaviour. This approach therefore uses theoretical model of ritual to make sense of death-related practice.

Third, there are social scientists who question the model of 'impoverished' and 'over-stark' Western disposal, arguing that this is limited to middle-class, white and Anglican funerals, which should not be taken as the norm. In their view, working-class funerals and those conducted for and by members of Western ethnic minorities are marginalized in such debates. Howarth, for example, in her ethnography of an East End undertaking business, challenges John Fry's claim that the funeral ceremony is now 'a minor disposal service' (cited in Howarth 1996: 199). Her work demonstrates the persistence of traditional practices at white working-class funerals: the undertaker's black silk top hat; 'walking' the cortege; bowing to the coffin. She describes the funeral cortege leaving the funeral director's shop to travel slowly to the home of the deceased, a reflection of the belief that in the East End community 'returning the deceased to the place they knew as home was "only right and proper"' (Howarth 1996: 177). In one case, a detour was even made to the former home of the deceased and his wife. On arrival at the family's current home, a group of neighbours often gathered on the pavement to watch the 'spectacle', a practice rare in more middle-class parts of London but in evidence where there are strong links between family and local working-class community.

In this example, the East End funeral director and the local community are bound by an identity of interests: the slow drive around the locality, followed by 'walking' the cortege from the home of the deceased, both satisfies family and friends that respects have been paid in full *and* allows the funeral director to advertise his business by demonstrating its quality (Howarth 1996: 181). By contrast, Hindu mourning ritual (see Chapter 16) is at odds with the professional agendas of hospital staff and funeral directors in that death should take place on the ground followed by rapid cremation. Yet, as Firth argues, 'priests are evolving their own rituals, negotiating with each family within the constraints of time and the family tradition' (see p. 239). Elements from the various parts of the ritual as performed in India are condensed in home-based practices: recitation of religious verses, circumambulation of the open coffin, the placing of flowers, butter, herbs and balls of rice or barley in the coffin. This is not the depersonalized, minimalist death ritual that we recognize as a focus for criticism; neither is it a set of minority practices, Firth's data being gathered from among a community of 3000 Hindus living in a British city. Finally, the use of clairvoyants needs to be included here as an example of a mourning custom, which fails to be recognized within more middle-class analyses. Audiences at the public performances of spirit mediums often arrive in family groups and have an explicit intention to contact a bereaved member of their family. Such events reveal the strong emotions which are invoked in the process, as well as the social relationships through which they are managed (Hallam *et al.* 1999)

This approach therefore questions the database of many critiques of contemporary death ritual and asks whether it constitutes an implicit reflection of the experiences of middle-class white researchers. In this respect it could be said to mirror the correspondence between the initial bereavement database and the everyday experiences of psychiatrists, the metaphors of symptomatology, disease and healing being evident in their analyses (for example, Engel 1961, cited in Worden 1991). A related critique is one which questions the evidence that Modernist funerals are experienced as attenuated and unsatisfying. D. Davies (1996) presents data from two studies which show that within one sample only nine per cent of those surveyed thought the cremation service was too short and within the other only 13 out of 533 individuals shared this view. Marris (1958, cited in Walter 1994: 18) describes how East End widows in the 1950s were prepared to abandon traditional rituals and resist the enforced wearing of black for long periods.

Fourth, there are those who do not just demand that a broader range of behaviours be brought under the rubric of 'ritual' but raise questions about the purposes of ritual and how they are achieved. In line with critics who condemn the 'empty' and therefore purposeless funeral, anthropologists define ritual as an event that 'makes change' and 'moves' participants, emotionally, ideologically and structurally (Turner 1969). It therefore contrasts with ceremony that merely 'marks' a change which has been effected elsewhere. Thus initiation rituals make adolescents into adults (Richards 1956; La Fontaine 1966); anti-sorcery rites cure victims (Kapferer 1995); funerals change the formerly living into the dead and so transform the structural position of survivors, with wives becoming widows, sons and daughters becoming family heads (Van Gennep [1909] 1960). Accounts of the Bemba girls' initiation ritual illustrate this point (Richards 1956; La Fontaine 1966). The Bemba say 'We do the rite to grow the girl' (La Fontaine 1966: 121); the girls themselves may or may not have begun menstruation. It is their seclusion for a period of demanding ritual activities that 'grows them' into women who are available for marriage. Looked at in this way, ritual can be described as a series of events which not only 'moves' individuals, but also makes them understand the world, and how individuals should operate within it, in a particular way.

Knowledge is therefore key to ritual power and practice. As Small notes in Chapter 1, it is a site for strategies, conflicts and struggles for control. Faced with the unknowable prospect and event of death, it is aspects of the known world that are brought into play through embodied sets of metaphors, to provide a culturally-specific account of what is occurring when someone has died. Rather than annihilation, common Western metaphors include sleep, the cycles of growth and decay in the natural world, and journeyings – that is, either the peaceful stillness of rest or transition or transformation into a new form. Thus, the familiar experience of rest and sleep is metaphorically transposed in the recumbent position of the corpse as it moves through rituals of disposal, the bed-like form of traditional graves with their 'headboard' tombstones, and the repeated written and spoken references to 'rest' and 'peace' in funeral liturgy, on gravestones and in In Memoriam notices. Equally familiar are the natural cycles of growth and decay, in evidence as embodied metaphors in traditional Christian and alternative woodland burial practices, the scattering of ashes in gardens, at sea or in the countryside, and the Christian funeral liturgy's references – 'earth to earth' and 'man cometh up and is cut down like a flower'. The known experience of travel also becomes a metaphor which implies transition or transcendence, embodied in the ritual transportation of the corpse in the slow-moving hearse and on the shoulders of funeral directors. Cremation is popularly referred to through the metaphor of the conveyor belt, a concept that more accurately describes the passage of mourners in and out of the chapel's different doors than the actual committal of the coffin to the furnace (D. Davies 1996). The transition evoked by this metaphor may therefore refer more to the changes wrought among the bereaved, rather than the deceased. It is echoed in the stages theories of grief, which imply a time of disorientation followed by arrival at an end-stage of recovery (see Chapter 1).

In sum, rest, the organic cycles of nature and journeying are examples of embodied or three-dimensional experiences drawn from the known world of everyday life. In Fernandez's words they provide 'organising images which ritual action puts into effect' (1977: 101). If ritual involves the articulation of an organizing image, however, there remains the question of how this process actually produces change in participants. Why should an Anglican funeral with its repertoire of metaphoric imagery and acts be experienced by some participants as an 'empty ordeal' (Ter Blanche and Parkes 1997)? Victor Turner's extensive work on ritual stresses the multi-vocality of religious symbols. By bringing together the physiological/emotional and abstract/conceptual domains, primary experience reanimates abstract thought, which in turn gives meaning to mysterious or frightening experiences such as death. Ter Blanche and Parkes suggest that even regular churchgoers may no longer share the 'enthusiastic commitment' of earlier generations of Christians (1997: 134). In Turner's view, the capacity of ritual to 'make' change occur rests on participants' willingness to submit to the authority represented by ritual specialists and to participate in the particular construction of reality that the ritual puts forward. Evidence of survivors' willing participation in ritualized or routinized behaviours has already been detailed (see, for example, Chapter 11).

Fifth, and in line with the anthropological notion of ritual as an event that makes rather than just marks change, are postmodern approaches to death ritual. These advocate that individuals can – and should – personalize their experience of loss, making it meaningful through self-selected images and practices, which help them manage their loss as they see fit. Evidence that postmodern death ritual is actually taking place alongside the much critiqued 'contemporary' Modernist funeral can be found in the personal accounts of individuals who have tailored their own, quite specific ritual practices (for example, Partington, 1996). Further evidence can be found in the Christian clergy's expressed desire to make funerals as personal as possible, for example by incorporating secular music and contributions from family, friends and colleagues (Naylor 1989, cited in Walter 1994; Hockey 1992). Postmodernist theorists of death and dying would therefore argue that those who despairingly search contemporary society for collective rituals, orchestrated in line with dominant religious ideologies, are blindly following a Modernist agenda. They are neglecting to recognize the diversity and the choice which are the hallmark of contemporary society where individuals are constructing their own lifecourse narratives, both in health, sickness and, currently, in death.

As Walter (1996) notes, it is in the construction of postmodern death rituals that we most clearly see the reanimation of ritual forms from other societies or from our own pasts. However, as he points out, 'in traditional deaths documented by historians and anthropologists, the dying or grieving person is the chief actor but not the writer of the script' (1996: 199). Here we see the chief contrast between traditional and postmodern funerals – and also the most ambiguous aspect of more recent approaches to death ritual. Whereas the field-working anthropologist valued an opportunity to be present at a death ritual since it was believed to represent the most unequivocal expression of a society's dominant set of values (Kalsi 1996: 31), the postmodern funeral may be highly idiosyncratic with an emphasis on supporting the individual in making whatever choices most express them and their lifestyles. However, as Walter (1996) argues, many Westerners encounter bereavement for the first time in adult life. Whilst wishing to take up the challenge – or injunction – to express themselves rather than submit to an external authority, there is a need for advice, whether from a counsellor, from the media or from a group of others who have shared a similar loss. The result of this ambiguity is what Walter terms the late modern and the postmodern revivals of death (1994: 39–46). In the former, the needs of individuals who lack the support of traditional beliefs and practices are identified by experts; psychiatrists, counsellors and other healthcare professionals. In the absence of religious and community deathways, therapeutic theories are devised. While these put the needs of the individual at the centre, they constitute a set of injunctions – that the individual shall express their emotions, shall acknowledge the reality of their loss and shall share their thoughts and feelings with appropriate others. In Walter's view, this approach remains Modernist in that it attempts to control the experiences of individuals via overarching theories and institutionalized agencies. In contrast, postmodern approaches are more likely to value individual choice, even if it flies in the face of the most recent theories. Using Jencks notion of 'double-coding', he argues that postmodern death ritual freely incorporates elements of traditional rituals, selects items of Modernist expertise such as pain-control and orients the whole in a person-centred cocktail of support.

References

Adams, S. (1993) A gendered history of the social management of death and dying in Foleshill, Coventry, during the inter-war years, in D. Clark (ed.) *The Sociology of Death*. Oxford: Blackwell Publishers.
Albery, N., Mezey, M., McHugh, M. and Papworth, M. (1995) *Before and After; The Best New Ideas for Improving the Quality of Dying and for Inexpensive, Green, Family-organised Funerals*. London: The Natural Death Centre.
Ariès, P. (1981) *The Hour of Our Death*. London: Allen Lane.
Árnason, A. (1998) 'Feel the Pain': death, grief and bereavement counselling in the North East of England. Unpublished PhD thesis, University of Durham.

Bloch, M. (1971) *Placing the Dead: Tombs, Ancestral Villages and Kinship Organisation in Madagascar*. London: Seminar Press.

Bloch, M. and Parry, J. (1982) *Death and the Regeneration of Life*. Cambridge: Cambridge University Press.

Bluebond-Langner, M. (1978) *The Private Worlds of Dying Children*. Princeton, NJ: Princeton University Press.

Bourke, J. (1996) *Dismembering the Male: Men's Bodies, Britain and the Great War*. London: Reaktion Books.

Cannadine, D. (1981) War and death, grief and mourning in modern Britain, in J. Whaley (ed.) *Mirrors of Mortality. Studies in the Social History of Death*. London: Europa Publications.

Clark, D. (1982) *Between Pulpit and Pew: Folk Religion in a North Yorkshire Fishing Village*. Cambridge: Cambridge University Press.

Cohen, A.P. and Rapport, N. (eds) (1995) *Questions of Consciousness*. London: Routledge.

Collick, E. (1982) *Through Grief*. Mirfield: Mirfield Publications.

Davidoff, L., L'Esperance, J. and Newby, H. (1976) Landscape with figures: home and community in English society, in J. Mitchell and A. Oakley (eds) *The Rights and Wrongs of Women*. London: Penguin.

Davies, C. (1996) Dirt, death, decay and dissolution: American denial and British avoidance, in G. Howarth and P.C. Jupp (eds) *Contemporary Issues in the Sociology of Death, Dying and Disposal*. Basingstoke: Macmillan.

Davies, D. (1996) The social facts of death, in G. Howarth and P.C. Jupp (eds) *Contemporary Issues in the Sociology of Death, Dying and Disposal*. Basingstoke: Macmillan.

Du Boulay, J. (1982) The Greek vampire: a study of cyclic symbolism in marriage and death. *Man*, 17: 219–38.

Durkheim, E. ([1912] 1965) *The Elementary Forms of the Religious Life*. New York: Free Press.

Evans, M. (1982) *The Woman Question*. Oxford: Fontana Paperbacks.

Fernandez, J.W. (1977) The performance of ritual metaphors, in J.D. Sapir and J.C. Crocker (eds) *The Social Use of Metaphor*. Philadelphia: Universily of Pennsylvania Press.

Foucault, M. (1977) *The Archaeology of Knowledge*. London: Tavistock.

Fox, N. (1997) Is there life after Foncault? Texts, frames and *differends*, in A. Petersen and R. Bunton (eds) *Foucault, Health and Medicine*. London: Routledge.

Freud, S. (1917) Mourning and melancholia, in J. Strachey (ed.) *The Standard Edition of the Complete Psychological Works of Sigmund Freud*, Vol. 14. London: Hogarth Press and Institute of Psycho-Analysis.

Froggatt, K. (1997) Rites of passage and the hospice culture. *Mortality*, 2(2): 123–36.

Gorer, G. (1965) *Death, Grief and Mourning in Contemporary Britain*. London: Cresset Press.

Hallam, E., Hockey, J. and Howarth, G. (1999) *Beyond the Body: Death and Social Identity*. London: Routledge.

Helman, C. (1990) *Culture, Health and Illness*. Oxford: Butterworth Heinemann.

Helman, C. (1991) *Body Myths*. London: Chatto and Windus.

Hertz, R. ([1907] 1960) *Death and the Right Hand*. New York: Free Press.

Hockey, J. (1992) *Making the Most of a Funeral*. Richmond upon Thames: Cruse – Bereavement Care.

Hockey, J. (1996a) 'The view from the West': Reading the anthropology of non-western death ritual, in G. Howarth and P.C. Jupp (eds) *Contemporary Issues in the Sociology of Death, Dying and Disposal*. Basingstoke: Macmillan.

Hockey, J. (1996b) Accounting for the time of bereavement. Paper given at the Time, Space and Health Conference, Queen Mary and Westfield College, London.

Howarth, G. (1996) *Last Rites: The Work of the Modern Funeral Director*. New York: Baywood.

Howarth, G. (1997) Death on the road: the role of the English coroner's court in the social construction of an accident, in M. Mitchell (ed.) *The Aftermath of Road Accidents: Psychological, Social and Legal Consequences of an Everyday Trauma*. London: Routledge.

Huntington, R. and Metcalf, P. (1979) *Celebrations of Death. The Anthropology of Mortuary Ritual*. Cambridge: Cambridge University Press.

Illich, I. (1975) *Medical Nemesis: The Expropriation of Health*. London: Caldar and Boyars.

James, N. and Field, D. (1992) The routinisation of hospice: charisma and bureaucratisation. *Social Science and Medicine*, 34(12): 1363–75.

Jupp, P.C. (1993) Cremation or burial? Contemporary choice in city or village, in D. Clark (ed.) *The Sociology of Death*. Oxford: Blackwell Publishers/The Sociological Review.

Kalsi, S.S. (1996) Change and continuity in the funeral ritual of Sikhs in Britain, in G. Howarth and P.C. Jupp (eds) *Contemporary Issues in the Sociology of Death, Dying and Disposal*. Basingstoke: Macmillan.

Kapferer, B. (1995) From the edge of death: sorcery and the motion of consciousness, in A. Cohen and N. Rapport (eds) *Questions of Consciousness*. London: Routledge.

Kellehear, A. (1990) *Dying of Cancer*. Chur: Harwood Academic Publishers.

Komaromy, C. (2000) The sight and sound of death. *Mortality*, 5(3): 299–315.

La Fontaine, J. (1966) *Chisungu*. London: Faber.

Lawton, J. (1998) Contemporary hospice care: the sequestration of the unbounded body and 'dirty dying'. *Sociology of Health and Illness*, 20(2): 121–43.

Lewis, C.S. (1961) *A Grief Observed*. New York: Seabury Press.

Littlewood, J. (1993) The denial of death and rites of passage in contemporary societies, in D. Clark (ed.) *The Sociology of Death*. Oxford: Blackwell Publishers/The Sociological Review.

Lofland, L. (1985) The social shaping of emotion: The case of grief. *Symbolic Interaction*, 8(2): 171–90.

Lovell, A. (1997) Death at the beginning of life, in D. Field, J. Hockey and N. Small (eds) *Death, Gender and Ethnicity*. London: Routledge.

Lupton, D. (1998) *The Emotional Self*. London: Sage.

Marris, P. (1958) *Widows and their Families*. London: Routledge.

Martins, H. (1983) Introduction Tristes Durees, in R. Feijo, H. Martins and J. de Pina-Cabral (eds) *Death in Portugal, Journal of the Anthropological Society of Oxford*, Occasional Papers, no. 2 (v–xxii).

Morley, J. (1971) *Death, Heaven and the Victorians*. London: Studio Vista.

Parkes, C.M. (1972) *Bereavement: Studies of Grief in Adult Life*. Harmondsworth: Penguin.

Partington, M. (1996) Salvaging the sacred, *The Guardian Weekend*, 18 May, 14–23.

Prior, L. (1989) *The Social Organization of Death*. Basingstoke: Macmillan.

Richards, A. (1956) *Chisungu: A Girls Initiation Ceremony among the Bemba of Northern Rhodesia*. London: Faber.

Richardson, R. (1984) Old people's attitudes to death in the twentieth century. *Society for the Social History of Medicine Bulletin*, 34: 48–51.

Riches, G. and Dawson, P. (1996) Communities of feeling: the culture of bereaved parents. *Mortality*, 1(2): 143–61.

Riches, G. and Dawson, P. (1997) 'Shoring up the walls of heartache'; parental responses to the death of a child, in D. Field, J. Hockey and N. Small (eds) *Death, Gender and Ethnicity*. London: Routledge.

Rosaldo, R. (1989) Introduction. Grief and the headhunter's rage, in R. Rosaldo (ed.) *Culture and Truth. The Remaking of Social Analysis*. Boston, MA: Beacon Press.

Sudnow, D. (1967) *Passing On: The Social Organisation of Dying*. Englewood Cliffs, NJ: Prentice-Hall.

Ter Blanche, H. and Parkes, C.M. (1997) Christianity, in C.M. Parkes, P. Laungani and B. Young (eds) *Death and Bereavement across Cultures*. London: Routledge.

Thompson, N. (1997) Masculinity and loss, in D. Field, J. Hockey and N. Small (eds) *Death, Gender and Ethnicity*. London: Routledge.

Turner, V. (1969) *The Ritual Process*. Harmondsworth: Penguin.

Van Gennep, A. ([1909] 1960) *The Rites of Passage*. Chicago, IL: University of Chicago Press.

Walter, T. (1990) *Funerals and How to Improve Them*. London: Hodder and Stoughton.

Walter, T. (1994) *The Revival of Death*. London: Routledge.

Walter, T. (1995) Natural death and the noble savage. *Omega*, 30(4): 237–48.

Walter, T. (1996) Facing death without tradition, in G. Howarth and P.C. Jupp (eds) *Contemporary Issues in the Sociology of Death, Dying and Disposal*. Basingstoke: Macmillan.

Wilson, G. (1939) Nyakyusa conventions of burial. *Bantu Studies*, 13: 1–31.

Winter, J. (1995) *Sites of Memory, Sites of Mourning*. Cambridge: Cambridge University Press.

Worden, J.W. (1991) *Grief Counselling and Grief Therapy*. London: Tavistock/Routledge.

Wright, M. (1981) Coming to terms with death: patient care in a hospice for the terminally ill, in P. Atkinson and G. Heath (eds) *Medical Work*. London: Gower Press.

13 Funeral ritual past and present

PHIL GORE

This chapter explores the changes that have occurred within the funeral industry in east Kent since the 1920s and is focused on the responses of retired local funeral directors. There is no special significance to this area, but it is broadly reflective of the changes that have occurred over the rest of England during this period. The chapter starts with a brief look at funeral ritual and customs of the past, the impact of changes follow and a brief summary of their implications in current practice concludes this section.

In the past, funerals were organized by industries that provided the craft skills for casual undertaking: carpentry, building and timberwork. Due to the largely rural nature of east Kent in the 1920s and 1930s, all the firms concerned were engaged wholly in their craft occupation and only marginally in their death-related activities. William in Wingham said: 'Most funerals were local, not like the building work. It was nice to have somebody personally they knew in the parishes around Wingham'.

Personal contact appeared to guide many people to the local firm, as Jack confirmed: 'Well it was a Deal family and they always went to that firm to get their repairs done therefore they went there to get the funerals . . . We lived in Duke Street for 40 years, in that street we knew everybody around Wingham'.

There were several reasons for this 'part-time' occupation, summarized under the areas of rural deathways, craft practice and transport. The sparsely populated rural areas of the countryside and smaller towns accounted to a large extent for the sporadic nature of funeral needs, which invariably meant burial, usually in the local churchyard, an activity ubiquitous to east Kent in many parts into the early 1960s. Parochial burials required local involvement because the local grave-digger would know the correct grave location and would be familiar with the terrain: what sort of soil, if the grave was liable to flood, how long it would take to excavate, etc.

Community-based rural deathways at this time focused on the home, where the individual would have died, or (if the death occurred elsewhere) the body would be returned home with the greatest urgency. So the funeral would inevitably start from within the community, the body would remain within the community and communal funeral rituals would play a role in community deathways. A large factor in pre-funeral logistics therefore concerned the delivery of the coffin to the house for the ritual 'lying in' of the body. The 'last look' for friends, neighbours and family was a vital social duty. Ernie in Ramsgate said: 'All the neighbours would have to come in, that was quite normal, the whole street would eventually have paid their respects to the dead. And all the curtains would be drawn in the rest of the street as well as the boarding up at the windows. That lasted right into the 1960s, but it doesn't happen now'. Because the 'last look' was important, some people planned their funeral attire in advance, as this was something that the neighbours would see. Violet, a local layer-out in Minster between the wars, said: 'Well you always had to ask somebody what they wanted to put on. You always asked the neighbour. I can remember my mum saying "In that drawer there is what I want put on when I die." They leave something ready'.

'Laying out' in the front parlour at home usually required some special fitments. Many firms furnished a carpet, candlesticks and pall-cloth besides the usual coffin trestles and equipment case, as Chris in Canterbury said:

> Just this case used to go with us and possibly a pair of trestles and a big oval carpet. The furniture was cleared usually in the bedroom, the coffin was placed on the trestles on this carpet by the window. We had two different effects in palls, one that we took home was much thicker, almost like a blanket, a deep mauve with gilding upon it. We did have candlesticks as well, they were only taken home where there was room for them.

Some areas, such as Deal, had access to a temporary mortuary in a converted cemetery chapel. But usually the practice of taking home meant that few firms had any sort of mortuary accommodation, as Tom mentioned about Margate, a seaside resort: 'Some people, especially hotels, you had to bring the body out, you had to keep them here. But as I say, the locals, it was unheard of to take them away from the house. After the war, well I suppose there were more people starting to live in flats then'.

Local funeral customs such as flowers, boarding and walking provided community support, which was an important part of local, communal ritual. Bright displays of funeral flowers outside the house contrasted with the drawn curtains of neighbouring houses, as Tom in Margate told me: 'Going back when nobody was ever moved from the house, when we took the coffin to the house the flowers were always at the house because the body and the coffin was there'.

Boarding the windows further underlined the fact of death, as Don in Whitstable recalled: 'Early on when I first went (1936) they used to keep a series of these black boards that we used to have to run round and put up at people's windows. A black board was about four inches wide, piece of flooring actually painted black. People would know there'd been a death in the household'.

Walking the funeral, with its associated slow gait, emphasized its ceremony and solemnity. Don commented: 'When I first started funerals you used to walk all the way to the cemetery. We used to walk all the way, didn't matter if it was raining or flipping snowing, we used to walk all the time. Immediately after the war that stopped'.

The craft nature of early practice focused on coffin making. Hand making a bespoke coffin was a time-consuming task from hand-seasoned virgin boards specially cut for this purpose. Ernie in Ramsgate reckoned on seven to eight hours from start to finish, Grace's husband in the 1950s at Garlinge would have taken about a day and Chris in Canterbury told me that to convert inch and a half oak boards, by hand into a coffin took 'a day and a half and damned hard work'! Virtually every respondent could give their firm's formula for construction, which had lain dormant for 30, 40 or 50 years within the minds of the respondents. This effortless recall underlined just how important this act was and explained why funeral conducting was invested into this particular craft occupation. Jack in Deal explained how to set out a coffin board, which formed the base of the coffin: 'Put a centre line down and put a line at the top across with your half square, then one down about 20–22 inches and another line across, then the (length for) legs, you could mark the foot. You got the width of the body, that would be the width of the shoulders, you'd allow for an inch side for rounding'.

The visible nature of funeral ritual explained the pre-occupation with the coffin, where thickness of timber and the type of handles and finish (oiling, waxing, brush polishing, French polishing) conveyed something of the salubrity of the funeral. In Woodnesborough and Birchington between the 1930s and 1985 it was common practice to have different handles on the coffin according to sex: bar handles for men and ring handles for women. The nameplate might have been painted in Margate or 'wriggled' in Canterbury. (Wriggling was a form of hand inscribing.) By contrast Parish ('pauper') funerals were often left 'in the white' – unfinished, underlining the deep divide between the poor and others. This example of Victor's concerns Hampstead early on in this century: 'Black boxes was the people who couldn't afford a real burial, you know, so they was put into what was called a black box, you see, it was only painted black, that's all it was and the inside of it had no lining'.

Before the war transport in east Kent was limited. Most localities had a carriage master who possessed a hearse, which would be hired to the local undertakers when the need arose. Early funerals involving horse transport were cumbersome and labour intensive. As Ernest from Herne Bay mentioned, in the 1920s: 'We used to get up at five in the morning and I'd come home perhaps at ten o'clock at night and I was too tired to eat. You never finished, from early morning you had to clean the horse before you put them in the stable . . . we never had a holiday, Christmas, Easter, they had to be looked after every day'.

This does not mean that early motor vehicles were easier to use. Chris in Canterbury outlined the challenges in driving the earlier vehicles at walking pace with no automatic transmission or power steering: 'Our first hearse was a Rolls Royce hearse. You had a gauge and you had to get the revs just right and you had to double de-clutch in and out of gear all the way and that wasn't always successful'.

This is not to say, however, that there was a uniform progression from horse to motor. Charles, an early 1930s chauffeur in Ramsgate, was driving an early motor funeral hearse when Bernard, in nearby Minster, walked on some of his village funerals with a wheel bier.

This broad picture of past times conveys a centuries-old pattern of funeral rites. However this tradition was under growing pressure through the 1950s and onwards. The growth of small towns in east Kent in this period meant that the local death rate rose. This had significant repercussions for the local man engaged in funeral work. To 'drop everything' and make a coffin became an increasingly common feature, when building the new estates to a time-scale meant that sudden switching of men from building or harvest to funerals was very awkward. Don in Whitstable recalled:

> Quite often when it did get a bit haywire we used to start at five o'clock in the morning, coffin making, because you hadn't got to interfere with your day. I mean we'd got umpteen bricklayers, at one time there was 90 of us on the firm. We have started at four o'clock and then once the normal day started, drop that and go back onto our normal day's work and then when normal day work was over, work evenings.

Prolonged overtime became a strain, so an obvious answer was to create a special funeral 'department'. However, the movement to a permanent core of men wholly engaged in funerals produced its own problems: how to balance times of low demand with times of peak demand. The answer involved a radical disruption of the craftsmen concepts of bespoke coffin making. The carpenter built up a stock of general coffin sizes, the nearest size furnishing the appropriate coffin. John in Ashford told me: 'I know when I went to Woods to have ready-made coffins was a great boon, and the slack time you could get some ready and then (when needed) an hour and you could sail'.

Another effect of growing population density was the growing demand for burial spaces, which severely taxed the part-time local churchyard grave-digger and started extending the normal three-day funeral into at least a week. George told me about the strain of part-time grave digging in Birchington during the 1960s:

> I used to come in of a night-time, we were having our tea and somebody knock knock at the door, oh it was the old church warden. We'd up and go and that was your job. Six or seven hours, whenever you've got the time, a couple of evenings work . . . that used to get me, working bloody evening and then you got to go to work of a morning. Saw a great big pick and shovel looking at you.

As churchyards filled and closed this prompted a transition to more distant burial sites run by the local borough, which also contributed to delay as local areas were focused into one central cemetery instead of more numerous Parish churchyards. The factors of delay created problems with the 'front parlour' at home and the growing popularity of cremation contributed to the radical move to distance death from the community into the local 'funeral parlour'. Consequently from a period roughly within the 1960s, the practice of accommodating the dead at home started to dwindle and so the premises of funeral firms had to alter and accommodate the dead. Few undertakers felt any responsibility towards the body while the front parlour at home was used, but as habits changed, so the need to upgrade premises became more urgent. Les in Deal recalled:

> We discarded this chapel in the yard at Pittocks and adapted what was the machine shop into a new chapel in about '65. I think we got, you know, people started to complain about it. You can imagine you're going through a builders yard, which in the winter was all mud, and you got to make your way to this chalet sort of thing. One felt embarrassed by it. I think most people began to upgrade about that time.

Population concentration and growing preference for more distant cremation (some Kent crematoria were as much as 30 miles away in the 1930s) prompted investment in rolling stock by funeral directors, as numbers of funerals grew. This rationalizing, converting of premises and purchase of vehicles served to further concentrate the industry. Local funerals might now not be so local and therefore involved more time. Timings had also to correspond with the schedules of bureaucratic crematoria instead of the vagaries of the churchyard. Paperwork and organizing became a major feature of funerals, which also contributed to the growth of specialized funeral firms. Smaller firms had either to invest in funeral directing or move out of this occupation.

Walter in Faversham told me: 'I bought Fullers, the builders who were undertakers. Well undertaking distracted you from your building, it distracted you from what your main task was and also there wasn't much money in it really'.

This shrinkage of casual undertaking had an impact on the firms hiring to small undertakers: the carriage masters. An excellent example of this change concerns John in Faversham and Peter, the local motor carriage master.

> Well at the same time, Peter, the one who described himself as a carriage master, 'cause we used to hire his hearse and car, he was finding more and more of the builder undertakers, carpenter undertakers was disappearing . . . so one very cold winter's day I went to see him and we was sat on an upturned a bucket, each one and we said 'You know, this is silly, we'd better work together, you'd better act as an undertaker.'

The transition from part-time undertaker to full-time funeral director, which started in the late 1950s, was virtually complete by the mid-1980s. John, the village undertaker outside Faversham told me that in the 1960s: 'Faversham was a big expansion for us. I could see a change in the trade, it was turning into a profession'.

A feature of modern funeral practice is the rationalized nature of funeral firms, which are now specialized establishments almost wholly focused on funeral organizing. East Kent is now covered by 12 private companies, the Co-op and the recent American entrants, SCI. Conversely oral respondents could between them remember well over 100 small firms, each doing a small number of funerals in their own parishes during the past.

Urban people need to be aware of the array of modern funeral choices; this has produced a highly organized and specialized occupational group of funeral organizers. Local burial has been submerged by the growth of population and efficient motor transport has enabled distant crematoria to replace local burial.

In contrast to the parish-based organization of funerals in the past, the scheduling of contemporary funerals involves coordination of many different agencies: local authorities, florist, coroner, clergy, registrar and the general workings of a complicated and bureaucratic urban system. Today the physical distancing of mortuary accommodation and crematoria has meant that local community ritual had dwindled. Boarding windows, ringing bells, curtain drawing and walking funerals are rare. Bland cremation has encouraged plainer coffins. Neighbours and friends must now 'pay their respects' at the funeral firm, but this is for personal need, not as an act of support from the community to the family at home, thus eroding the community-based funeral support of the past and replacing local customs with distant, attenuated ritual.

14 Forget me not: memorialization in cemeteries and crematoria

MARY BRADBURY

I am always struck by the vast array of memorial artefacts on display in crematoria and cemeteries. We remember our dead with bunches of flowers, pot plants, bulbs, rose bushes, trees, wall plaques, niche space, urns, benches, statues, entries in the Books of Remembrance (large tomes in which the name, date of birth and date of death are inscribed) and poems. Memorials are often thoughtfully chosen and lovingly maintained, reflecting the cultural heritage, status and values of the deceased and his or her surviving family members. Until recently, contemporary Western memorialization has not attracted much attention within the social sciences. In an environment of positivism, in which the social sciences were keen to emulate the natural sciences, the study of something as apparently old fashioned or 'primitive' as rituals and customs in a contemporary Western setting was not attractive. If considered at all, the sale of memorials was viewed as an example of the exploitation of vulnerable clients by a greedy and manipulative funeral industry (Mitford 1963). Further, at a time when the manifestations of grief had been likened to a disease (Lindemann 1944), the ailing next of kin (Parkes 1964, 1975; Parkes and Weiss 1969, 1983; Glick *et al.* 1974) were presumed to be in no fit state to make sensible decisions about money and the extravagant expenditure on plants or stone could all too easily be inferred to be a representation of 'pathological grief' (Lindemann 1944; Volkan 1970) – a failure to let go, move on and get better.

Drawing on a qualitative study that took place in the early 1990s in London (Bradbury 1999), I argue that contemporary memorialization represents a flourishing custom in which people find a welcome conduit for the expression of the many complex emotions of grief. During my research, which involved interviewing 'deathworkers' (such as the nurse, doctor, registrar, coroner, funeral director and cemetery manager) and their bereaved 'clients', as well as observing the day-to-day activities involved in the disposal of our dead, I was surprised to find that the grieving women who talked to me were generally enthusiastic about the memorials they had purchased for their loved ones. This stood in stark contrast to their more ambivalent descriptions of the moment of death, their interview at the funeral parlour, their trip to the parlour to view the corpse, or the committal service at the crematorium or cemetery. Choosing between a rose and group of croci is likely to be a lot less stressful than viewing the embalmed and encoffined corpse of your partner of many years, but this in itself does not explain why buying a memorial is so often felt to be positive.

The cemetery and the crematorium

I imagine everyone has driven past forlorn bunches of flowers tied to a railing, marking a fatal traffic accident. While temporary memorials may be placed at the site of death, most long-term memorials are built at the final resting place of the body and this is usually within the walls of crematoria or cemetery. Most crematoria and cemeteries, or 'crems' and 'cems' as they are commonly known within the death industry, are found on the outskirts of towns and cities. Generally offering ample parking and generous open hours, these are accessible sites that may be pleasant to visit. A striking feature of a crematorium in particular is the strong delineation between public, 'front stage', area and private, 'backstage', work sites (Goffman 1959). The areas for public use are the churchy waiting rooms, the committal chapels, the chapels of remembrance and commemorative gardens. Backstage, are the office, the stark cremator anterooms (which hold coffins until a cremator is free) the busy cremating room, and the room in which the 'cremains', as they are called, are ground up before being put into urns. The change in décor between front stage and backstage is as absolute as could be found in any theatre. Most visitors are unlikely to pass into the backstage working areas of these sites, although some crematoria hold 'open days' in which they invite interested members of the public to explore their grounds.

The committal service

In the ancient rite of burial, the friends and family watch the coffin being lowered into the ground. This is a dramatic moment. In contrast, cremation takes place backstage. Instead, the survivors watch a 'false committal' in which the coffin disappears from view behind a mechanically controlled curtain. In my research I found a great deal of interest focused on what happens behind this curtain. Is the body taken out of the coffin? Do the cremator operators whip off the brass handles? How long does the coffin wait until it is put into the cremator? These questions often remain unanswered. 'He always wanted to be cremated. But, I don't know what those ashes are, to be quite honest. I mean, you see your husband go through, in a box, and they give you box of ashes. Do they actually take the body out, is that all that the ashes are? I don't know. And I still don't know whether they are his ashes in that thing' (Janet).

The 'cremains'

'I felt nothing for the ashes. I just felt "This is not my husband" because you know, they can mix them up. My friend told me they get them all mixed up' (Kate).

The cremation of a body creates a by-product, the ashes. Understandably, relatives were often intimidated by the prospect of being reunited with this altered form of the deceased. Their uncertainty was often focused upon the composition of the ashes. Still more questions begged to be answered: How much ash does a body create – a spoonful or a bucketful? What is the real make-up of the ashes – does it include wood from the coffin or bones or a mixture of both? Is there an obscene mixing of ashes from the day's intake of funerals? Many respondents were highly sceptical about the integrity of the ashes with which they were presented. How on earth could they prove that these remains were those of their beloved relative? In fact, I found that cremator staff did make every effort to keep the ashes of each body separate. From the moment the unadulterated coffin is pushed into the cremator furnace to the time that a label is stuck on the plastic pot of ground up bones, the staff have kept tags on whose remains they are handling. Indeed, their efforts to maintain the 'individuality' of the remains appear something of a point of honour.

There is nothing neutral about a pot of ashes and many relatives wait months before they can face the prospect of seeing it. Aware of the often-emotional response to the 'cremains', most crematoria offer to store the ashes, for a small weekly fee, until relatives feel ready. Other people are able to pick up the ashes quite soon after the committal service and keep their urn at home. One of my interviewees found a certain charm in storing her husbands ashes at the bottom of her wardrobe; she liked being close to him. She reassured me that she was careful not to tell her offspring however, fearing they might think this was 'crazy'.

Choosing the final resting place

Unless one is going to keep the ashes at home, in pride of place on the mantelpiece or tucked away in a cupboard, one has to decide where these remains will ultimately reside. I found that some people are not always prepared for this second rite of disposal.

Since time immemorial, people have wanted to bury their dead in family plots or sites. The exact site of the final resting place of the dead often involves family members in much discussion. Some people care a great deal about this issue, finding solace in the thought that deceased family members are physically reunited. Of course, not everyone can afford to keep family plots and the stress of sharing a gravesite can be intense. I was told of a 'terrible row' that developed when one woman discovered that her husband's remains were to be included in a 'common grave'; she had not understood that her husband was to be buried above a 'foreign' stranger.

The democratic spirit of cremation, in which everybody gets to use the same cremator, can also threaten that reassuring sense of exclusivity. To compensate for the cremator's fiery promiscuity great emphasis is placed on the location in which the ashes are finally buried or scattered. Crematoria keep precise records of the disposal site of ashes on site. As other relatives die they can be strewn on the same spot, even many years later when any trace of ash could not be expected to remain. Alternatively, relatives may wish to scatter the ashes at a place that has particular sentimental value, such as a mountain-top, out at sea or simply in a much loved garden. The significance and location of these sites are unlikely to be forgotten by the family for at least a generation.

In a culture that traditionally buried its dead, the custom of scattering ashes is, of course, relatively new. After all, cremation is scarcely over a century old (Davies 1997). Precisely because these are usually private ceremonies, the importance of this rite is often underestimated by both the media and academics. These personal rituals of secondary disposal are often creative and highly idiosyncratic, reflecting the tastes and emotions of the family involved. People read from religious text, recite poetry, sing, play instruments or simply give impromptu speeches to express their feelings of love and loss and to acknowledge a life well lived. I found that many people viewed these activities as symbolically powerful and important. Sadly, in the aftermath of a death some fail to appreciate the possible significance of this moment until much later. One of my respondents felt cheated because she had followed her funeral director's advice, prompted by misplaced kindness, and did not attend the scattering of the ashes in the crematorium's grounds; later, she wished she had been there. For others the prospect of going through another mortuary ritual was simply too much for their frayed emotions and, to protect themselves from further distress, they avoided this final rite of disposal.

Choosing the memorial

I have made a little plaque. I am very pleased with that, because he was a good man.

(Kate)

There is a whole field of them croci. Oh, it really is beautiful. It really is. We'd rather have them than a rose bush. And, as I say, he was against flowers. He couldn't see any point in them. He didn't believe in having memorials. But, I could not do it. I couldn't just wipe it out all together.

(Doris)

Having disposed of the body, people now have to choose a suitable memorial. They may be helped in this decision by a 'memorial counsellor', essentially a salesperson who presents the grieving relative with brochures of memorial artefacts, complete with price list. Having another point of view, even from someone who clearly has a commercial motive, can be gratefully accepted. Difficult choices have to be made, such as between a wall niche and an urn, between burying the ashes under a tree or rose bush and scattering on 'commemorative lawns' colourfully planted with spring bulbs. What would the deceased have liked? What phrase in a book or on a stone says it all? Not all memorials are bought in perpetuity; cemeteries and crematoria are busy places and space is always in demand. Many mourners are well aware that they will not live for long themselves and so it suits them to rent their niche space, stone, rose or bench by the year. It should be noted that not everyone likes to buy or rent memorials from the crem or cem. Some feel no need to remember their dead at the site of disposal or final resting place. Their memorials, just as powerful, are to found in the home in the shape of a chair, a cardigan, a photograph or a letter.

Visiting memorials

To me, that little bit, there, is him. In a sense. It is something for you to go up to and lay a flower on, just for remembrance, you know.

(Janet)

Having purchased a suitable memorial and having endured the apparently inevitable wait until it is finally installed, the relatives can now visit the completed site. Most people develop a pattern of visits structured around certain anniversaries particular to the deceased and their family, birthdays, 'deathdays' (the anniversary of death), and wedding anniversaries, as well as respecting various public ceremonies such as religious festivals and holidays. Some people visit their memorials according to days of the week. Others may respond to the impulse to be physically close to the deceased, reacting to repetitive waves of loss. Certain family members or close friends of the deceased may visit the site more frequently than others. There may also be occasions when the close and extended family choose to visit together. Over the years the frequency of visits may reduce, although some people maintain a steady pattern of visiting throughout their lives.

I like to go. I take up my little gloves, and my bits, you know. And just walk over there and make sure it is all tidy, make sure that the roses are okay.

(Paula)

Visiting a memorial is an intensely personal activity. Once at the grave or memorial site people do different things. Some people come armed with tools and spend their time quietly gardening. Others adorn the site with flowers, fresh or dried, bought from florists or gathered from their own garden. They may leave notes and cards. A child's grave may be covered with toys. Still others visit their memorial to talk to the deceased, to weep, or simply to sit and contemplate their life.

Why do people remember their dead?

There is little doubt that those people who find memorials attractive and are able to afford them find solace in memorialization. In my small sample of bereaved women who had purchased a memorial there were many satisfied customers. I found that people seem to benefit from visiting these sites as it gives them a physical focus around which they can centre their grief. A trip to the memorial can give people the opportunity to contemplate the life they shared with the deceased and to come to terms with the new life without the person. It can even help them to forge a relationship with their dead (see Hallam *et al.* 1999).

There are other reasons why memorialization may be so popular in this culture. In the first hectic days after a death many people find themselves adopting the role of bystanders. For all too many, their experience as 'the next of kin' is a series of interviews by a series of professionals and pseudo-professionals in windowless or heavily curtained rooms. The doctor, the registrar, the coroner, the police and the funeral director all may wish to ask questions in offices filled with dried flowers, social security leaflets and boxes of tissues. Having spent so much time waiting and answering questions, it is not so surprising to find that choosing a memorial which reflects the personality and character of the deceased and then taking the initiative about when to visit that memorial is experienced as a good thing. At last, the relatives can take control of events.

Another explanation for the current popularity of memorialization possibly lies in the fact that the bereaved relatives finally have access to the remains. In contrast to pre-industrial mortuary practises, in which the body remained at home with the family until the day of burial, most families are now separated from the corpse for at least a week. From the moment of death, the body usually remains firmly in the hands of the professionals: doctor, nurse, morgue attendant, coroner or embalmer. As it is kept backstage in the hospital morgue or funeral parlour, access to the body is often limited to one or two emotionally charged meetings. The body is presented and represented in altered forms (laid out, embalmed, encoffined) and the professionals are always on hand to subtly orchestrate the response of the grieving next of kin. After this, one can see how memorialization may come as a relief; finally the bereaved family have unquestioned and unlimited access to what remains of the body where they can freely express their anguish. As any cemetery manager will confirm, relatives are singularly demanding in their requests that the cemetery gates be kept open throughout the year.

Commerce or custom?

Without doubt, the sale of funeral artefacts is big business. I can still remember my astonishment when attending a crems and cems annual conference. A large hall was packed with stands selling every imaginable artefact associated with the disposal of the dead. At each stand genial sales representatives displayed their funerary urns, cremators, commemorative benches or wall plaques. Apparently, they were blissfully unaware of the incongruity of this modern-day meeting of death and commerce. Memorials are expensive and although it is true that we invest more on our weddings than our funerals, people still spend a great deal of money remembering their dead. It appears that, however satisfying memorialization may be, the exchange of money can leave people feeling slightly ashamed. I certainly detected an air of sheepishness as some of my respondents told me about their pleasure in purchasing extravagant memorials; a couple of my respondents were even aware that their deceased partners would probably have disapproved, but they had gone ahead nevertheless. Often, this was the first independent financial decision they had made in decades. If one lacks the funds, however, one is not even given the luxury of feeling duped. One woman, whose husband's funeral had been paid for by the Department of Social Security, was devastated because she could not afford to buy an entry in the book of remembrance. Without this concrete representation of her husband, whose ashes had been scattered, she felt there was no point in visiting the crematorium. She was adrift in grief.

In this short chapter, I have tried to emphasize the generally positive experiences of remembrance. Since the 1960s, there has been a fashion in deriding Western mortuary practices as somehow empty or shallow. Locked in cross-cultural envy and nostalgia we seem to imagine that other people do it better or that we used to be able to throw a good funeral but have somehow lost the knack. I am not sure whether this is always so true. During my research it became clear that memoralization is a flourishing custom from which participants extract meaning. A memorial, in whatever shape or form it takes, can not only represent a recognition of the reality of a loss and the finality of death, but also provide an opportunity to celebrate life itself.

Perhaps we should have more faith in our cultural ingenuity. Think, for example, of the eco-friendly development in memorialization in which mourners plant trees, rather than erect headstones. These 'woods for the dead', which make oxygen for the living, beautifully illustrate the fluid and flexible nature of our mortuary customs.

References

Bradbury, M.A.I. (1999) *Representation of Death: A Social Psychological Perspective*. London: Routledge.

Davies, D. (1997) *Death, Ritual and Belief: The Rhetoric of Funerary Rites*. London: Cassell.

Glick, I., Weiss, R. and Parkes, C. (1974) *The First Year of Bereavement*. New York: Wiley.

Goffman, E. (1959) *The Presentation of Self in Everyday Life*. Harmondsworth: Penguin.

Hallam, E., Hockey, J. and Howarth, G. (1999) *Beyond the Body: Death and Social Identity*. London Routledge.

Lindemann, E. (1944) Symptomatology and management of acute grief. *American Journal of Psychiatry*, 101: 141–8.

Mitford, J. (1963) *The American Way of Death*. New York: Simon and Schuster.

Parkes, C.M. (1964) The effects of bereavement on physical and mental health: a study of the medical records of widows. *British Medical Journal*, 2: 274–9.

Parkes, C.M. (1975) Determinants of outcome following bereavement. *Omega*, 6(4): 303–23.

Parkes, C.M. and Weiss, R.S. (1983) *Recovery from Bereavement*. New York: Basic Books.

Parkes, C.M., Benjamin, B. and Fitzgerald, R. (1969) Broken heart; a statistical study of increased morality among widowers. *British Medical Journal*, 1: 740–3.

Volkan, V. (1970) Typical findings in pathological grief. *Psychiatric Quarterly*, 44: 231–50.

15

The cemetery: the evidence of continuing bonds

DORIS FRANCIS, LEONIE KELLAHER AND GEORGINA NEOPHYTOU

Cemeteries are public spaces for the collective disposal of the dead. Because of their unrestricted and communal nature, English cemeteries provide a unique focus for considering the attributes and meanings of the connections between the deceased and the bereaved.[1]

In England, there are four key visual characteristics that define a cemetery. These elements provide the textuality of memory and endow the burial landscape with the significance of mourning (Bowdler 1996): the first is the memorial, marking the physical remains of the deceased. Often stone, these memorials are costly and enduring, though subject to weathering and decay. Second are the words, epithets and images carved on the stone. Third is the presence of mourners, their disposition and behaviour legible across the landscape, providing clues to psychological states and intensity of feeling. Nature is the fourth element; the trees and plantings with their seasonal cycles of birth, maturation, death, decay and regeneration record, which confound the linear time of the human life cycle (Leach 1961) and provoke an examination of life by direct reflection on relationships with the dead (Miller 1993).

In linking the study of the cemetery landscape with current bereavement theories, this chapter shows how people engage with and act on the sacred, sculptural space of the cemetery to generate customs of memorialization and mourning through which to express grief. Recent arguments in the thanatological literature (Littlewood 1993; Stroebe and Schut 1995; Klass et al. 1996; Walter 1996) and that of landscape design (Hunt 1997) offer theoretical insights into these processes.

Bereavement studies are increasingly challenging the orthodox Freudian paradigm, where death in Western society is perceived as a loss from which the mourner is expected to recover, severing attachment and moving on to form new relationships. The components of such extended models of grief, which this cemetery data[2] documents as significant dimensions of bereavement behaviour are:

- The continuation of close bonds between the living and deceased.
- The persistence of normal grief throughout a lifetime.
- The closely interwoven processes of memorialization and the reformulation of identity for the survivor and the deceased.
- The concurrent letting go and continued attachment of grief work.

After death, the deceased no longer provides a mirror in which the mourners view their own reflections and realize themselves as social beings (Warner 1959). For survivors to continue to see themselves still living in, and related to the 'other', they must reconstruct the image of the deceased, and in so doing, rethink their own identity. The garden historian John Dixon Hunt (1997) suggests how the bounded, liminal space of the cemetery becomes a privileged site for the re-creation of the identity of both the bereaved and the deceased. In selecting the stone, composing the epithet and/or creating the small garden plot with the memorial, the mourners project their own self-image, which is often realized and reflected in the process. These materially manifest tasks also allow the living to re-work the deceased's identity, and in so doing, to appropriate attributes of the departed for themselves.

A further link between the cemetery landscape and the processes of bereavement is suggested by Walter (1996), who notes the public performance dimensions of grieving. Building on Gorer's work (1965) on mourning customs, Walter argues that, whilst death has become a private affair in England, public – though limited – displays of bereavement are required to demonstrate affection for the deceased. Issues of gender and contrasting strategies for dealing with loss and adjustment are introduced by Stroebe and Schut (1995), who combine the theoretical concept of grief work with research on stress to delineate two types of coping and grief. Coping contains times when people confront loss and focus on bereavement experiences, and times when this is avoided and new roles are learned. The authors suggest that men 'typically' employ more problem-focused strategies to eliminate sources of stress, while women are likely to confront loss more directly.

In the research that informs this chapter, the public, non-clinical setting of the cemetery presented opportunities to understand how grief may take its place in 'ordinary' life. The data, gathered through empirical observation and discussion of meaning at the graveside with a wide range of persons who generally do not seek bereavement counselling, speaks for itself. Conversations with 1500 mourners in London cemeteries show how people act in and on the burial landscape as a public theatre for the creation and continued expression of relationships with the deceased. Here, case studies focus selectively on four kinds of loss: loss of a baby; death of a wife; courtship and remarriage after death of both former spouses; and the death of parents. While each individual's case is unique, common themes emerge that permit analysis to support an expanded paradigm of grief.

The death of a baby

Parents who, three years earlier, had a full-term, but stillborn infant convey the memories, feelings, hopes and expectations that maintain their dead son as a presence in their lives. The cemetery, especially the children's memorial plot chosen for the burial, and their weekly visits, reveal and engender the rituals through which the grounds become a physical extension of their relationship with their baby. The father explains: 'We come because we need the continuity of a relationship and fulfilment in it. We chose an area where the children's graves are together – a community. Here we do not have to speak. It is a shared experience. The other parents know our story and we know theirs'.

In the cemetery, their grieving is sanctioned and validated through the experiences they share with other parents. They describe how they exchange gifts with other bereaved parents on the anniversary of a child's death.

> People remembered our son's anniversary. They sent flowers and cards and presents, little books. Another couple, like us, bought their child a whole set of Beatrice Potter books, and wrote 'For B on his first anniversary'. With our son, he is 'more adult'. We bought a fossil and put it on the grave . . . the things for him are not baby things.

A sense of the deceased infant is thus constructed, and a shared inner representation of their son as a person, is nurtured. The obstacles to such a construction are also acknowledged by the mother.

> When a baby is stillborn, it does not have a proper existence . . . not really here. We wanted to say he was our son . . . take pride . . . make sure everyone knew about him. Otherwise, he would just disappear. If we did not make something of him we would have been left with nothing. We have a sense that others do not consider him a person. We had to make him one, for us.

The role of the cemetery is central:

> I feel I need to come to the cemetery for J to be part of my life, still. And coming to the cemetery is a way to do that. To still look after him. It would be neglectful if we did not come. He's stuck here. Family and friends want you to move on. They can't understand that he is still a part of my life now that I have given birth to another child.

The ongoing interaction with the terrain, notably the grave, emerges as pivotal:

We planned a garden on the grave. The scheme is white and small; it is a small plot; everything is low growing. Originally, the plan was to plant it permanently; but with such a small space, it is impossible to choose. We keep changing it all the time; so now it is a combination of permanent and temporary; there is always something nice and different to plant there. At Christmas, we have a little tree. I want it to look really nice for myself, for J, and for other people. I get upset if I see dead strewn flowers, which are sorry for themselves ... there is so little I can do for my child. I feel we're doing it for him and it gives me pleasure.

Three themes emerge from the account given by these parents; these recur amongst other groups and amplify the argument for continuing bonds as valid and productive facets of grief. First, this example of a stillborn child poignantly demonstrates the links between grief, memorialization and identity construction of both the deceased child as a person with attributes and characteristics, and of bereaved parents building and developing an identity for themselves as the caring parents of this child of whom they can be proud.

Second, the cemetery garden plot is a living memorial to their son. It symbolically expresses his constructed identity as a small, fragile, pure baby through the purposely selected colours of cream and white, and the diminutive size of the plantings. The permanence of the box border containing the seasonally changed plant scheme expresses the persistence of memory alongside its iteratively evolving content as the parents raise a second child and continue to reflect on the changing meaning of their loss.

Third, the cemetery offers a supportive community of fellow mourners who condone and endorse such ongoing connections and the continued need to grieve. Whereas the everyday world of work, leisure and family is perceived as uneasy with the powerful and ongoing emotions of grief and loss, the cemetery provides a retreat to express bereavement in freedom.

Loss of a wife

Much of the research on bereavement is based on women in clinical settings. This cemetery data, however, suggests a high proportion of older men – relative to those surviving into the upper age groups – who visit the cemetery on a weekly basis. Men in their 70s and 80s are often visible across cemetery landscapes making their way to their wife's grave. They say they have 'come to see the wife', to 'tidy' the grave. Despite poor health and public transport deficiencies, these men try to visit regularly and, often, frequently. Fresh flowers are brought, along with gardening and cleaning things, usually in a special, old, shopping bag. The mourners weed, plant, water or arrange the flowers and wash the stone; and at the same time, they recall memories and reflect on their married life: 'At the cemetery, I think of different things – in the old days; things come back into your memory'.

Many also use the occasion to tell the deceased about their week's activities and to share the news of family events. 'I need to put flowers, it's nicer to look at. It makes you think of her all the time. It makes you come to do the flowers and to keep it tidy, and you are thinking more when you come over . . .'. His granddaughter adds: 'and it lets everybody know you're thinking of her'.

In the cemetery, people engage in the active construction of new, public ways of connecting and caring. In describing the meaning of his present visits, a widower emphasizes continuity in the context of his previous efforts to nurse his wife: 'It would be no good doing this if I never looked after her in life'.

For older men, the maintenance of the role of spouse and the salience of the bond with the deceased remains a significant personal resource in old age (Lopata 1996; Moss and Moss 1996). Visiting the cemetery allows continued expression and expansion of this identity: 'I am proud of her grave and my part in creating it and writing the inscription, which keeps her memory'.

Importantly, this continuity of interaction between spouses in the cemetery extends to, and is also reinforced by, domestic activity. For many elderly men, the family home is symbolically linked with their wife. The husband often continues to live in the same house, carefully maintaining the routines established by the wife, keeping things just as they were when she was alive: 'The house is the same, I follow the same cleaning routine she followed. I keep it up to scratch'. Domestic tasks provide a ready structure of activities for the week and bring the wife into the present by keeping her memory current. Cemetery visits become part of the ordinary, an extension of the everyday domestic routine through which the deceased is re-incorporated in daily living. 'I look forward to coming to the cemetery on a Thursday and a Sunday. It's visiting the wife; visiting her memory.'

Tending the grave in the peaceful atmosphere of the cemetery can be an emotionally therapeutic strategy – and simultaneously, a minor distraction from the very grief it is expressing: 'If I start thinking, I get something to do'. Visiting the cemetery allows mourners to hold on to memories, engendering review and integration of a whole life with a shared past. Looking up and seeing other people with their private thoughts contextualizes and legitimates feelings of loss by defining the experience as normal. 'I feel at ease, I feel better for coming. That's how you cope, you do not feel so alone.'

The themes that emerge from observations of widowers might be regarded as facets of the motifs identified through the very different life span which is being commemorated at the grave of a stillborn child. First, in the sacred space of the cemetery, there is no dichotomy between the natural and supernatural as both are tended simultaneously. As already noted, the ongoing, but changed, relationship between the living and the deceased is often expressed through the small commemorative gardens planted in the cemetery. Information about the ongoing meaning of the deceased and about the quality of the past and present relationship between the self and other must be registered and conveyed publicly. This figurative language, using the poetic vocabulary of flowers and plants, allows the articulation of emotions that are not always easy to verbalize; yet the symbolism is understood and can be visually interpreted by the community of mourners. The working and re-working of the soil where the body is interred and/or the particular choice of plants that the dead person favoured, bring the mourner into physical and psychological contact with the deceased. The removal of weeds, the tidying and watering of the plot make the mourner, rather than nature, the keeper of the memory and nourish the connection. At the same time, tending the plot and/or inspecting and washing the stone allow the deflection and dissipation of the emotional shock of seeing the name of the deceased inscribed in stone. Study participants state that these powerful feelings necessitate quickly turning to some physical task to reduce the stressful impact of realization.

Courtship and remarriage

While a continuation of the bond with the deceased can be significant for identity reconstruction, affirmation of ties with the former spouse also impacts on emergent relationships and adjustment to new roles (Moss and Moss 1996). Such oscillation – between loss and restoration – may be witnessed at the cemetery. Standing in front of her husband's memorial stone, a 70-year-old woman shared her internal dialogue. Her conversation and voiced thoughts – merging rather than alternating – touched on memories shared with her deceased husband and her feelings for the new partner: 'I had a lovely birthday . . . the girls made me a lovely birthday. You were so gorgeous . . . your lovely red hair, your lovely face. You're always in my heart'. As the commentary moved to the immediate she continued: 'I hope L. (the deceased husband) is pleased that I'm friendly with S. (the new partner). I've done nothing wrong. I did not take a man away from his wife. My daughters are pleased. S. makes me laugh. It's lovely. Even if I remarry, I will never forget you L. I will always come to the grounds . . .'

New partners may also accompany each other to the cemetery where they are introduced to the deceased spouse: 'B, not that you don't know already, this is S, I'm sure its OK with you'. Much of the discussion as the new partnership is negotiated deals with letting go and holding on to the two deceased persons also in their relationship. While finding a new partner is generally seen as a sign that the person has moved on, grieving continues and allows the survivor to manage the unfinished and the emergent relationships. A widow explained, with particular clarity, how the meaning of her first husband's death continues to change throughout her second marriage:

> There is an air of permanence about the cemetery, which forces you to accept that the person is gone in that form. However, this is the tip of the iceberg, and the other nine-tenths is the way you see the thing within yourself. It is an ever-changing scene, not constant. Seamless, but it changes as our own circumstances change.

She further elaborates on the memorial stone as a symbol of the continuing bond which is constant in memory but mutable in remarriage; how the deceased is both present and absent at the same time:

> The memorial for your husband is necessary. It's having a home to go to. It's the same difference as having your own home and living in a hotel. You built and organized it . . . a source of pride and sorrow. It's a manifestation of 30 years together. I even improved the stone. I would visualize his body lying there, and I did not want to hit it with a spade. So I had chipping's put there, where I could lay flowers. It was an alteration. I improved it. I did it when I got remarried and was going to live in the country and would not be coming as often to attend to it. It symbolized the end of one chapter and the start of another. Marriage is a four-way split relationship. You are an amalgam of your own personality and what came from living with another person for a long time. There are four of us welded together. Remarriage is a four-way relationship, a quadratic equation.

The value of separate pasts is acknowledged, as is the benefit likely to accrue to a new relationship through remaining connected to a deceased spouse. Rather than a sign of pathology, enduring bonds appear to be an ongoing part of adaptation to change in the later years.

Unlike interviews in a clinical research setting, observations in the cemetery show that the psychological states of grieving and distraction to other tasks, of remembering the past spouse and thinking about a new romantic partner, may be concurrent. The ongoing bond validates that past and the accompanying meanings, recollections, roles and statuses that are part of the sense of self.

Death of parents

Study participants who lost parents 40 or more years ago suggest that ongoing visits to the cemetery focus grief and are an expression of reciprocal, interdependent bonds. Such close attachments provide a mirroring of the self (Rosenblatt 1996; Stroebe *et al.* 1996): 'We will always come here. Coming to the cemetery is a mechanism to hang on to them, to hang on to the past. I get a picture of them when I visit the grave. I feel closer when I am physically closer to what was them'.

In visiting the cemetery, adult children identify with aspects of the deceased and renegotiate the bond with their parents. In describing parents as role models and behavioural guides, they incorporate admired qualities into their self-representations: 'My father was wonderful and took over being the head of the family. He was unselfish, and everyone came to him with their troubles. Now I'm the person who visits the sick and keeps in touch with the family. I do it for my father's sake'.

Parents continue as helper, supporter and confidant, but the changed content and connection leads to new dimensions and possibilities for adult children, who are themselves now at the top of the generational ladder. The mechanisms by which this interaction is achieved may be unique to the cemetery:

> I've come to work out family problems and to relate back to my ancestors and wish they were here. I ask: How would they have dealt with it. I'm the only one left. You come to the cemetery when something is wrong with you. You come to discuss things with someone, someone who can't talk back. My relationship with my mother was not good; she was a difficult woman, but there is something deeper, or else I have no one else to turn to to ask.

Many adult children continue to confide in parents and seek their endorsement and support:

> To visit the cemetery is healing. This is the last thing that the departed do for us. We feel their presence. I tell them about what's happened and the news and about unfinished matters and its healing. Our conversations have changed, they are more confidential now. When she was alive, I protected her. Now, I feel she knows everything. I can tell her intimate things, which I never shared before.

For others, whose experiences with parents were less supportive, visiting the grave may allow the working through of unfinished business, and by providing opportunities for reconciliation, bring the past into the present so that identities can be positively reshaped: 'I had a word with her today. I whispered about the years when we were estranged, and that it was for a reason. She knows now why it happened, and that I am glad I was able to love her again before the end, in her latter years. And I said I am glad she's at peace and happy now'.

As with the other three groups discussed, these parental examples show how the cemetery and its rituals engender and sanction the maintenance of an ongoing relationship with the deceased. Accompanying dialogues appear to clarify thoughts and to deal with unresolved relationship issues. The cemetery is a place where issues of self-identity – of who we are and what we are – may be worked out through an ongoing bond with the deceased. These processes further assist survivors to reintegrate their own lives and prepare for the future, and possibly for older mourners to anticipate their own deaths: 'This is my last visit to see my mother's grave. I am very ill and will not come again. I want to leave everything in order'. Finally, whilst grief encountered in previous years does not evaporate, recurrence can be affirming.

Summary and discussion

This chapter has argued for an expanded view of the bereavement process, which takes account of information about the behaviour of people in cemeteries. The data collected through study of a range of people facing major losses suggest that the purposeful establishment and maintenance of a continuing bond with the deceased aids grief work by allowing the survivor to confront the loss, while at the same time moving forward to new tasks. Grieving people in cemeteries acknowledge their pain and bereavement and appear to 'dose' the amount of emotional suffering they carry to consciously avoid despair. Paradoxically, the very acts of expressive mourning – such as gardening and washing the stone – also serve as distractions. The creation and retention of close bonds with deceased persons does not obstruct the acceptance of the death by the bereaved. Rather, it suggests that people live in a web of relationships, which include the deceased (Silverman and Klass 1996), and that this bond remains a significant and developing personal resource throughout life. 'They're with you all the time, they haven't gone.'

The 'major challenge to grief work is to come to terms with a loss, while honouring and holding on to meaning, precious memories, investments and identities connected to the deceased in such a way that the past is validated' (Rosenblatt 1996: 53). For many cemetery visitors, the cleaning of the stone, the careful arrangement of flowers, the putting in of spring bulbs and/or the planting of summer and autumn bedding plants are physically and psychologically therapeutic. These tasks encourage concentration on memories as an important aspect of grieving, and provide a legitimate reason for visiting: 'I need to do something for them. I like to work over here, to polish, to weed. It's the only way I can still give to them physically – I already give to them emotionally'.

In English burial grounds, the evolving customs of cemetery gardening help to maintain contact with the deceased and provide material evidence of the complex psychological processes of grieving. Study participants affirm that remaining connected facilitates their ability to cope with the loss and that this 'connection' provides comfort, consolation and support (Klass *et al.* 1996). Cemetery landscapes reveal ritualized efforts to maintain plants that look vibrant in every season, and endeavours to keep the memorial stones pristine. These labours also work to construct and project the identity of both the deceased and the mourner. Surviving family members explain these publicly visible practices as showing private respect and care for the deceased. They also demonstrate the tension of maintaining ongoing contact while accepting the loss. The area above the soil is required to belie the reality of decay and decomposition beneath. These flourishing cemetery garden plots and well-washed memorial stones signify that bonds with the deceased do not end with death, but continue through memory and action.

Notes

1 Data for this chapter is drawn from a 14-month ESRC sponsored research project, Cemetery as Garden, Reference No. R00236493, exploring behaviour in six London cemeteries, which were selected for their cultural/ethnic diversity, managerial structures and horticultural/landscape type.
2 Visitors at the graveside were approached at random, at different times of the day and week and in different sections of the cemetery. After an explanation of the project and a guarantee of confidentiality, most people consented to speak with us while they pursued their intended activities. These conversations tended to be intense, intimate, immediate and often anonymous. The refusal rate to approaches was low. Study participants were generally willing and welcoming of the opportunity to talk, whilst being able to indicate clearly when they wished the encounter to finish. Only a small number of newly bereaved were approached.

References

Bowdler, R. (1996) Gardens of death: the importance of London's burial grounds, in *London Cemeteries and Churchyards: A Dying Legacy?* Proceedings of the 1996 Conference of the London Historic Parks and Gardens Trust.

Gorer, G. (1965) *Death, Grief and Mourning in Contemporary Britain*. London: Cresset Press.

Hunt, J.D. (1997) Come Into the Garden Maude: garden art as a privileged mode of commemoration and identity, in J. Wolschke-Bulmahn (ed.) Places of Commemoration: The Search for Identity and Landscape Design. Dumbarton Oaks Colloquium on the History of Landscape Architecture 19, Washington, DC.

Klass, D., Silverman, P.R. and Nickman, S.L. (eds) (1996) *Continuing Bonds: New Understandings of Grief*. Washington, DC: Taylor & Francis.

Leach, E.R. (1961) Cronos and Chronos: two essays concerning the symbolic representation of time, in *Rethinking Anthropology*. London: Althone Press.

Littlewood, J. (1993) The denial of death and rites of passage in contemporary societies, in D. Clark (ed.) *The Sociology of Death*. Oxford: Blackwell.

Lopata, H.Z. (1996) Widowhood and husband sanctification, in D. Klass, P.R. Silverman and S.L. Nickman (eds) *Continuing Bonds: New Understandings of Grief*. Washington, DC: Taylor & Francis.

Miller, M. (1993) *The Garden as an Art*. Albany: SUNY Press.

Moss, M.S. and Moss, S.Z. (1996) Remarriage of widowed persons: a triadic relationship, in D. Klass, P.R. Silverman and S.L. Nickman (eds) *Continuing Bonds: New Understandings of Grief*. Washington, DC: Taylor & Francis.

Rosenblatt, P.C. (1996) Grief that does not end, in D. Klass, P.R. Silverman and S.L. Nickman (eds) *Continuing Bonds: New Understandings of Grief*. Washington, DC: Taylor & Francis.

Silverman, P.R. and Klass, D. (1996) Introduction: what's the problem?, in D. Klass, P.R. Silverman and S.L. Nickman (eds) *Continuing Bonds: New Understandings of Grief*. Washington, DC: Taylor & Francis.

Stroebe, M. and Schut, H. (1995) The dual process model of coping with loss. Paper presented at International Work Group on Death, Dying and Bereavement, Oxford, June 26–9.

Stroebe, M., Gergen, M., Gergen, K. and Stroebe, W. (1996) Broken hearts or broken bonds?, in D. Klass, P.R. Silverman and S.L. Nickman (eds) *Continuing Bonds: New Understandings of Grief*. Washington, DC: Taylor & Francis.

Walter, T. (1996) A new model of grief: bereavement and biography. *Mortality*, 1(1): 7–25.

Warner, W.L. (1959) *The Living and the Dead*. Chicago, IL: Free Press.

16

Hindu death and mourning rituals: the impact of geographic mobility

SHIRLEY FIRTH

Hindus in Britain have probably had more drastic changes to their traditional ways of dealing with death and bereavement than any other new
immigrant group. The formal and informal rituals are being adapted because of the professionalization of death, legal and bureaucratic requirements in Britain, the difficulties of obtaining ritual specialists and the
fragmentation of families. Women's roles are altering with Westernized
education, so that some are now challenging the tradition that only men
should perform death rituals. They are taking a more proactive ritual role,
influenced by pragmatism, reformist Hindu traditions and feminism. This
also influences the position of younger widows who can live independently
and work. However, there are also powerful forces of conservatism reinforced by the priests and elders, often women who Menski describes as
'vigilant guardians of family and caste customs' (1991: 49). This chapter
explores the impact of geographic mobility on the above issues in one British
Hindu community, with particular reference to women. The research was
based chiefly on fieldwork in a British city with about 3000 Hindus, with
three months in India living with relatives and caste peers of British Hindu
informants.

Death for Hindus is a process lasting at least 12 days. Viewed as an
example of Van Gennep's (1960) model of rites of passage, it becomes
apparent that there is a disruption of this pattern in Britain. In India there
is a seamless flow of ritual activity from before the death up to the cremation (rites of separation), followed by ten days in which a new body is
ritually created for the disembodied ghost, *preta* (rites of transition). On
the twelfth day (symbolizing the completion of twelve months), a new
ancestor is generated who is located in heaven or reborn, followed by a
ceremony legitimating the new heir. Until then the family is severely polluted

and withdraws from the world. There are strict gender divisions of activity. This structure provides a socially acceptable framework for grieving and religious and cognitive meaning in death.

This pattern is ruptured in Britain. Death is professionalized. The changes in the time, place and format of funerals alters the structure of the mourning period, which now begins *before* the rites of separation are complete, instead of afterwards. Some rituals have disappeared with the rites of transition, or are reinvented and condensed. Without the familiar ritual framework there is less certainty, since the beliefs no longer make sense outside their original context. The 12-day period is difficult to maintain with work obligations, but the final rites of reincorporation (*shraddha*) are still considered essential, and are often supplemented in India.

Many Hindus are 'twice migrants' via East Africa (Bacchu 1985). Mourning may be complicated by earlier losses, of country, familiar religious and cultural milieu, and wider family networks. Eisenbruch (1984b) observes that uprooting affects whole communities. Some compensate by clinging to the past, while others adapt and 'modernize'. Both extremes, of resistance to change and the desire to adopt the customs and behaviour of the host community can prevent adequate mourning at the time of death.

Rituals at death

The good death is a conscious death at the right place (at home), and time, having dealt with unfinished business, said goodbye, performed an act of penance and offered meritorious gifts.[1] Attention is focused on God (*Bhagavad Gita* 8, 5–6). Death should take place on the floor, with Ganges water and a *tulsi* leaf in the mouth to purify sins (Firth 1997: 66, 68). Facilitating this is a sacred duty, ensuring the soul moves on. With an untimely or violent death the unsatisfied soul hangs around, necessitating remedial rituals (Parry 1982: 83–4, 1994: 162; Madan 1987: 126–7; Firth 1989: 69–71, 1997: 60ff).

In Britain most deaths occur in hospital. There is a low take-up of hospice places by South Asians (Hill and Penso 1995). Rituals are difficult to perform on a busy ward, and death on the floor is impossible in most hospitals (Firth 1989: 71). The priests rarely visit. Sometimes the family are excluded, or are not told death is imminent; consequently, the most fundamental rites of reincorporation may not be possible (Firth 1993: 28–30, 1997: 53ff, 119–29). This creates guilt, distress and anxiety that the attached soul will create disturbances. One Gujarati couple who were not permitted to give a dying aunt Ganges water at the point of death believed the family would be haunted by her for seven generations, causing their infertility (Firth 1997: 117).

Preparation of the body and procession to the cremation ground

In India, the corpse is bathed and dressed according to caste traditions immediately after death by same-sex relatives. Purifying substances are placed on the body to prepare it as the last sacrifice (*antim sanskar*) to the god of fire, Agni. It is then carried on a stretcher by male relatives to the cremation ground. During the ritual procession the chief mourner (the eldest son or nearest male relative) offers balls of wheat, barley or rice (*pindas*) at strategic locations to protect the soul and the corpse from dangerous spirits (Parry 1994: 175–6; Firth 1997: 74–6). Some Punjabi women attend the cremation; Gujarati women do not on the grounds that it may be too upsetting.

In Britain the body is removed to the undertakers and bathed just before the cremation, usually one week later. Laying out a refrigerated body in impersonal surroundings creates great distress. Some families leave this to the undertaker, simply sprinkling it with Ganges water and saying a few mantras. It is placed in a coffin and taken to the family home. The ritual procession has vanished, and the *pindas* are only offered at home.

Funeral rites

After the body is placed on the pyre, the pandit recites Sanskritic texts as the chief mourner circumambulates the body with water and then with a fire brand before lighting the pyre. Half-way through the cremation he may break the skull (*kapala-kriya*) to release the soul (Firth 1991: 70–1, 1997: 78–9; Parry 1994: 177). Afterwards the mourners bathe and return home. The women purify the house, bathe and change. Food, prepared by relatives, is eaten for the first time since the death. At this point mourning proper begins.

In Britain there may be a week before the funeral, raising questions about the fate of the soul, although British pandits stated that it would not suffer if the rituals were performed with faith (Firth 1997: 193). If no pandit is available a senior family or community member recites some Sanskrit verses. Priests are evolving their own rituals, negotiating with each family within the constraints of time and the family tradition. There can be prolonged arguments with senior members of the community, particularly the women. (Firth 1991: 54–5, 1997: 193; Menski 1991: 48–9).

At the house, the ritual contains condensed elements from the preparation of the body, the ritual procession and the pyre. As Vedic verses are recited, the coffin is opened and the mourners, led by the widow, circumambulate it with flowers, butter and herbs, placing them on the body. Incense sticks may be used as a substitute for the fire (Firth 1991: 73–4, 1997: 81–7). If *pindas* are offered at all, they are placed in the coffin. Viewing the body gives *darshan* and the entire family, including children, participate. The coffin is then closed and taken by hearse to the crematorium.

Gujarati women are discouraged from attending, although younger ones may go, as do Punjabi women, sitting separately from the men. The service contains a few prayers and readings, and a homily intended to enlighten and comfort the mourners (Firth 1997: 87ff). The National Council of Hindu Temples has produced a standardized service, which is criticized by some pandits as being for the consolation of the mourners instead of the progress of the deceased.

It is impossible to circumambulate the body in most crematoria, although some new ones have Hindu needs in mind. The chief mourner presses a button, or pushes the coffin into the cremator. Returning home, relatives bathe and change, often at a friend's house. Other mourners sprinkle themselves with water from a bowl outside the house, and then sit with the bereaved, the men and women often in separate rooms.

Reincorporation

Complex rites incorporate the deceased as an ancestor and reincorporate the mourners into society. A new ethereal body is ritually formed over ten days, before the twelfth day ritual, *sapindikarana*, creates a new ancestor (Knipe 1977; Firth 1997: 93ff).[2] The chief mourner is then given a turban by his wife's or mother's family, acknowledging his new role as heir and head of the family, and the widow embarks on her new marginalized role in society (see below).

The ancestors, now *ritually* located in *pitr-loka*, the abode of the ancestors, are *thought of* as being in heaven with God or reborn, often within the family (Firth 1997: 40ff, 93ff). They are in a symbiotic relationship with their descendants, giving progeny protection and safety in return for offerings. They can be demanding and capricious. Dreams of the deceased indicate that they are unsatisfied, and relatives hasten to make offerings to pacify them. Those who have had premature or bad deaths can create great mischief. This, and the danger from pollution, may reflect ambivalent feelings in the bereaved. Anger against parents is taboo and it would not be appropriate to express negative feelings after death; only the best things are remembered and discussed in an effort to view the death as a good one.

In Britain there is a combined, condensed ritual on the twelfth day. Its significance as an act of regeneration seems to be disappearing and is often seen as 'giving a send-off'. However, it remains fundamentally important and may be done in India by proxy or when the family take the ashes back to India. Brahmins, as surrogates for the deceased, are given gifts of money, food and clothing, although some families prefer to give to charity.

Mourning in Britain

Mourning is set in a ritual framework of purposeful activity for the deceased. This period provides a setting for expressing grief and an opportunity to review the life of the person who died in a wider framework of meaning relating to the ultimate purpose of life. The sophisticated rituals provide a means of sharing and dissipating grief within the entire community (Roger Ballard, personal communication). Scripture readings, hymn singing, homilies and shared narratives of good deaths are ways of assuring the bereaved that there is meaning and significance in the death even if the death was sudden, forcing the mourners' attention away from themselves. The periods of talking and weeping for limited periods gradually bring the death home to the family.

For 12 days, chairs are removed from the living room and sheets spread on the floor. The bereaved relatives sit on the floor to receive the condolences of the relatives, friends and neighbours who pour into the house. Their ascetic lifestyle, sleeping on the floor, eating simple food, and having only religious music, reflects their liminal status, as they are dead to the ordinary world. They are in a ritually impure state (*sutaka*).[3] They would not normally offer food or drink to anyone not in *sutaka*, although it is being relaxed because mourners come from considerable distances (Firth 1997: 136, 139–40). *Sutaka* seems to be associated with danger from the half-formed *preta* (ghost), which can cause injury to the family if it has not moved onto its new life (Parry 1994: 215ff; Firth 1997: 135ff). One Gujarati woman even hesitated before accepting food at her brother's home following their mother's funeral, but decided her own mother's ghost would not injure her if she did accept food there.

Grief is expressed in gender-specific ways; men are expected to be stoical while the women express their grief openly (Parry 1994: 152ff). However, in Britain, with one exception, I noted restraint among educated Hindus. Young Hindu informants were often critical of expectations to show grief for distant relatives. They felt that grief got 'switched off and on' artificially, and some of the visitors were hypocritical. Public expression of grief in Britain occasionally causes problems in hospitals and at crematoria, although informants sometimes said that it was good to 'get it out of your system'.[4]

The loss of children is particularly distressing, especially a son on whom one's material, emotional and spiritual future depends. Infants under two are buried with a few prayers; as they are not yet social beings, they are considered too pure to warrant normal funeral rituals, and there is little social mourning (Parry 1994: 220; Firth 1997: 175ff). This can leave the mother without a sense of completion, and one mother has taken the unusual step of arranging for annual prayers at the temple for her daughter, who died as an infant.

Women's roles

In India gender roles are clearly demarcated in religious activities. Only male priests officiate at Sanskritic life-cycle rites and an eldest or youngest son, grandson or brother of the deceased normally acts as chief mourner, although a woman can perform mortuary rites for a husband or father if there are no male heirs, according to some texts.[5] This is linked to patrilineage and inheritance. Daughters are given away on marriage (*kanya-dan*), joining their husbands' lineage, whereas sons inherit the property, guaranteeing security in old age and the parents' salvation by performing funeral and ancestral rites. At her death a woman's husband, son or grandson performs her rites.

In Britain several pandits allow daughters to perform their father's rites if there is no heir or if they insist on participating, seeing no valid scriptural reason to exclude them; other pandits insist this is inappropriate. Women have to negotiate with the formidable combination of the pandit, relatives and elders. In one Gujarati family with no sons, the dying father insisted that the daughters acted as chief mourners, as they were to inherit the property and should have equal rights with men. The rest of the family were outraged, but they could do nothing about it because his preference was stated in his will. His widow was blamed for 'leading him on and twisting him around her little finger', and also blamed for not having had sons. Some of the relatives boycotted the funeral, and for years afterwards treated the wife coolly. She has now made the same provision in her will.

As Menski observes, older women are the guardians of family and caste traditions (1991: 48–9). They know about the cremation rites even if they have never seen them. Their memories are reinforced by videos of, and visits to India. They visit the bereaved, sharing the narratives of their own experiences, reading scriptures for consolation and teaching, explaining beliefs and customs, and leading the *satsangs* (hymn singing). In one city, a Gujarati Brahmin woman with some knowledge of Sanskrit conducted temple and domestic rituals when there was no priest, including funeral rites in the Chapel of Rest, and she continues to be the recipient of the gifts on the anniversary of the death in lieu of the priest (Parry 1994: 119ff; Firth 1997: 107–8). The fact that she was a knowledgeable Brahmin outweighed the fact that she was a woman, and now she is widowed she still takes an active role in the community, saying that as she has adult sons she can hold her head up with self-respect.

Widows

A married upper-class woman is part of her husband's body, with a sacred obligation to pray for and perform rituals to protect and preserve his life.[6] She is extremely fortunate if she dies first (*sahagamana*), and is honoured by the community (Leslie 1991a, 1991b; Firth 1999). If he dies first, she has failed in this task because of her bad karma. Her only option is the life of an ascetic (Firth 1999: 100). As half a body she is permanently impure and inauspicious (Bayly 1981: 175). If she has no sons to protect her, she may be abused by her husband's family and blamed for his death. The higher the caste the less likely she is to contribute to the family economy apart from her dowry; and is of little economic value. She may be thrown out, as evidenced by the large number of widows in Banaras (Eck 1983: 329; Parry 1994: 51). Younger educated women can support themselves, and some remarry, although it is uncommon in higher castes. Lower caste women can remarry, often to a younger brother to keep property and labour in the family, in a traditional but not religious ceremony (Firth 1997: 146–8, 1999).

The change of status for Hindu widows is less extreme in Britain, but they are still regarded as inauspicious and criticized if they deviate from social norms or do not show enough grief. They are expected to perform *puja* daily for their husbands, honouring them on their death anniversaries and during the ancestors' fortnight, *pitr-paksha*. In some Gujarati families there is a reversal of the marriage rite, in which older widows demonstrate their power by claiming her as one of their own (see Stevenson 1920: 204). One informant had to dress as a bride. Her nose ring was removed, and her bangles forced off by a senior widow and placed in the coffin. She had to bathe and change into a white sari and carry a lamp, *diva*, to place before her husband's photo in the living room. All the married women turned their backs on her so they did not have to see her face, signalling that she was now bad luck. She could never wear make-up or a *bindi* (red marriage mark) again, or red, green or yellow saris or coloured bangles; because she was young she could wear beige or blue instead of the traditional white. Her mourning period was shortened from a year to three months so that the family could arrange auspicious events such as marriages (Firth 1999). A Lohana widow suggested that such rituals only occur if the mother-in-law is alive, suggesting a punitive element legitimized by custom and indicating the pressure placed on the widow at her most vulnerable to conform to a view of herself as inauspicious and marginalized. Several older informants had internalized this negative view. One Gujarati woman refused to go out of the house for ten years because she felt so inauspicious, despite her status as the mother of sons, and still does not take an active part in ritual activities (Firth 1999: 104–5). Other older widows, particularly Arya Samaji Punjabis, maintain an active temple role, taking part in the weekly Vedic *havan* (fire ritual) at the temple. A more active religious and prayer life becomes a channel for their energies, which hitherto were focused on their husband and children. Some find new roles helping with grandchildren and the family business, or work. Others prefer to live independently, grateful for the safety net provided by social services. Those who refuse to conform to stereotypes are open to gossip and criticism, especially if they wear make-up and colours, or are seen talking to men.

Widows without children or kin can be very isolated. There are reports of 'Granny dumping', where upwardly mobile families abandon a widow, ostensibly because of space (Daly 1997). Although, traditionally, the sons take care of their mother, in Britain an increasing number are living with their daughters. A growing number of schemes throughout the country are providing housing for Asian elders.

Conclusion

For British Hindus the tension between tradition and change often leads to creative compromises in death rituals and practices. Pandits are adapting rituals appropriate to the circumstances, but whether there is eventually a standardized form or a variety as at present remains to be seen. The purpose of the funeral is shifting towards the consolation of the mourners in this world, rather than the welfare of the dead in the next. The entire family is more involved and delays allow overseas relatives to come. The biggest loss is failure to perform the appropriate rituals at the deathbed, which creates guilt, remorse and anger, complicating normal reactions to loss, adding anxiety about the ghost of the deceased disturbing the family and bringing bad luck. It is important for professionals to recognize the religious and psychological importance of these rites of separation.

For women the tension between conservative attitudes reflected in the ritual for the new young widow, above, and those of younger educated women living and working in a Westernized society can lead to alienation unless their nearest kin are supportive of change. Many care for their own elderly parents, traditionally the sons' domain. They can inherit property. Some insist on taking part in the funeral and cremation rites even at the risk of antagonizing the community. If these younger women become widowed they will have enough economic independence to determine their own future. Some pandits fiercely resist these changes, but others are cooperative, which will influence community attitudes. The tension between the maintenance of continuity of tradition and the development of new rituals and roles both reflects and creates changes in beliefs and in gender relations. The question is whether the price will be the loss of important beliefs that give death meaning and of community cohesion and support, which are so important at times of loss.

Notes

1 Death in Varanasi or near the Ganges is an ideal available only to a few (Parry 1994; Justice 1997).

2 Arya Samajis complete their mourning in India on the fourth day only with the Vedic fire ritual, *havan*. In Britain this follows cremation.
3 *Sutaka* rules vary according to caste, and for lower castes extends up to 30 days. There are further rituals up to a year.
4 Eisenbruch notes that many immigrants to the United States have to be seen to grieve, and show extremes of emotion: 'Yet Anglo-American hospital staff may feel bewildered, threatened, hostile or derisive when faced by these behaviours, which are often treated by them as pathological' (1984b: 509).
5 Kane 1973: 256–9; Parry 1994: 183–4; Firth 1997: 71–2.
6 In the top three twice-born classes boys undergo the *upanayana*, the investiture of the sacred thread.

References

Bacchu, P. (1985) *Twice Migrants: East African Sikh Settlers in Britain*. London: Tavistock.

Bayly, C.A. (1981) From ritual to ceremony: death ritual and society in Hindu North India since 1600, in J. Whalley (ed.) *Mirrors of Mortality: Studies in the Social History of Death*. London: Europa.

The Bhagavad Gita, translated by F. Edgerton (1972) Cambridge, MA: Harvard University Press.

Daly, M. (1997) *The Big Issue*, 26 May–1 June, No. 234.

Eck, D.L. (1983) *Banaras, City of Light*. London: Routledge and Kegan Paul.

Eisenbruch, M. (1984a) Cross-cultural aspects of bereavement I: a conceptual framework for comparative analysis. *Culture, Medicine and Psychiatry*, 8(3): 283–309.

Eisenbruch, M. (1984b) Cross-Cultural aspects of bereavement II: ethnic and cultural variations in the development of bereavement practices. *Culture, Medicine and Psychiatry*, 8(4): 315–47.

Firth, S. (1989) The good death: approaches to death, dying and bereavement among British Hindus, in A. Berger, P. Bedham, A.H. Kutscher *et al.* (eds) Perspectives on Death and Dying: Cross-cultural and Multi-disciplinary Views. Philadelphia, CA: The Charles Press.

Firth, S. (1991) Changing patterns of Hindu death rituals in Britain, in D. Killingley, W. Menski and S. Firth *Hindu Ritual and Society*. Newcastle-upon-Tyne: S.Y. Killingley.

Firth, S. (1993) Approaches to death in Hindu and Sikh communities, in D. Dickenson and M. Johnson (eds) *Death, Dying and Bereavement*. London: Sage.

Firth, S. (1997) *Dying, Death and Bereavement in a British Hindu Community*. Leuven: Peeters.

Firth, S. (1999) Hindu widows in Britain: continuity and change, in R. Barot, H. Bradley and S. Fenton (eds) *Ethnicity, Gender and Social Change*. Basingstoke: Macmillan, pp. 99–114.

Hill, D. and Penso, D. (1995) *Opening Doors: Improving Access to Hospice and Specialist Palliative Care Services by Members of the Black and Ethnic Minority Communities*. London: National Council for Hospice and Specialist Palliative Care Services.

Justice, C. (1997) *Dying the Good Death: The Pilgrimage to Die in India's Holy City*. Albany, NY: State University of New York Press.

Kane, P.V. (1973) *History of the Dharmashastra*, Vol IV, 2nd edn. Poona: Bhandarkar Oriental Research Institute.

Knipe, D.M. (1977) *Sapindikarama*: the Hindu rite of entry into heaven, in F.E. Reynolds and E.H. Waugh (eds) *Religious Encounters with Death: Insights from the History and Anthropology of Religions*. University Park, PA: Pennsylvania State University Press.

Leslie, J. (1991a) Religion, gender and *dharma*: the case of the widow ascetic. British Association for the Study of Religion, Occasional Papers 4.

Leslie, J. (1991b) Suttee or Sati: victim or victor, in J. Leslie (ed.) *Roles and Rituals for Hindu Women*. London: Printer.

Madan, T.N. (1987) *Non-renunciation: Themes and Interpretations of Hindu Culture*. Delhi: Oxford University Press.

Menski, W. (1991) Change and continuity in Hindu marriage rituals, in D. Killingley, W. Menski and S. Firth *Hindu Ritual and Society*. Newcastle-upon-Tyne: S. Y. Killingley.

Parry, J. (1982) Sacrificial death and the necrophagous ascetic, in M. Bloch and J. Parry (eds) *Death and the Regeneration of Life*. Cambridge: Cambridge University Press.

Parry, J. (1994) *Death in Banaras*. Cambridge: Cambridge University Press.

Stevenson, M.S. (1920) *Rites of the Twice-Born*. London: Oxford University Press.

Van Gennep, A. ([1908] 1960) *The Rites of Passage*, translated by M.B. Vizendom and G.L. Caffee. Chicago, IL: University of Chicago Press.

17 Grieving in public

⬜ GLENNYS HOWARTH

It is frequently observed in Western societies that throughout the twentieth century grieving has increasingly taken place in private. The elaborate mourning rituals of the nineteenth century carried the expectation that people would adhere to the etiquette of mourning paraphernalia (such as the wearing of 'widows weeds') and resulted in an outwardly public expression of grief. By contrast, the twentieth century has been marked by a reluctance to indulge public demonstrations of grief. If death has been the taboo subject for many decades (Ariès 1981; Walter 1991), bereaved people have been the pariahs, unwilling, and largely disabled from openly displaying the extent of their grief.

This chapter suggests that the imperative for private grief is changing as bereaved people, especially those, who are affected by sudden or violent death, find new avenues for the public expression of grief. The placing of floral tributes at the site of a sudden death, most commonly by a roadside, is one instance of a relatively recent innovation in public mourning ritual that is rapidly popularizing. A further example of public grief is found in the ritual of the coroner's court – a system designed to explain sudden death. This chapter examines the manner in which the coroner's inquest has become a setting for public grief work for many bereaved people. In previous centuries, 'fate' determined the nature of a death; the hand of God was seen to be at work, deciding when the earthly existence of an individual was to end. During this century more scientific explanations have been sought to define and account for sudden death and it is the purpose of the inquest to produce an objective, scientific account of death. It is during the inquest, however, that relatives and friends of the deceased also try to make sense of what happened, especially if the death was not only sudden but also of a violent nature. In so doing, the public ritual in the courtroom is becoming more central to the grieving process with families demanding more information from which to construct their own understanding of the death and any associated blame. Consequently, and in similar ways to those who insist on greater participation in funeral rituals, people are now beginning to use professional and expert rituals to play out their own grief. Indeed, findings from a study of the coroner system[1] show that bereaved families and friends are now publicly questioning the nature of evidence and the interpretation of findings and as such, are demonstrating dissatisfaction with a singularly private, individualized approach to grief.

The discussion will begin by briefly considering the impact that sudden death can have for survivors. The coroner's inquest will provide the focus for the chapter. It will concentrate on the way in which bereaved people use the public inquest to undertake grief work (Lindemann 1944; Freud 1917). Grief work may be defined as the emotional work that individuals undertake to assist them to manage their experiences of grief. A satisfactory outcome of grief work is the ability to cope, adjust to, and live with the loss of the deceased person. When set within the coroner system, this work may involve gathering information, formulating interpretations, making sense of, filling in the gaps, and restoring biographical continuity for the deceased (Howarth 2000).

Sudden death and responsibility

What is specifically characteristic about the bereaved people who encounter the coroner system is the sudden and often violent nature of the death and this explains their lack of preparation. As Yates *et al.* (1993) point out 'the impact of a sudden death on relatives is often more pronounced than that of a death after a prolonged illness, during which the relatives have had time to prepare themselves' (p. 279). The sudden and often *violent* nature of the death exacerbates the trauma.

Sudden death poses distinct problems when people come to undertake grief work. In keeping with the nature of grief generally, there is often a sense of disbelief. When the death is sudden this is commonly exacerbated by a lack of knowledge or information about the event. Bereaved family and friends are often absent when the death occurs and this results in them searching for answers to a series of questions about the factors that precipitated the death, the time between injury and death, other persons involved, the procedures adopted by emergency service personnel, and so on. There may be bewilderment and anger, particularly in cases of accidental death, murder or manslaughter. The unexpected nature of the death may also lead people to question how it could be that someone so recently alive and vibrant can now be dead. People also rue the lack of an opportunity to 'say goodbye' (Weber and Marcus 1996). Others may bemoan the deceased's age at death, especially if this upsets the popular assumption that death now occurs in old age (Stedeford 1984).

Perhaps the most frequently posed question is, 'could the death have been averted?' Linked to this is the question of blame or responsibility. This is sometimes self-focused, taking the form of personal guilt, most noticeably in cases of suicide. By trying to make sense of such forms of sudden death bereaved people increasingly appear to be seeking an explanation that leads to the apportioning of blame. In modern society, where the vagaries of luck and chance are no longer accepted as sufficient explanations for tragic events, rationalization is commonly sought in terms of responsibility. Indeed, an opinion poll conducted in 1970 noted that three-quarters of respondents thought that a function of the coroner should be to discover whether 'anyone was responsible for the death' (Brodrick Committee 1971: 124). Yet, there is no longer any provision within the coroner system to allow a legal verdict that cites either an individual or organization as being responsible for the death. Perhaps in virtue of this, bereaved people are frequently criticized for their desire to apportion blame or responsibility (Matthews and Foreman 1993). This tension between the coroner's practice and the needs of survivors will be examined shortly. It is important to note here, however, that in their grief work, the question of blame may have to be addressed and resolved if survivors are to move on. Although at one extreme, the allocation of responsibility may demand a public inquiry or criminal prosecution subsequent to the coroner's inquest, many families seek no more than a recognition of fault and an apology. A woman whose mother was killed on the road commented: 'It's like being in a car crash when the insurance company insists that even if you know it's your fault you don't ever say so. I don't want compensation or anyone prosecuted, I just want someone to say they're sorry'.

For a minority of bereaved people, resolving the issue of blame may actually require that an individual or organization is legally held responsible for the death. Survivors, especially of large-scale disasters, may establish campaigning groups where bereaved people can draw public attention to their grievances and openly discuss the problematic issues surrounding the death of their loved ones. Such groups function to generate public sympathy and support and so to exert pressure for a favourable outcome to an inquiry.

This form of grief work provides a sharp contrast with more privatized approaches to grief resolution that may involve private communication between a bereaved person and their counsellor. It is a site for systematically working through the meaning of the death for the individual and trying to locate the key to a future without the deceased person. Although private grieving may well take place in parallel with public grieving, activity in campaigns and self-help groups can be public ways of managing grief. Let us now consider the role of the coroner's inquest in providing a public forum for the expression and resolution of grief.

The coroner system

The coroner system exists to investigate sudden death: road, rail, sea and air fatalities; suicide; death at work; death from industrial disease; death in custody; in disasters; from homicide; manslaughter; and so on. This encompasses any death that is deemed to be unexpected in so far as the deceased had not seen a doctor within the last 14 days of life. The role of the coroner is to distinguish between natural and non-natural death (see Prior 1985, for a discussion on the concept of 'natural' death).

The purpose of the investigation is to determine *who* the deceased was, *how*, *when* and *where* he or she came by their death (Coroners Act 1988). How an individual met their death is determined in relation to medical categories and legal verdicts. For example, death could have been caused by kidney failure resulting from the individual committing the act of suicide. The inquest is an inquisitorial rather than adversarial process in that the proceedings are not designed to apportion blame: 'there are no parties, there is no indictment, there is no prosecution, there is no defence, there is no trial, simply an attempt to establish facts' (Matthews and Foreman 1993: 6). In cases where criminal prosecution is to be pursued and an adversarial process demanded, for example in instances of homicide, the inquiry will be passed to the Criminal Prosecution Service. When this occurs an inquest will be opened and immediately adjourned pending the verdict of the criminal court.

The inquest

Not all sudden death necessitates a public inquest. If the pathologist's examination of the body, carried out shortly after death, reveals that the death was attributable to natural causes then an inquest will not be deemed necessary. In all other cases where the cause is non-natural or uncertain, the inquest provides a public forum for the ritualized reconstruction of death. Both expert and lay witnesses are called to give evidence about the circumstances of death. Expert witnesses are relied on to supply legal and medical evidence and lay witnesses provide information about the social circumstances surrounding death. When all witness testimonies have been heard and questioning is complete the coroner must reach a legal verdict. Examples of these are accidental death, suicide, unlawful killing, misadventure and so on. This verdict stems from the coroner's interpretation of the synthesis of the medical, legal and social discourses presented in the courtroom. When the verdict is reached, however, some families may be bewildered if the outcome fails to coincide with their expectations of a statement apportioning responsibility. Indeed, many assume that the inquest will be productive in either assigning blame or, at the very least, demanding that a dangerous system or situation be changed.

Grief work in the inquest

Clearly the experience of bereavement differs among individuals and will vary according to their relationship with the deceased and to the nature of the death. With that in mind, there continues to be a growing tendency for survivors to question their experiences within the coroner's court (Matthews and Foreman 1993: vii). The system and procedures during the inquest are not experienced in the same way by bereaved people and the professionals who organize and control them. The needs and purposes of these two groups are disparate. Whilst coroners have largely come to view their role in the investigation of sudden death in terms of legal and medical criteria, many bereaved people perceive the purpose of the inquest in terms of discovering the social causes and implications of death. This clash of interests provoked one coroner (now retired) to remark that among the public, 'There is quite the wrong idea of inquests. That in some way they are provided, as it were, for the delectation of the relatives of the deceased' (Chambers 1994).

Asking questions and gathering information

More than ever, the inquest is being utilized by bereaved people as a mechanism for the public expression of grief and the resolution of personal questions related to the death. The reconstruction of the circumstances of the death that is undertaken within the coroner's court is an important postmortem compensation for families' lack of preparation. As they are denied access to official documents such as witness testimonies and expert reports, they look to the courtroom reconstruction to provide the information they require. Listening to the testimony of experts reporting the 'facts' of the death, and witnesses describing the scene, they are able to reconstruct the death for themselves. This experience may prove painful and traumatic as they hear evidence for the first time; for example, a pathologist's report of detailed physical injuries sustained by the deceased. Nevertheless, working through their grief in this public domain, they are accessing information that provides answers to questions and helps them in their attempt to make sense of the death.

Although some coroners are opposed to greater involvement by families during the inquest, preferring survivors to adopt observer rather than participant roles, others make conscious provision for their needs. The latter spend time with the family before the inquest, explaining procedures and encouraging them to formulate and ask questions of witnesses during the proceedings. In cases where the death may be especially contentious, such as a death in custody, families may employ a solicitor to ask questions on their behalf. Many such questions are focused on the issue of whether the death could have been avoided. Ascertaining a satisfactory answer to this question is clearly fundamental to any eventual grief resolution. This is poignantly illustrated by the experience of one respondent who performed resuscitation on his father following a heart attack. The father had died but the man needed the information contained in the pathologist's report to satisfy himself that the attack had been fatal and all attempts at resuscitation futile. If a death could have been avoided by some act or omission, this then leads to the question of responsibility – an issue that may need to be resolved, either personally or publicly, before the individual can emotionally adapt to their loss.

Interpreting outcomes

When the courtroom reconstruction of the death is complete the coroner must reach a verdict. Whilst many families can accept the verdict as an appropriate outcome, others may question it. Victim Support, for example, note that, 'Many families object strongly to the words "accident" and "compensation"; they feel that road crashes, often caused by illegal driving behaviour, are *not* accidents, and certainly nothing can compensate them for their loss' (Victim Support 1994: 3). Having sat through the inquest, and being equipped with personal knowledge of the deceased person, bereaved families arrive at their own interpretations, which help them to make sense of, and so to manage, their perceptions and adjustment to the death. When survivors' interpretations do not coincide with the legal verdict they may challenge it through judicial review and/or register their disapproval by seeking media publicity.

Using the media

Bereaved people often perceive the media as intrusive and sometimes feel that newspaper reports aggravate their grief by presenting sensationalist and distorted narratives of their personal tragedy. The media desire for newsworthy stories, however, also makes them an ideal source of publicity for people who wish to criticize or overturn a verdict. In such cases initiating a media campaign may provide a further avenue for the public expression of grief.

Public recognition and the right to grieve

The experience of grief work in the context of the coroner's court is significantly distinct from a private counselling consultation that puts emphasis in grief resolution on the need for the grieving individual to change either their behaviour or thinking in order to accommodate to their loss – to 'accept' the realities of the death. In the inquest the interaction is not between individuals in a private communication, but takes place in the public domain. It is a form of grief work, which involves asking social questions and demanding answers of public officials. Rather than trying to bend to the inevitable, bereaved families question the possible need to change systems.

It is important to acknowledge, however, that not all people respond in this way. Not all ask questions or reject the coroner's verdict. Some neither need nor desire public rituals, preferring private communication. Nevertheless, in the courtroom, the coroner will usually note the tragic circumstances, the terrible loss and will openly express sympathy for the family and friends of the deceased. In this way their right to grieve, and the particularly intense nature of their grief, can be publicly acknowledged. Identification of tragic loss and the recognition of the severe and possibly prolonged nature of their grieving is an important feature of the social management of grief.

Conclusion

This chapter has considered some of the ways in which bereaved people engage with the coroner's inquest to gather information and secure public recognition to assist them in their grief work. For many, the opportunity to grieve in public may be crucial. If it cannot find expression in other forms, such as the prolonged wearing of mourning clothes, then bereaved people may seek other avenues through which to publicly express their grief. In cases of sudden death, especially that which is violent and 'untimely', survivors may be particularly keen to achieve public recognition of their loss and their 'right' to grieve intensely – even more so in a society that discourages lengthy and public mourning rituals. Moreover, when bereaved people actively pursue information during the coroner's inquest and demand the allocation of responsibility, they are attempting to address the apparently random nature of death and this too, can be a central aspect of grief work.

It is often assumed that when professionals and experts are involved there is a danger that a bureaucratic and rational system will effectively subjugate bereaved people. In the case of the coroners, this is a system designed to ascertain the medical and legal causes of death. Information may be withheld; the body of the deceased may be inaccessible to the family until the coroner decides otherwise, the voice of the survivors silenced by the professionals within the courtroom. This description of the system is in large part true in that bereaved families have little or no impact, power or control over the investigative process. On occasion conflict may therefore occur between officials and families and in some instances relatives may not even be informed of the date and time the inquest is to take place. It is sometimes argued by the professionals involved that such tensions arise because the families do not understand the nature of the inquest (Matthews and Foreman 1993; Chambers 1994). Whilst this is likely to be the case, the difficulties are exacerbated by the lack of congruence between the official purpose and the needs of the bereaved. Nonetheless, what this chapter has demonstrated is that it does not necessarily follow that bereaved people become victims of the system. By considering only the dominant discourse of the experts, and by attributing primary 'value' to professional processes and effects, the way in which the coroner's system is utilized by bereaved people is far less visible. As shown here, many seek to actively engage with the public ritual of the inquest to meet their own needs to acquire knowledge, to ask questions, to make statements and to gain public recognition for their tragedy. In this way, they are undertaking essential grief work.

Acknowledgements

I am grateful to the *British Journal of Sociology* and the Nuffield Foundation for funding the research on which this chapter is based.

Note

1 This discussion is based on a study of the coroner system in three distinct geographical regions of England. Data were collected through in-depth interviews with coroners, their officers, police officers, bereaved families, and other expert and lay witnesses. Lengthy courtroom observations were also undertaken.

References

Ariès, P. (1981) *The Hour of Our Death*. New York: Knopf.
Brodrick Committee (1971) *Report of the Committee on Death Certification and Coroners*, Cmnd. 4810. London: HMSO.
Chambers, D. (1994) cited in *The Times*, 26 April.
Freud, S. (1917) Mourning and melancholia, in J. Strachey (ed. and trans.) *The Standard Edition of the Complete Psychological Works of Sigmund Freud*, Vol. 14. London: Hogarth Press and Institute of Psycho-Analysis.
Howarth, G. (2000) Dismantling the boundaries between life and death. *Mortality*, (2): 127–38.
Lindemann, E. (1944) Symptomatology and management of acute grief. *American Journal of Psychiatry*, 101: 141–8.
Matthews, P. and Foreman, J. (1993) *Jervis on the Office and Duties of Coroners*, 11th edn. London: Sweet and Maxwell.
Prior, L. (1985) The good, the bad and the unnatural: a study of coroner's decisions in Northern Ireland. *The Sociological Review*, 33(1): 64–90.
Stedeford, A. (1984) *Facing Death: Patients, Families and Professionals*. London: Heinemann.
Victim Support (1994) *Assisting the Victims of Serious Crime*. London: National Association of Victim Support Schemes.

Walter, T. (1991) Modern death: taboo or not taboo? *Sociology*, 25: 293–310.

Weber, A. and Marcus, J. (1996) *No Chance to Say Goodbye: Traumatic Bereavement and its Management*. Video and accompanying notes produced by Jo Marcus Productions, London.

Yates, D.W., Ellison, G. and McGuiness, S. (1993) Care of the suddenly bereaved, in D. Dickenson and M. Johnson (eds) *Death, Dying and Bereavement*. London: Sage.

18 Post-disaster rituals

ANNE EYRE

The 1980s in the UK might be termed the 'decade of disasters'. A series of tragedies unfolded in relatively quick succession, many having a major impact not only on those directly affected but also on the nation as a whole. The disasters included the fires at Bradford Football Club, Kings Cross Underground Station and Manchester airport, as well as the Clapham train crash, the Lockerbie air disaster, the capsize of the *Herald of Free Enterprise*, the sinking of the *Marchioness Pleasureboat* and the Hillsborough Football Stadium Disaster (see Table 18.1). The tenth anniversaries of these disasters have now passed; yet many are still deeply affected as the attendance and responses at anniversary events have shown.

Table 18.1 Summary of some of the major disasters that occurred in the 1980s

Date	Location	Incident	No of Fatalities
11.05.85	Bradford	Football stadium fire	56
22.08.85	Manchester	Aeroplane fire	54
06.03.87	Zeebrugge	Ferry sinks	193
08.11.87	Enniskillen	Terrorist bomb	11
18.11.87	Kings Cross	Underground fire	31
06.07.88	Piper Alpha	Oil rig explosion	167
21.10.88	Greece	Cruise ship sinks	4
12.12.88	Clapham	Train collision	36
21.12.88	Lockerbie	Air crash	270
08.01.89	Kegworth	Air crash	47
15.04.89	Hillsborough	Overcrowded stadium	96
20.08.89	Marchioness	Riverboat sinks	51

This chapter examines various forms of death ritual following disasters. After first discussing definitions of disaster and the different types of victims, the chapter examines ritual responses forming part of the grieving process and shows how the organization and content of these can reflect and influence the feelings of the bereaved. A theme running through the chapter is the practical implications of grief and bereavement responses for those involved in disaster management, whether it be as members of the emergency services or those dealing more directly with victims in the aftermath, either as members of debriefing teams, the clergy or longer term counsellors. Although the main focus of this chapter is humanly caused disasters affecting UK citizens, many of the issues here relate to those affected by other types and locations of disasters.

The meaning of disaster

In order to understand the nature and meaning of grief following disaster, a clear definition of disasters is needed. This can be either a simple or very difficult task. In general parlance the term 'disaster' is applied loosely to any event with what for some might be negative consequences: the splitting up of a teen pop group, spilling red wine on a favourite outfit; we might describe these as personal 'disasters'. On a collective level it is easy to give examples of disaster situations: the news media daily feature major incidents, such as sudden large-scale accidents, transport crashes, other humanly-caused events such as shootings and terrorist attacks and slower onset 'complex emergencies', such as war and its aftermath, often entailing secondary 'humanitarian disaster'. All these examples would involve injuries or fatalities.

Within an academic and practitioner context a more specific, consistent definition of disasters is needed. The more complex task here is to identify those key features of disasters that enable us to distinguish which types of events and incidents should be included or excluded in analysis. For practitioners, this is particularly important because definitions have operational implications: for example, the response of the emergency services is quantitatively different in a major incident or disaster (in terms of deployment of resources) and may have qualitatively different effects (in terms of the psycho-social impact on personnel).

Much debate has been dedicated to defining and measuring disasters (Quarantelli 1998). They have been categorized according to cause and type (for example, humanly-caused as opposed to natural disasters) and according to the length of warning ('slow onset' or 'sudden impact'). The suddenness of the events covered in this chapter, which involve unexpected deaths, often of very young people, have had an impact on the nature and intensity of grief (Eyre 1998). Scale of event is also a defining characteristic of disasters; they are regarded as a level beyond relatively small-scale, ordinary accidents. The emergency services reflects this emphasis in defining a major incident as:

> any emergency that requires the implementation of special arrangements by one or all of the emergency services for:
>
> 1 The rescue and transport of a large number of casualties.
> 2 The involvement either directly or indirectly of large numbers of people.
> 3 The handling of a large number of enquiries likely to be generated, both from the public and the news media usually to the police.
> 4 Any incident that requires the large-scale combined resources of the three emergency services.
> 5 The mobilisation and organisation of the emergency services and supporting organisations e.g. local authority, to cater for the threat of death, serious injury or homelessness to a large number of people.
>
> (Association of Chief Police Officers 1990: iii)

This definition is also useful in highlighting the typical features in a disaster situation, including the role of the media, which may have an impact on the psycho-social response of the bereaved. This will be discussed later.

For our purposes it is of significant interest that some definitions of disaster rest on the number of deaths; for example, Westgate and O'Keefe refer to a disaster as 'a sudden event which kills 10 or more people' (1976: 7). One of the potential difficulties with such comparative definitions is the implication that an event with a larger number of fatalities is necessarily more 'disastrous' than one with a lower number. In quantitative terms this may be so, but in qualitative terms this is a complex area. Great caution needs to be exercised in adopting a comparative approach to the psycho-social impact of any event. The effect of any disaster is likely to reflect not just the nature and scale of the incident but a range of other factors too, relating both to the event itself and to the personal circumstances and personality factors of the persons involved.

The definition of disaster is, therefore, not just an academic exercise; it affects the allocation of resources and whether full-scale emergency plans are activated or not. By way of example, members of disaster debriefing teams (those called on to provide psycho-social support) may only be called on to assist in the aftermath of an incident if the situation is deemed to be one where the normal services are overwhelmed and where it is considered that there are enough victims for a formal disaster plan to be applied. This is an important point because disaster management historically has tended to reflect quantifiable, tangible and pragmatic elements of disasters. Understanding of the psycho-social impact of disaster and its subjective meaning for those involved, including the nature of grief and its expression, is only gradually being understood and given appropriate recognition in disaster planning and response.

Who are the victims?

Who are the victims of disaster, what are your assumptions about them and how would you expect them to behave? In terms of the impact of disasters and the experience of multiple loss and bereavement, it is important to have a clear understanding of who the victims are and what being a 'victim' can mean. The term can conjure up images of passivity, helplessness and power-lessness, all of which may apply, but there is also much more to being a disaster victim than this and responses to victims based on inappropriate stereotypes can be both insulting and unhelpful. Anyone working with vic-tims of disaster needs to understand that a whole range of emotions occur, of which grief may be just one. Let us therefore consider who the victims of disaster are and what it means for them.

The most immediate or direct victims of a disaster are easy to identify; they include those killed or injured, the rescued survivors, relatives and friends and direct witnesses. An individual might fit into more than one of these categories, which might well have implications for the psychological impact of the event on them in the aftermath. Stephen Homewood (1989) gives a moving account of this based on his experience as a crew member surviving the Zeebrugge disaster.

Proximity to an event is often regarded as a criterion of victim status; we assume that those most closely involved in an event are likely to be more severely affected. This may or may not necessarily be so and has both psy-chological and legal implications. Indeed proximity was one of the criteria for dismissing the claims for compensation for post-traumatic stress dis-order of some relatives of those killed at the Hillsborough football stadium disaster. Although they witnessed the horrific scenes of this disaster live on television, it was assumed in law that physical presence at the event deter-mined the degree of psychological distress (Kelly 1998).

The victims of disaster might also include those involved either officially or unofficially as rescuers (indeed, in most disaster situations victims are involved in helping each other before representatives of emergency and other external agencies arrive (Tierney 1989: 23)). In the past official res-cuers were not always recognized as potential or actual victims of disaster in terms of the impact of traumatic stress, loss and bereavement, partly because of the stereotyping referred to earlier and the expectation that this was part of their professional role (despite the police's definition of dis-asters as extraordinary events). Today these potential victims of disaster are less 'hidden' and more proactive measures are taken to prepare rescuers and aid workers for the impact of disaster work and to debrief them after-wards (Hodgkinson and Stewart 1998: 196–229; IFRCRCS 1998: 32–43).

Taylor (1990) has identified six categories of victim and discusses their relative needs. They are (1) those directly exposed; (2) those with close family or personal ties to primary victims who themselves have vicarious grief reactions; (3) rescue and recovery workers who may need emotional help and support throughout the rescue period; (4) concerned people in the community who may emotionally identity with victims or feel guilt and responsibility for having caused the disaster; (5) those not directly involved but with underlying psychopathology who act in a disorderly way during times of social breakdown; and (6) a miscellaneous group including those who, but for chance, might have been primary victims. The emotional relationships with other victims and the particular needs of those in this group make it difficult to place them in other groups.

Taylor's work is useful because it reminds us not only of the various types of victim experience but also of their differing needs and the implications of these for levels of psycho-social support following disaster. Given this, it is interesting that research into provisions for psycho-social care has shown an emphasis in most regional plans on first level survivors and staff care, but includes little mention of relatives and communities (Adshead *et al.* 1995: 9). Taylor's typology also challenges the assumption that all victims should be treated in the same way. Such distinctions may have implications not only for treatment but also for assumptions about the nature of losses and grieving. The notion of a hierarchy of grief, for example, is a further consequence of the distinctions made between different groups of victims. On the tenth anniversary following a disaster one survivor stated: 'There is undoubtedly a hierarchy of grief. People accord me a certain amount of importance when they find out that I was (directly involved). My experience gives what I feel is a kind of legitimacy, but the fact that no one close to me died also makes others assume that I should be over it by now' (Eyre 1999).

As the next section illustrates, a further feature of disasters is the impact they have on the community at large, including the national or even international community, depending on the nature of the disaster. One indication of the impact of disaster on society is the involvement of the public in post-disaster rituals. While these can facilitate the grieving of the public at large, the public profile of what for many victims are private and deeply personal moments can be distressing and may even reinforce the traumatic impact of disaster.

Post-disaster rituals

Following the shooting of 16 children and their teacher at a primary school in Dunblane in 1996, scores of bouquets of flowers and large sums of money were poured into the disaster-struck community. It was an example of a pattern now common following disasters, which includes both formal and informal popular rituals. These include visits to disaster sites, the laying of flowers and other symbolic mementoes, official memorial services, the setting up of permanent memorials and anniversary events. Elements of such disaster ritual are not new; many remember the poignant scenes surrounding the tragedy at Aberfan in 1966. This was the scene of the first live television outside broadcast following a community tragedy. Since then high profile media coverage has transmitted and helped to mould the nature of both 'spontaneous' and organized expression of disaster ritual. What is new is the increasing recognition and, arguably, acceptance of this sort of ritual and emotional display. Though not strictly a 'disaster' under the terms discussed above, the death of Princess Diana in 1997 and its aftermath instigated much debate about the national sense of mourning, which would also apply here. Those involved in planning for disasters recognize the important functions served by such commemorative acts: 'Public and community recognition of disaster, marked by such things as religious services, memorials, anniversaries and appeal funds will be helpful' (Emergency Planning Society 1998: para 8.1.8).

Though beyond the scope of this chapter, a cross-cultural approach highlights some interesting similarities and contrasts in the symbolism and function associated with the commemoration of disaster across time and place.

Informal popular rituals

Rituals following a disaster are often spontaneous and start within hours of the disaster becoming public knowledge. They include members of the public visiting a disaster site or other significant sites associated with the event as well as places of worship. At these venues there is the laying of flowers, toys (where children are involved) or other mementoes; candles are often lit in houses or places of worship. It is now also common to see flowers by the side of the road at the site of a fatal accident. Walter (1998) has argued that the place where flowers and other tributes are laid reflect a new way of mapping the sacred sites of contemporary culture. For example, after the death of Diana flowers were left at town halls, war memorials and in some supermarkets.

Some see these as religious forms of expression addressing the unanswerable question of 'why?' in the face of human powerlessness and mortality. By way of example, in the *Estonia* disaster over 800 people died following the sinking of a Baltic Superferry. On the day of the disaster over 500 churches in Sweden (a traditionally secular society) were opened for individual prayer and lighting of candles and visits and memorial services took place over a number of weeks (Pettersson 1996).

Other instinctive responses during the first few days include public contributions to disaster funds. This is still one of the most instinctive responses by members of the broader community. People feel they want to *do something* to express their sorrow and to acknowledge both their individual and shared sense of grief – even when may not know those killed or injured.

Although much further grief is often caused by disaster funds (Miller 1974; Coleman *et al.* 1990; James 1998), this is a response that needs to be recognized and is increasingly planned for (at least the Disasters Working Party recommend this (1991: 14)). Following the problems that have been associated with the management and distribution of such funds, trustees have learned much and have adapted the nature, status and communication of appeals. One of the continuing ironies of such giving, however, is that it does not necessarily reflect the needs of the bereaved. The large influx of toys was a symbolic but inappropriate arrival into the village of Aberfan, which had just lost a generation of its children (Austin 1967: 178; Miller 1974: 30–31).

As well as the signing of official books of condolence, poignant messages accompanying flowers and other gifts also reflect the depth of grief following disaster and can be of much comfort to the bereaved. Personal and/or collective messages from those bereaved by other disasters can suggest that there are others who have some understanding of the pain, while messages from key public figures such as the Queen or Prime Minister may be heartening. An example of the former was a floral tribute at the Dryfesdale Cemetery, Scotland, on the tenth anniversary of the Lockerbie Disaster with the simple message: 'To the bereaved families of Lockerbie and Flight 103 from the bereaved families of Dunblane'.

Funerals

One of the most vivid ways in which disasters stand out in comparison to more ordinary forms of death is the number of funerals that have to take place. As well as the usual decisions to be faced regarding a funeral's form, the bereaved following disaster may be asked whether they prefer an individual or collective funeral and whether they would prefer the funeral to be private or public. Collective funerals reflect the community impact of an event; after the Aberfan Disaster, over half of the families opted to participate in the collective service; this was a community faced with 144 disposals:

> The Sunday following the disaster it was decided in Merthyr that there should be a communal burial, since there was only one cemetery for all the different churches and chapels in Aberfan. The ministers met in Aberfan on the Monday and agreed that the service should be taken by a Roman Catholic, an Anglican and a nonconformist . . . Parents were not very happy about the idea of a communal burial, nor did they necessarily want the children buried according to classes in the school. Finally it was agreed that a mass burial should be held with two strip graves which allowed each one an individually-named grave. Eighty-one children and one adult, a mother with her two sons, were buried at the mass funeral.
>
> (Miller 1974: 28–9)

An important issue following any such disaster is the role of the media and the need for the privacy of mourners to be respected. However, such respect is not always accorded the bereaved, particularly following an event deemed newsworthy, and the sense of national mourning is often regarded as a legitimate reason for the media to focus on the bereaved following disasters. Guided by a voluntary code of practice, a marked feature of the media's response following Dunblane was the stated decision not to film at the funerals. However, media intrusion and insensitivity is still identified by disaster victims as a distressing feature of participation in rituals in the days, weeks and years afterwards.

Formal memorial services

Some weeks after a disaster there is usually a planned official memorial service, which, depending on its local, communal or national significance, is usually held in a cathedral or church. (This can be politically sensitive as the debate about the location and commemorative nature of the service following the Falklands War testifies; this included debate about whether the service should include reference to Argentinian military victims.) The degree and nature of religious content in such services is also a complex topic. These are important events for the various types of victims, including emergency service workers and other helpers, who may be joining together with the bereaved for the first time after the event. Given the recentness of the event and the fact that people are still in shock, these are very emotional occasions. One survivor (of the sinking of the *Jupiter* cruise ship) comments thus on the community impact and solidarity she felt at a thanksgiving service: 'The church was absolutely packed and we were amazed that all these people had turned out on a cold November night to church. And there was the caretakers and the dinner ladies and neighbours, not only, you know, VIPs like the local MP and the mayor. There were so many people and it was absolutely packed'.

Although these events are often attended by key national figures such as members of the royal family and politicians, the question of which dignitaries do and do not attend can be sensitive. Many of those who attended the official memorial service following Hillsborough were upset that a senior royal did not attend and were upset by the attendance of the Prime Minister, Mrs Thatcher, whose relationship with the city both before and after the disaster was not warm. Those planning official memorial services need to be sensitive to this and plan accordingly. Following the Hillsborough Disaster, the association of bereavement with Liverpool Football Club was symbolized by the attendance of players at many of the funerals and the impact of the whole disaster on them was publicly discussed, including a debate about when would be the appropriate time for them to start playing football again.

An important question is whether dignitaries should be given priority over those most deeply affected? One relative from the Lockerbie Disaster feels memorial services are 'appalling occasions because the most important people at them are the PM and/or the royal people, the local dignitary; they are the ones who get to sit in the front pew, who get to read a lesson or something like that. So my family chose absolutely not to go in the immediate aftermath'. Statements such as this show that great sensitivity is needed in planning the form, content, attendance and broadcasting of such services. There are obvious implications here for the training of clergy and others involved in planning and delivering these high profile events. Sadly, as with much disaster management, these are seen as sufficiently rare events and are not part of the regular training of religious and other professionals.

Anniversary events

The first anniversary is particularly important after a disaster but subsequent ones are also significant, and often have high attendance. On the 30th anniversary of the Aberfan Disaster, more than 100 villagers attended the annual commemoration service led by five ministers from eight churches and chapels (*Timewatch* 1996). As well as anniversaries being opportunities for relatives and survivors to reunite, bereavement and grief can resurface at this time. For some these events and their media coverage may even trigger the beginning of grief work and the onset of post-traumatic stress. 'Many existing crisis counselling services have received phone calls at times of anniversaries, birthdays, holidays, resolution of court cases and publications of reports about the disaster – all occasions when the memory of the disaster is evoked' (Disasters Working Party 1991: para 3.5).

Support workers need to be aware of this. Although practical information and support is planned for in the first few weeks and months following disaster, to whom will the distressed turn should the tenth, twentieth or thirtieth anniversary be the occasion of the first feelings of flashback and other symptoms of post-traumatic response? Optional helpline support may pick up some of these at anniversary and other significant points in the longer term, including the conclusion of inquest and inquiry procedures. As well as their therapeutic potential, planners need to be responsive to the fact that anniversary events themselves can cause resentment. They may reinforce, for example, anger at media intrusion or divisions among or between relatives, survivors and organizers.

For those more actively involved after disasters, for example members of relatives and/or survivors' action groups, anniversaries can be used to raise the public profile of outstanding issues and injustices. For such campaigners, the media coverage of events can be positively used. As an example, the Hillsborough Families Support Group used the tenth anniversary to highlight the 'unfinished business' of the disaster and the ongoing search for justice through the prosecution of senior police officers in charge on the day (HFSG 1999).

Elsewhere I have argued that the public and 'complicated' nature of death through disasters has a significant impact on grieving processes and emphasized the inability of the bereaved to find 'closure' while fundamental questions relating to the deaths of their loved ones remain outstanding (Eyre 1998). This theme in the aftermath of humanly caused disasters is a reflection of unsatisfactory and unsympathetic procedures in inquests, inquiries and court cases and their outcome. The persistence of unresolved issues relating to responsibility, accountability and justice can be a source of ongoing trauma for relatives and survivors. For them, anniversaries are far from a rite of passage to 'moving on' but a painful reminder of the little that has been achieved after so long. Further distress is sometimes caused when these appropriate feelings of anger are dismissed as 'unresolved grief'. Rather, grief is just one of the complex emotions experienced after disaster that needs to be understood within the broader psycho-social and legal aftermath of disasters and their unfinished business.

This chapter has examined various forms of post-disaster acts and services and explored their significance for those affected and those involved in managing and responding to post-disaster events. Not only are informal and official commemorative events occasions for remembering those killed and injured, they are also ways of expressing personal and collective grief. Disaster workers need to be aware that commemorative sites and services can also be political sites of consensus and conflict. There is a range of social, religious and political issues surrounding disaster commemoration itself, reflected in decisions about where, when and how it takes place and who has the authority to make such decisions. In the longer term there are often also outstanding issues surrounding the causes and consequences of disaster which anniversaries and memorials may be used to highlight.

Those interested in understanding and addressing the nature of grief following disaster have an important and valuable role to play. They also need to understand that for the victims the psycho-social impact of disaster relates both to the event itself and also to the secondary disasters associated with processes of inquest, inquiry, accountability and compensation for as long as they remain unresolved.

References

Adshead, G., Canterbury, R. and Rose, S. (1995) Current provision and recommendations for the management of psycho-social morbidity following disaster in England, *Disaster Prevention and Management: An International Journal*, 4(4): 5–12.

Association of Chief Police Officers (1990) Emergency Procedures Manual.

Austin, T. (1967) *Aberfan: The Story of a Disaster*. London: Hutchinson.

Coleman, S., Jemphrey, A., Scraton, P. and Skidmore, P. (1990) *Hillsborough and After: The Liverpool Experience*, First Report. Liverpool: Liverpool City Council.

Disasters Working Party (1991) *Disasters: Planning for a Caring Response*. London: HMSO.

Emergency Planning Society (1998) *Responding to Disaster: The Human Aspects*. Guidance Document produced by Emergency Planning Society Professional Issues & Public Information and Welfare Group. Liverpool: Brodie Publishing.

Eyre, A. (1998) More than PTSD: proactive responses after disaster. *Australasian Journal of Trauma and Disaster Studies*, http:www.massey.ac.nz/%7Etrauma/welcome.htm

Eyre, A. (1999) I've learnt a lot from Hillsborough (interview with Caroline Scott). *The Daily Telegraph*, 15 April, p. 22.

HFSG (1999) Hillsborough Families Support Group website – http://www.hfsg.org. faqs/why/htm

Hodgkinson, P. and Stewart, M. (1998) *Coping with Catastrophe: A Handbook of Post-Disaster Psychosocial Aftercare*. London: Routledge.

Homewood, S. (1989) *Zeebrugge: A Hero's Story*. London: Bloomsbury.

IFRCRCS (1998) *World Disasters Report*. Oxford: International Federation of Red Cross and Red Crescent Societies/Oxford University Press.

James, B. (1998) The new tragedy of Dunblane. *The Mail on Sunday*, Night and Day Section, 19 July, pp. 22–4.

Kelly. G. (1998) An Examination of the Law on PTSD in the light of the Irish Supreme Court decision in Kelly *v* Hennesy (1995) 3 I.R.253; third of a series of papers by G. Kelly BL http://www.telecoms.net/lawlptsd3.htm

Miller, J. (1974) *Aberfan: A Disaster and its Aftermath*. London: Constable.

Pettersson, P. (1996) Implicit religion turned explicit: a case study of the *Estonia* disaster. Paper presented at the XIX Denton Conference on Implicit Religion, Denton, Yorkshire, 10–12 May.

Quarantelli E.L. (ed.) (1998) *What is a Disaster?* London: Routledge.

Taylor, A.J. (1990) A pattern of disasters and their victims. *Disasters*, 14: 291–300.

Tierney, K. (1989) Social and community contexts of disaster, in R. Gist and B. Lubin (eds) *Psychosocial Aspects of Disaster*. New York: Wiley & Sons.

Timewatch (1996) Remember Aberfan, BBC TV, October.

Walter, T. (1998) Presentation at Death, Dying and Bereavement Symposium, The Open University Milton Keynes, November.

Westgate, K. and O'Keefe, P. (1976) *Some Definitions of Disaster*. University of Bradford Disaster Research Unit, Occasional Paper No. 4, June.

Conclusion

JEANNE KATZ

In this book we have explored the meanings and consequences of loss through death for a variety of populations. In contrast to many other books in this subject area we have not tried to develop one particular theoretical or disciplinary framework into which to bind what we find to be very different experiences. Further, despite dividing this book into sections that artificially separate the internal world of grief from attempts to repair suffering and also external manifestations of mourning, one of our primary aims has been to demonstrate the links between these different domains and to question the received wisdom of separating them.

At the level of overarching theory, therefore, this book shares Walter's view that the contemporary Western distinction between internal emotion (grief) and external behaviour (mourning) is problematic (Walter 1996). We have argued that as social scientists we should not allow our internally differentiated disciplinary boundaries to replicate these divisive categories. For example, the assumption that psychologists look at people's internal reality whereas anthropologists observe what people actually do can undermine the potential insights of both these disciplines. Instead this book has recognized the pervasiveness of the social when it comes to examining private feelings. Anderson's chapter on cultural models of the emotions explores this area for example. The book has also acknowledged the agency of the individual within collectivities and offered a sustained emphasis on diversity and individual innovation.

Each of the volume's three sections began with a long chapter that examined the historical, social and cultural contexts within which social scientists and practitioners have been developing the theories of grief, mourning and death ritual, which now have a 'popular' status. The shorter chapters provide more substantive, in-depth accounts of grief and mourning practices.

Although our primary focus is human relationships and their rupture through death, these shorter chapters testify to the importance of material culture and practice, an aspect of bereavement that often gets overlooked or trivialized when emotions and beliefs are at stake. Chapters of particular relevance here include Mary Bradbury on memorials; Phil Gore on coffins; Miriam and Sydney Moss on siblings who keep family identity via deceased's possessions; Doris Francis *et al.* on the cemetery garden and the gardening work that takes place there; and Anne Eyre on post-disaster practices such as signing books of condolence. As Lunt and Livingston (1992: 65, cited in Lupton 1998) have commented, research in the social sciences has tended to be directed at the relationships people have with each other, or with social institutions, rather than with objects or things. Miller has similarly identified this suspicion of objects among critics of mass culture. He argues that they have tended to be dismissive of attempts to analyse objects culturally, assuming 'that the relation of persons to objects is in some way vicarious, fetishistic or wrong; that primary concern should lie with direct social relations and "real" people' (Miller 1987: 11, cited in Lupton 1998).

In its longer chapters, this volume explores the strengths and shortcomings of the postmodern theories that have been used to explain responses to loss and death, a project which is also taken up in the recent publications by Payne *et al.* (1999) and Walter (1999). Among the 15 shorter chapters we have contributions from social scientists who offered an additional layer of theorizing, providing 'knowledge about knowledge' via disciplinary perspectives, which extend beyond a more specific focus on death and dying: for example, medical sociology (Currer) and the anthropology of metaphor (Anderson). Alongside their chapters we have placed the accounts of practitioners who have articulated the models that underpin their work in a reflexive manner (Heslop and Simons).

Brought together in this way, the diverse contributions that make up this volume centre around a number of key themes. The first is that of making sense of suffering. In the first long chapter we explore the psychiatric theories of grief that have predominated in this arena, from Freud to Klass *et al.*'s theory of continuing bonds (1996). Two shorter chapters that exemplify this theme are those of Howarth, who investigates how coroners' proceedings try to understand how a death came to take place, and Komaromy and Hockey, who demonstrate how staff in residential homes try to categorize residents' deaths.

A second theme is that of finding a relationship with the dead, in particular the material objects and practices through which this is achieved and the implications for survivors' identities. This includes the role of the deceased within ongoing and new interpersonal relationships. The chapters by Littlewood and Heslop describes ways in which the living sustain their relationships with dead spouses and children. The work of Moss and Moss shows how loss is incorporated into family identity, whilst the chapters by

Francis *et al.* and Bradbury demonstrate active, materially-grounded ways in which relationships with the deceased can be nurtured.

A third theme relates to the *social* experience of grieving and mourning practices. The substantive data presented include examples of shared experiences that have led to community action in different forms. The chapter by Katz refers to public action following mass deaths through shooting. Miriam and Sidney Moss describe how family members make sense of a parent's death and their evolving relationships with the deceased parent. This links in to the systemic approaches cited by Small and Hockey who note how this focus differs from the traditional attachment theory and client-centred perspectives. Yet we know that for many, grieving and mourning is a very lonely experience in the English-speaking world. Small and Hockey quote Abrams (1995) who, following the publication of her book, was made increasingly aware of the loneliness of people bereaved of parents.

Experiences of this kind have therefore been a focus for analysis and interpretation throughout the volume. A historical perspective has been important here and we have taken the First World War and its aftermath as the catalyst for change in attitudes towards modern death. This period witnessed a shift in the funeral and mourning practices which arguably had been dominant in the UK for several centuries. It was also the springboard for developing expert theories about grieving and it was a spur to the development of changing concepts of what constituted appropriate health and social care provision. These developments occurred within the context of massive changes in society, which in their turn impacted on approaches to death and bereavement. For example, the twentieth century witnessed hitherto unfamiliar patterns in social and geographic mobility in the UK and the US. (The impact of large migrations was familiar in other parts of Europe and indeed elsewhere.) As Firth has demonstrated in her chapter, immigration has resulted in challenges to those services that provide care for dying and bereaved people. In broad terms, therefore, the host white Anglo-Saxon population in the UK has now been confronted with a variety of responses to death from different migrant populations, some of whom, in turn, have had to adapt their death rituals and even experiences of grieving to a Western context. At the end of the twentieth century repeated exposure to different kinds of rituals that *apparently* provide solace and structure to immigrant groups partly contributed to a re-evaluation of the attitudes and practices of the host society and a strengthening of the belief that structural support for bereaved people is a good thing.

By the end of the Second World War, the Holocaust and other mass murders had created populations with complex bereavement needs, with 'survivors' not only having 'lost' the people in their lives, but also their history, their culture, their home, their language, their society, their livelihoods, their education and so forth. Tragically these situations have been repeated across the globe and our understanding of the ramifications of these losses can be applied to those experiencing disasters of all kinds, whether caused by nature or human beings. Ann Eyre's chapter explores this area. Core to this book, therefore, is a recognition of the special and invisible needs of evermore diverse categories of bereaved people and categories of death. We present a non-comprehensive list, which includes bereaved children and school teachers (Katz), parents bereaved of children (Heslop and Simons), female members of an ethnic minority (Firth), adult children bereaved of parents (Moss and Moss) and, finally, those whose bereavement has been central to theory and practice in this area, widows and widowers (Littlewood, Francis *et al.* and Bradbury). In relation to categories of death, we look at concepts of timely and untimely death (Komaromy and Hockey), a good death (reviewed in Small and Hockey), sudden death (Howarth) and violent deaths in accidents, disasters and war (Howarth and Eyre).

Alongside national and international events such as these, the break-up of local communities has left gaps in care-giving and other tasks formerly managed within communities. This has been demonstrated in David Clark's study of Staithes in Yorkshire (1982) and Sheila Adams' study of inter-war Foleshill in Coventry (1993). Here we add additional force to the argument that 'expert', 'professional' others have stepped in to provide otherwise unavailable care for bereaved people. Chapters by Gore, Árnason, Anderson, Heslop and Simons contribute here.

However, we have retained a critical perspective in relation to professionalization, scrutinizing the ways in which death has been removed from the control of the client for their perceived benefit. Mary Bradbury describes the mystique of cremation, as evidenced in the media's speculation about what goes on behind the scenes. We note that bereavement too can be simply taken out of ordinary people's hands. As Small suggests, the professionalization of grieving can disempower people (particularly those who are not linked into religious or cultural contexts) and remove their 'natural' coping mechanisms. His quote 'if the professional moves in does the neighbourhood move out?' sums up this concern. We have therefore questioned some of the models of professional practice and attempted to develop new models. Katz on school teachers' needs to be reassured that they have expertise, and Simons on the criteria for selecting helpline counsellors contribute to this debate.

Whilst charting the processes of professionalization, we have also highlighted the agency of individuals who have been bereaved, identifying innovative and often invisible practices such as memorialization at the site of the grave and the private scattering of ashes (Bradbury). Another example of individuals bucking the trend is the rejection by widows of conventional bereavement counselling models (Littlewood) through their confidence in sustaining relationships with their dead spouse. Additionally, bereaved people have created communities of sentiment, through, for example, the Candle Service (Heslop) in Liverpool, volunteering for the Child Death

Helpline (Simons) or meeting regularly with other groups of similarly bereaved people, for example, in Cruse – Bereavement Care's friendships groups or among the Compassionate Friends.

Alongside the process of medicalization and its associated identification of specialized forms of grief, this volume has aimed to foreground hitherto unacknowledged sites and practices of mourning. These include courtrooms and classrooms, which were not previously seen as appropriate places for the expression of emotion. Whilst cemeteries have always been recognized as traditional sites for commemorating the deceased, gardening practices that link the deceased with their perceived individual characteristics (preferences and interests) and their former domestic environment demonstrate the imaginative ways in which bonds between the living and the dead can be strengthened. Even more so since the death of Diana, Princess of Wales, roadside memorialization has become commonplace, whether at the site of an accident or on the road outside a school (as in Dunblane).

Detailing practice has therefore been central to our account of grief, mourning and death ritual. It not only indicates the dynamic nature of responses to death but also demands that we continue to reflect on many of our theoretical assumptions. As in Walter's recent publication (1999), this volume has similarly provided a critical examination of the range of ideologies and beliefs that abound in this area. Small and Hockey, for example, follow a Foucauldian model and represent bereavement services as a set of discursive practices, so providing a different perspective on Walter's notion of 'policing grief' (1999). The shorter chapters in this second part of the book illustrate this point. Heslop shows how the secularization of emotion has precipitated the development of new practices for bereaved parents who found a vacuum in this area. Simon's chapter demonstrates how the unavailability of services, be they local or parochial, for parents who had experienced the death of a child in the distant past could stimulate positive action through their contributing to the staffing of the Child Death Helpline.

Pushing forward some of the concepts introduced in a previous edited collection (Field *et al.* 1997), Hockey and others in this volume show how changing masculinities have opened up the possibility of a new site and style of emotional expression. Once again these changes, as described by Simons, Anderson and Eyre, were exemplified in national mourning patterns following the death of Diana, Princess of Wales. It was an occasion when members of the public made their need for visible emotional expression paramount, the restrained, stiff upper lip of the nineteenth century being explicitly overthrown as a result of popular opinion.

In her long chapter, Hockey cited modernism as a critical historical and theoretical perspective that can help make sense of the cult of the expert. This point is also evidenced in the chapters by Howarth and Anderson. Small and Hockey's long chapter first raised this point when it emphasized the way in which each 'generation's' understanding and responses to grief and bereavement both contributes to and is moulded by contemporary values and attitudes. Within modernity we expect to rationalize and categorize every aspect of our lives within a sequential, comprehensible discourse. Small notes the dangers of modernist ideas of this kind in that they seek a solution to the 'problems' posed by and for bereaved people. He quotes Klass *et al.* (1996) who do not believe in imposing a structure for healthy grief, and Stroebe *et al.* (1996) who note the importance of reflexivity.

Alongside this focus on modernism, Hockey has also highlighted the links between death ritual and romanticism. The chapter written with Komaromy showed how the status of natural death links with Romanticism's privileging of the world of nature. By drawing on a construction of 'nature' which is set in opposition to modernity and industrialization, care staff legitimate an emotionally low-key, non-interventionist management of death in later life. Romantic constructions of 'nature' represent a pervasive theme within the management of death and the aesthetics of death ritual throughout the twentieth century. Winter (1995), for example, identifies a traditional vocabulary of mourning that flourished after the First World War. Classical, romantic or religious forms are evident in memorials and practices that positioned bereaved people, and indeed the nation as a whole, towards past stability rather than present chaos and future uncertainty.

In summary, the wide variety of descriptive accounts and theoretical perspectives that have been gathered together in this book are offered to the reader as a way of informing them about contemporary practices and understandings of what loss through death means to human kind. The question of the future direction of thought and practice in this area nonetheless remains pressing. Although gaps in the ethnographic data detailing the mourning practices of the host Western population are now being filled, anthropologists still have much to offer through describing 'smaller' populations. In turn, scrutinizing modernity and romanticism may help an understanding of what social forces are shaping responses to loss, but the richness inherent in different subgroups and in individual experience can best be uncovered via privileging small narratives and contingent meanings, a characteristic of a postmodern approach. This book offers theories, not a theory, and links them with reflective thinking derived from practise experience. It is this encounter between theory and practice, mediated through personal reflection, that offers the richest route by which to take studies of grief, mourning and death ritual into the new millennium.

References

Abrams, R. (1995) *When Parents Die*. London: Thorsons.
Adams, S. (1993) A gendered history of the social management of death and dying in Foleshill, Coventry, during the inter-war years, in D. Clark (ed.) *The Sociology of Death*. Oxford: Blackwell.

Clark, D. (1982) *Between Pulpit and Pew: Folk Religion in a North Yorkshire Fishing Village.* Cambridge: Cambridge University Press.

Field, D., Hockey, J. and Small, N. (1997) *Death, Gender and Ethnicity.* London: Routledge.

Klass, D., Silverman, P.R. and Nickman, S.L. (1996). *Continuing Bonds, New Understandings of Grief.* Washington, DC: Taylor & Francis.

Lupton, D. (1998) *The Emotional Self.* London: Sage.

Payne, S., Horn, S. and Relf, M. (1999) *Loss and Bereavement.* Buckingham: Open University Press.

Stroebe, M., Gergen, M., Gergen, K. and Stroebe, W. (1996). Broken hearts or broken bonds?, in D. Klass, P. Silverman and S.L. Nickman (1996) *Continuing Bonds, New Understandings of Grief.* Washington, DC: Taylor & Francis.

Walter, T. (1996) A new model of grief: bereavement and biography. *Mortality,* 1(1): 7–25.

Walter, T. (1999) *On Bereavement: The Culture of Grief.* Buckingham: Open University Press.

Winter, J. (1995) *Sites of Memory, Sites of Mourning.* Cambridge: Cambridge University Press.

Useful organizations and addresses

ACT Association for Children with life threatening or terminal conditions and their families
65 St Michael's Hill
Bristol
BS2 8DZ

Cancerlink
11–21 Northdown Street
London
N1 9BN
Telephone: 020 7833 2818

Child Death Helpline
Bereavement Services Department
Great Ormond Street Hospital NHS Trust
Great Ormond Street
London
WC1N 3JH
Telephone: 020 7405 9200, helpline: 0800 282986

Compassionate Friends
53 North Street
Bristol
BS3 1EN
Telephone: 0117 953 9639, helpline: 0117 953 9639

The Cot Death Society
Maple House
Unit 6 & 8
Padgate Business Centre Green Lane
Warrington

Cheshire
WA1 4JN
Telephone: 01925 850086

CRUSE – Bereavement Care
Cruse House
126 Sheen Road
Richmond
Surrey TW9 1UR
Telephone: 020 8939 9530

Hospice Information Service
St Christophers Hospice
51–59 Lawrie Park Road
London
SE26 6DZ
Telephone: 020 8778 9252

National Association of Bereavement Services
2nd floor
4 Pinchin Street
London
E1 1SA
Telephone: 020 7709 0505

Samaritans
10 The Grove
Slough
Berks SL1 1QP
Telephone: 01735 216500

SANDS (Stillbirth and Neonatal Death Society)
28 Portland Place
London
W1N 4DE
Helpline: 020 7436 5881

Terrence Higgins Trust
52–54 Gray's Inn Road
London
WC1X 8JU
Helpline: 020 7242 1010

INDEX

REFLECTIONS ON PALLIATIVE CARE

David Clark and Jane Seymour

Palliative care seems set to continue its rapid development into the early years of the twenty-first century. From its origins in the modern hospice movement, the new multidisciplinary specialty of palliative care has expanded into a variety of settings. Palliative care services are now being provided in the home, in hospital and in nursing homes. There are moves to extend palliative care beyond its traditional constituency of people with cancer. Efforts are being made to provide a wide range of palliative therapies to patients at an early stage of their disease progression. The evidence-base of palliative care is growing, with more research, evaluation and audit, along with specialist programmes of education. Palliative care appears to be coming of age.

On the other hand numbers of challenges still exist. Much service development has been unplanned and unregulated. Palliative care providers must continue to adapt to changing patterns of commissioning and funding services. The voluntary hospice movement may feel its values threatened by a new professionalism and policies which require its greater integration within mainstream services. There are concerns about the re-medicalization of palliative care, about how an evidence-based approach to practice can be developed, and about the extent to which its methods are transferring across diseases and settings.

Beyond these preoccupations lie wider societal issues about the organization of death and dying in late modern culture. To what extent have notions of death as a contemporary taboo been superseded? How can we characterize the nature of suffering? What factors are involved in the debate surrounding end of life care ethics and euthanasia?

David Clark and Jane Seymour, drawing on a wide range of sources, as well as their own empirical studies, offer a set of reflections on the development of palliative care and its place within a wider social context. Their book will be essential reading to any practitioner, policy maker, teacher or student involved in palliative care or concerned about death, dying and life-limiting illness.

Contents
Introduction – Part 1: Death in society – The social meaning of death and suffering – Ageing, dying and grieving – The ethics of dying – Part II: The philosophy and practice of palliative care – History and development – Definitions, components, meanings – Routinization and medicalization – Part III: Policy issues – Policy development and palliative care – The delivery of palliative care services – Part IV: Conclusion – The future for palliative care – References – Index.

224pp   0 335 19454 0 (Paperback)   0 335 19455 9 (Hardback)

AN INTIMATE LONELINESS
SUPPORTING BEREAVED PARENTS AND SIBLINGS

Gordon Riches and Pam Dawson

- What impact does a child's death have on family relationships?
- How might differences in the way mothers and fathers deal with bereavement contribute to increased marital tension?
- Why are bereaved siblings so deeply affected by the way their parents grieve?

An Intimate Loneliness explores how family members attempt to come to terms with the death of an offspring or brother or sister. Drawing on relevant research and the authors' own experience of working with bereaved parents and siblings, this book examines the importance of social relationships in helping them adjust to their bereavement. The chances of making sense of this most distressing loss are influenced by the resilience of the family's surviving relationships, by the availability of wider support networks and by the cultural resources that inform each's perception of death. This book considers the impact of bereavement on self and family identity. In particular, it examines the role of shared remembering in transforming survivors' relationships with the deceased, and in helping rebuild their own identity with a significantly changed family structure. Problems considered include: the failure of intimate relationships, cultural and gender expectations, the 'invisibility' of fathers' and siblings' grief, sudden and 'difficult' deaths, lack of information, and the sense of isolation felt by some family members.

This book will be of value to students on courses in counselling, health care, psychology, social policy, pastoral care and education. It will appeal to sociology students with an interest in death, dying and mortality. It is also aimed at professionally qualified counselling, health and social service workers, informed voluntary group members, the clergy, teachers and others involved with pastoral care.

Contents
Introduction – Order out of chaos: personal, social and cultural resources for making sense of loss – A bleak and lonely landscape: problems of adjustment for bereaved parents – What about me? Problems of adjustment for bereaved siblings – Connections and disconnections: ways family members deal with lost relationships – Difficult deaths and problems of adjustment – Things that help: supporting bereaved parents and brothers and sisters – Conclusion: professional support in a post-modern world – Appendix: shoe-strings and bricolage: some notes on the background research project

240pp   0 335 19972 0 (Paperback)   0 335 19973 9 (Hardback)

ON BEREAVEMENT
THE CULTURE OF GRIEF

Tony Walter

Insightful and refreshing.
Professor Dennis Klass, Webster University, St Louis, USA

A tour de force.
Dr Colin Murray Parkes, OBE, MD, FRCPsych, President of CRUSE

Some societies and some individuals find a place for their dead, others leave them behind. In recent years, researchers, professionals and bereaved people themselves have struggled with this. Should the bond with the dead be continued or broken? What is clear is that the grieving individual is not left in a social vacuum but has to struggle with expectations from self, family, friends, professionals and academic theorists.

This ground-breaking book looks at the social position of the bereaved. They find themselves caught between the living and the dead, sometimes searching for guidelines in a de-ritualized society that has few to offer, sometimes finding their grief inappropriately pathologized and policed. At its best, bereavement care offers reassurance, validation and freedom to talk where the client has previously encountered judgmentalism.

In this unique book, Tony Walter applies sociological insights to one of the most personal of human situations. *On Bereavement* is aimed of students on medical, nursing, counselling and social work courses that include bereavement as a topic. It will also appeal to sociology students with an interest in death, dying and mortality.

Contents
Introduction – Part I: Living with the dead – Other places, other times – War, peace and the dead: twentieth-century popular culture – Private bonds – Public bonds: the dead in everyday conversation – The last chapter – Theories – Part II: Policing grief – Guidelines for grief: historical background – Popular guidelines: the English case – Expert guidelines: clinical lore – Vive la différence? The politics of gender – Bereavement care – Conclusion: integration, regulation and postmodernism – References – Index.

256pp   0 335 20080 X (Paperback)   0 335 20081 8 (Hardback)